IS Wrestling FIXED?

IS Wrestling FIXED?

I DIDN'T KNOW IT WAS BROKEN!

MY INCREDIBLE **PRO WRESTLING JOURNEY...** AND BEYOND!

BY **BILL APTER!**

ECW

FOREWORD

by Jerry
"THE KING"
Lawler

During our time on Earth, there are people who come along and dramatically impact the course of our lives. Bill Apter is one of those people. He totally and positively changed the direction of my career— and changed my life for the better as well. I am flattered that he asked me to write the foreword of this book.

My career needed some fixing for sure, and Bill was quite the handyman, because he introduced me to "Andyman!" More about that below . . .

A lot of people don't realize this, but I always keep it in the back of my mind: if it wasn't for Bill, I would probably never have been part of WWE. I owe so much of my success and career to him.

At a time when our little Memphis-Nashville promotion was so obscure, so unknown, I would send Bill photos, trying to do some self-promotion to get me and the territory into the national magazines. He was kind enough, for some unknown reason, to take a personal interest in me and, along with the rest of the magazine staff, really helped to get my name out there.

The biggest thing that ever happened in my entire career, however, was the feud I had with Andy Kaufman. Bill was single-handedly responsible for hooking me up with Andy. If it were not for him, that entire classic adventure would never have happened. This incredible story became perhaps the most influential happening in the history of the business. It certainly changed the face of professional wrestling, and it really was the first time the sport experienced the involvement of a major celebrity. This *was* "Hollywood"—and the birth, even though no one knew it at the time, of sports entertainment. Our story revolutionized the business. Mainstream media couldn't get enough, and the fans showed their approval by setting record attendance numbers. And all of this happened because Bill "handed" Andy to me (the entire story in Bill's own words is in this book of course).

Back in the territorial days, whenever word got around that Bill Apter was coming to do interviews and shoot photos, the wrestlers upped their game, hoping that Bill would get a memorable picture or quote that would make it into a magazine. Remember there was no social media, no internet back then. If you were endorsed by Apter, you were something special, and you usually wound up somewhere in the magazines. He was the right guy to know.

Bill also knew how to play the game. He was smart in our business and quickly became accepted as one of us. If you confided in him or told him something that was to remain "kayfabe," you could rest assured he would never tell a soul.

Whether you were an iconic wrestler or an opening-match player, Bill was—and still is—always a welcome sight. The same is true for the promoters, business people and, of course, the fans. He is part of our fraternity and respected the world over. It's amazing that he has been doing his work with an undying passion for 50 years. That's half his life . . . (A little age humor doesn't hurt now, does it Bill?)

Bill, so many of us owe you so very much. I guess it's now time to crown *you* "King" of the wrestling magazine glory days (and online— when you include me in your reports, of course).

THE DISCLAIMER APTER WAS FORCED TO WRITE

!!!

I am proud to say I have no enemies in the sports entertainment/pro-wrestling business. It's amazing I can say that after a 45-year career in one of the most wonderful, colorful, intense, mad and unusual worlds around. Who else do you know has spent this much time reporting, photographing and befriending half-naked men in bathing suits who make like they're beating each other up?

As I write this, I'm astonished that millions of people from all over the world now witness this genre in full glory on their TVs, computers, cell phones and iPads. You will read about the happiest times of my career, interacting with the wrestlers, promoters, fans and critics, as well as the ugly times that no business can avoid.

This book is not about the various publishing companies I've worked for. There are stories about my time at those places, but this is not a representation of their business in any way.

If you're wondering why the "millions and millions" of photos I shot throughout my career are not in this book, the answer to that is quite simple: I was employed by the publishing companies—paid a weekly salary—and they own those photographs. I have no regrets. I was their employee and it's the way their business operated.

To the people who were part of this ride, no matter if it was a segment of the good or the bad, I thank you for being there on my incredible journey that continues onward.

In some stories, people may appear in an unfavorable light. During those periods, I didn't quite understand that we just did business in different ways. However, from each of them I learned valuable lessons that helped me make better choices as my career progressed. I do not think poorly of these people now; it's all a matter of history. But the stories do need to be told. I may have had heat with them in the past, but many are gone, and the others have settled peacefully on their perches and we are now in a friendly place.

Some of this book is about my

> **I learned valuable lessons that helped me make better choices.**

relationship with WWE and the McMahon family. It was a fun yet sometimes troublesome roller coaster. Despite many challenging times that were purely business based—not personal—today, World Wrestling Entertainment and the McMahon/Levesque family and I have an excellent relationship, which makes me very proud. I am delighted to be regarded as a "family member of WWE" (as one of the McMahons recently told me).

If, by chance, I somehow left out anyone who believes they should have been included in this book—wrestlers, promoters, former coworkers—please forgive me and bring it to my attention. Know that it was not intentional, I just cannot recall every step of the 45-plus years spent plying my trade.

To the fans who have made me a part of their lives—and asked for this book—thank you for your years of support. I enjoy meeting you on my trips around the wrestling world and love chatting about the old days, as well as the current sports entertainment scene.

Two final notes: I want to thank Greg Oliver for pushing me to write this book, sparkling up the chapters and mentoring me throughout the process. Authoring a book is totally different than writing magazine columns and stories; I had no idea how much of a newbie I would be at this craft. I could not have done this without him! Secondly, most of this book does not follow the chronology of my career. I wanted to make a book that you could just pick up and dip into—because that's the way I like to read. Yes, I am a "chapter jumper."

Enjoy the "Apter chapter" jumps . . .

IT'S NEVER TOO LATE TO START AGAIN

ONE

I was enjoying lunch with my wife and son at Philadelphia's XFINITY Live! restaurant on a beautiful, sunny Wednesday afternoon in early September 2014. Halfway though the meal I felt nature calling and excused myself. Down a long corridor leading from my table, I bumped into an acquaintance I had not seen in years.

"Bill Apter, how the hell are you?" he said. Then, before I could reply he asked, "I guess you retired? It's nice to see you again." I followed him as he rushed away. When I caught up, I tapped him on the back. He politely turned, and I could tell he was in a hurry, but I had to tell him, "I'm not retired. As a matter of fact I'm doing more now in the wrestling business than I ever did. I'm still with 1Wrestling.com, doing appearances on the WWE Network, writing semi-regularly for WWE.com, appearing at wrestling conventions, helping persons with disabilities find quality employment and entertaining at senior homes. I am not retired, and I never want to be retired. I love what I do."

"Really? You're doing stuff for WWE? Cool!" Then he shook my hand, patted me on the back and left.

This scenario plays out a few times a month. People can't fathom I've been in this business for 45 years. Even when I saw the Great Muta at a TNA show in New York City and did an interview with him, he asked, *on camera*, "You're still alive?"

Thanks to a guy named Eric Paulen, and another guy named Paul Levesque, I feel like I'm just getting started again in the world of sports entertainment.

* * *

Let me explain.

In late 2012, I took a huge slap in the face. No one *physically* did anything to me, but it still hurt. I was backstage at the Wells Fargo Center in Philadelphia at a WWE *Raw* show. Going up and down the corridors, I saw a few people coming out of a makeshift studio. One of them was Stu Saks, who is a dear friend and the publisher of my old home, *Pro Wrestling Illustrated*. Being curious, I asked

what he was doing. Stu explained that WWE was producing a DVD that would chronicle and celebrate its 50th anniversary, and he was interviewed for the project. To say I was envious is an understatement. I was happy about Stu's participation, yet deep down it really hurt that I wasn't included. I had been out in the trenches since 1970, photographing matches, conducting interviews and making relationships that would last forever. I was there when Bruno Sammartino lost the World Wide Wrestling Federation title to Ivan Koloff. I was there when WWWF became WWE. I talked regularly with Vince McMahon Sr. I knew everyone, I had no enemies—or at least none that I was aware of—so why wasn't I part of this historical DVD or even the book that came out to coincide with it? Hell, I'm a reporter—a journalist—so I decided to investigate.

I telephoned a few of my contacts in WWE, and one of them said he would contact the people who produced it and get back to me. In a matter of hours I had the answer. I was told whoever was working on the project really didn't know that much about what I had done in the business. The producers knew about *Pro Wrestling Illustrated* and went that route. I was told it was "an oversight," and I would be called upon for future projects. My name was now on their radar.

Around the same time, I received a call from a friend named Eric Paulen, who is a filmmaker, producer, director and anything else you can think of when it comes to moving images. I first met Eric when he produced some amazing footage for a few WrestleReunion conventions I hosted. Coincidentally, at the time of the call, he had recently been hired by WWE as a producer for the fledgling WWE Network. He was involved in putting together a few shows that included *The Monday Night War*, *WrestleMania Rewind* and *WWE Countdown*. They had a bevy of talent coming in for weeks and were doing on-camera "talking head"-style interviews for the show.

At one point, he asked one of the other producers, "Why haven't you had Bill Apter come in here yet?" He was met with, "Who?" They then said they had no idea where to contact me.

This is no knock, but these producers were not longtime "wrestling people," and they had no clue where I fit into the scheme of wrestling's history. They knew all the current talent base but not much about the time when I was in my

prime.

After looking at the thousands of Bill Apter bits on the internet, Eric called me and invited me to be a part of some of the shows. I was thrilled; I was finally working for WWE in a capacity I always wanted—on camera, as part of the WWE broadcast world.

The next day, I sent Eric a thank-you email. For some reason, I thought I should send one to Triple H (Paul Levesque), as I know he oversees almost everything in the company.

I expressed to Triple H that I always wanted to be on the broadcast end of WWE, and these appearances for the network made that dream come true. He shot an email back that read, "On that note, I have an idea and eventually we'll talk about it." I filed that away somewhere in my brain. I didn't know if it was a line or whether it might go somewhere one day.

Not long after that, the DVD department called asking me to come in and be part of a few upcoming projects. To date I have appeared in several of them. I was part of the Paul Heyman DVD. It was my first appearance, other than old footage of me presenting awards on behalf of *PWI*. Next I was brought in to tell my part of the Jerry Lawler versus Andy Kaufman story for a DVD

As editor-in-chief of *WOW Magazine*, I was proud to present Triple H with the World's Outstanding Wrestler award in 2000. No one could have predicted that he would go on to become a major force in every facet of the business.

called *It's Good to Be the King*, and I also hosted an entire segment about Haystacks Calhoun for the *True Giants* DVD. Forty-five years in the business and I was finally part of an official WWE DVD.

In mid-2013, I was back at the Wells Fargo Center for a live *Monday Night Raw*. I walked into the catering area to schmooze with the talent. While there, I noticed Rob Bernstein, the head of WWE.com. I had met Rob a few times in the past and we kept in touch, and

I always hinted that I would love to write or do video interviews for the site. He waved me over to his small table and asked if I had a minute to talk.

"Paul [Triple H] and I had a meeting about a few things a week or two ago, and he mentioned he would like you to contribute to WWE.com when you have time," he said. I couldn't believe it. I was on the network, appeared in a few DVDs and, not long after the meeting, started contributing to the website on a semi-regular basis. Another dream come true!

WWE doors seemed to be opening for me at lightning pace. Just days after author Brian Shields called me and asked for a quote he could use in the *30 Years of WrestleMania* book, a huge opportunity came. In late May 2013, I received a call from Randy Helms, Triple H's executive assistant at that time. He told me that "Hunter" wanted to personally invite me to the grand opening of the WWE Performance Center in Orlando, Florida. Although there would be a lot of other press there, Randy assured me that Hunter had only personally extended the invite to a chosen few. That incredible event happened in June and I was allowed to do interviews with Triple H, Stephanie McMahon and others. It also gave me face time with a lot of the top WWE brass and superstars.

A few weeks before *WrestleMania XXX*, I was invited by a few WWE executives to *WrestleMania* and the WWE Hall of Fame ceremony. One of the emails I received around this time was from Jane Geddes, Triple H's "right-hand person." A total professional, Ms. Geddes told me

My heart was beating.

that Paul wanted to discuss an idea with me. I told her that I would be at the *WrestleMania* press conference at the Hard Rock Cafe in New York City and perhaps we could talk there.

That day was a zoo, with tons of press and fans around. We connected only once. As he was leaving the stage at the end of the press conference, he saw me, walked over, shook my hand and said, "I'll call you in a few weeks. It was just too hectic to talk today."

In late May, I was driving on the Pennsylvania Turnpike one evening and my cell phone rang. It was Karra, one of Triple H's executive assistants. She told me Paul was on the line and wanted to talk. I pulled off the road and onto the shoulder as fast as I could. My heart was racing.

"Apter, listen, remember I told you I had an idea? Well here's what I'd like to do. I want to shoot a pilot show in Florida with you interviewing some of the legends. I'm not sure about the format, but I want to at least see what this looks like with you on our TV and how you interact with the talent." He went on to tell me that someone would arrange to send me to Orlando to tape the interviews on the day of the *NXT* taping. Before our conversation ended he said, "Let's do this and see what happens. It has to go through the proper channels and that could take some time after it's shot and edited."

In the early morning of June 11, I was picked up at home in a limo, brought to the Philadelphia airport and landed in Orlando a little over two hours later. Our pilot

show-taping was scheduled for June 12.

I was taken to the WWE Performance Center, where I spent a few hours hanging out with NXT and WWE talent and trainers. I was supposed to go to the hotel but was told that the taping would be one hour later (and one day earlier than the taping was scheduled) and that things had to be rearranged. I was told that I would be doing

In June 2014, I hosted a pilot show for a possible future series on the WWE Network. The format was me chatting with wrestling legends. Larry Zbyszko (rear left), Terry Taylor (center) and the late "American Dream" Dusty Rhodes were my guests.

three different segments: one with Dusty Rhodes (topic: *Starrcade*), another with Terry Taylor (subject: Mid-South Wrestling) and the final one with Larry Zbyszko (about: Bruno Sammartino). For the third one, Renee Young would be brought into the mix to see how a three-way interview would work, just in case the one-on-one wasn't smooth enough.

Before I could even think about what was happening, I was whisked into a makeshift studio with a dozen or more crew and the expert direction of Chris Chambers and Michael Cole. I changed from my jeans and shirt into a suit, was brushed with some makeup and then it was onto the set where I was seated face-to-face with Dusty Rhodes. I was told to spend about 10 to 15 minutes with Dusty.

Here was my moment. Chris Chambers pointed to me and I was on. I heard myself say, "For the WWE Network, this is Bill Apter"—and then I stopped suddenly. I wasn't nervous, and I hadn't frozen on camera. I just could not believe what I heard myself saying. I tried a second time and again it happened. Finally on the third take I got into my rhythm and was going full force. After about 15 minutes and a hearty round of applause from the crew, pilot segment number one was complete. This was followed by another good segment with Terry Taylor, and finally Zbyszko with my cohost Renee Young.

When it was all over, Michael Cole came over to say how good he thought the segments went. Then Chris Chambers and the other members of the crew all had nice things to say. It felt really good.

The next day I was a guest at the *NXT* taping. It was there I got to talk to Triple H. He told me he heard it went really well (as did his "gal Friday" Jane Geddes and WWE agent/talent scout Michael Hayes). Triple H told me he would be in touch. He added, "No promises, Bill. We will see what happens."

No matter what the decision is, I cannot thank him enough for making a real dream come true.

While people my age are retiring, I am just starting again.

"For the WWE Network, this is Bill Apter . . ."

I *really* love the sound of that.

ATTACKED!

TWO

Wrestlers are much bigger than me.

That doesn't stop them from manhandling me like I'm a heavyweight. Either spontaneous or planned, most of the attacks have not been much fun. They did, however, make for very colorful and highly interesting stories.

Abdullah the Butcher holds the record for number of attacks.

The first incident was in 1971, during a dressing-room visit at the Utica War Memorial Auditorium in Upstate New York. Abdullah was sitting on a bench taping his hands with long rolls of gauze. Standing near him was his manager for the night "Beautiful" Bruce Swayze.

"Hey, wrestling photographer," Swayze called as he waved me over. "Can I have your camera for a minute?" I introduced myself to him and he said, "Oh great. The magazine readers will love this." I had no idea what he was talking about until a moment later. He requested that I lie down on the floor, and told Abdullah to pose over me to make it look like the "Madman from the Sudan" was attacking me. "The readers will go nuts when they see this," he assured me. I was game. After all, it was a still photo.

I lay down on the hard, cold concrete floor near a set of lockers while Abdullah searched for something in the dressing room. Swayze moved back to make sure he would get both Abdullah and me in the frame. As I lay there waiting, I saw Abdullah approach me

> **Oh great. The magazine readers will love this.**

with a huge metal garbage can. He held it high above my head and looked like he was going to crash it right into me. Swayze yelled, "Freeze you two, this is a great shot!" The flash went off about three times as he shot the photo from a few different angles. He smiled and said, "Great!" At that moment, Abdullah followed through and tossed the can on me, full force, laughing as it hit. Damn, it really hurt. He put out his hand to help me get up and laughed as he said, "That was good, kid!" He

patted me on the shoulder, went back to the bench and put a huge cigar in his mouth. He looked like a gigantic bully sucking on a lollipop after beating up some nerd. Swayze gave me back my camera, I put it in my bag and was just about to leave the dressing room when Abdullah (in broken English, of course) said, "See you at ringside. Be careful. Sometimes I lose myself out there and even attack the ringside photographers!" I was absolutely terrified less than an hour later when his match against Tex McKenzie spilled out of the ring. Abdullah looked across the ring to where I was and began chasing me! Luckily, as I saw my entire life flash before me, I ran into the audience. I had never been so scared—until the next time he got me . . .

It was in Atlanta many years later. Abdullah was wrestling Tony Atlas. This time "Abby" not only chased me, he caught me. As I shot photos, Abdullah reached for me and pulled my head into the ring apron. His near 400-pound body was crushing as he punched me on the top of the head. I finally worked my way out and was about to run away when he grabbed my tie and pulled me back. Then, he

IS WRESTLING FIXED?

I thought wrestling was fixed! But it became all too real photographing the matches at ringside. Here an enraged Abdullah the Butcher tries to remove my head at the Omni Coliseum in Atlanta in the mid-'70s.

started eating my tie! I quickly untied it and it slipped from my neck, and he put the whole thing in his mouth. That was it. I ran back to the dressing-room area for safety. The few wrestlers who were watching the match from behind the curtain were laughing, but I certainly was not. He hurt me—and ruined a perfectly good tie. Another photographer around the ring, Emmy Yates, got a photo of him trying to yank my head off. On the way out of the arena, fans treated me as though I was a hero—just for being attacked by Abdullah! I was "over" in Atlanta.

In a Detroit hotel room in the early '70s, I was doing an audio tape interview with Pampero Firpo. I also had a photographer with me. Before I started the interview, Firpo was such a sweet, soft-spoken, pussycat kind of guy. As soon as I pressed the record button, he became the "superior animal" he always professed he was. Just five minutes into the interview I asked him if he thought he could beat the NWA, WWWF or AWA World champions. He growled, "What you mean do I tink? Meester Reporter, I could beat dem. I know I can beat dem!" At that moment, he grabbed my shirt and began tugging at it until a few buttons flew off. He held my shirt until he was sure the photographer got the right shot. I kept the recording going. When I finally ended the interview, he went back to that nice, soft-spoken guy. He apologized and offered to buy me a steak in the hotel restaurant. I turned him down. Those few minutes rattled me a bit, and I just wanted to go back to my room and put on a different shirt.

***

George "Crybaby" Cannon was another one who really got heated during interviews. In 1975, in a Florida hotel (Cannon was working as a manager there for Pedro Martinez's IWA promotion), we set up to record an audio interview. The plan was that eventually Cannon would get angry at one of my questions, grab a towel that happened to be on the couch and begin choking me with it. Referee Tommy Young, who was "in a room nearby and heard my screams" was then supposed to run in and pull the huge Cannon off me. It was all set, right?

Wrong.

With the recording started and a photographer taking photos, I asked "Crybaby" very innocently, "Why do you interfere in matches?" That was the cue. So he got the towel and began choking me—for real! Tommy Young took forever to get into the photo to stop Cannon. The photos were shot on black-and-white film, but if they were in color you would have seen my face turn red and nearly blue before Young got George to release the towel.

George was a jolly, great guy, but he didn't know his own strength. He apologized for weeks about that incident.

***

"Wild Bull" Curry was plain nuts. The first time I ever met him was in Detroit in 1973. I walked into the dressing room at Cobo Center, and he was being examined by the attending physician. While he was seated and getting his blood pressure checked, I asked if I could do an interview when he was finished with the doctor. The doctor told me not to bother him right now as it could affect his pressure. Fair enough. When Curry got up, I offered a handshake and he said, "In a minute." About half a minute later, I was ducking large floor-standing ashtrays being thrown at me! One, two, three ashtrays were thrown until I left the dressing room totally confused.

After interviewing a few "normal" wrestlers, I was at ringside shooting photos. Curry was in a brawl with Ed Farhat, the original Sheik, and Curry lost by disqualification (what a surprise). Stupidly, I climbed onto the ring apron to get a photo of him snarling at the fans. I figured it would be a great perspective. Moments later, Curry charged at me and began pulling my hair (I had such a nice head of hair in those days). My camera dropped to the floor with a thud, and he started punching me in the face. *Jeez, I thought this was supposed to be fixed, and no one really gets hurt*, was all I could think. Next he pulled me through the ropes, and I thought I was going to die. All of a sudden, babyface Tony Marino came to my rescue. As soon as Curry saw him head to the ring, Curry shot back to the locker room like a lightning bolt. Fans cheered as Tony raised my arm. I was over in Detroit then too.

> **He was convinced that wrestling was fixed.**

***

Here are a few other times I wondered how "fixed" wrestling really was . . .

Sometime around 1988, during a match in Memphis between Curt Hennig and Jerry Lawler, I got caught between them at ringside. Curt looked at me, grabbed a chuck of my thinning hair and got Lawler in the same position. He then cracked our heads together. I saw stars and fell to the ground as Lawler got right back up and into the battle. I sustained a nice lump on the head.

In Philadelphia in the mid-'90s, I brought my friend Joe Baum to an ECW match. He had been begging me for years to bring him to a live show, so one night I obliged. No matter what I would tell him, he was convinced that wrestling was fixed. "Bro-Joe," as I fondly refer to him, is one of those people you cannot convince otherwise. This night, the show was at the famed ECW "Bingo Hall," where the fans were as hardcore as the wrestlers! Joe was given a front-row seat, and as I was shooting photos I watched him smile—he really enjoyed the ECW action. During a match between

Terry Funk and Cactus Jack, I again got caught in the middle of two wrestlers. Funk looked at one of the regulars in the front row that had a real cast-iron frying pan in his hand. Why, you ask? Because this was ECW! Funk was offered the frying pan and instead of attacking Foley with it, he clocked me on the head. You could hear the "clang" throughout the arena and the chants of "EC-Dub" over and over as I nearly fell unconscious. They continued to brawl, and as I got up and backed into the guardrail, I could feel a huge lump forming on the side of my head. Joe was hysterically laughing as the cobwebs cleared and I began shooting the match again.

After the show the fans outside chanted for me as Joe and I got into my car.

I was over in ECW.

Joe laughed and said, "Billy that looked so real. You know how to fake it so well."

Even the lump on my head couldn't convince Joe the incident wasn't fixed! He even had the audacity to question if the frying pan was real!

* * *

Perhaps the most well-known attack perpetrated on me *was* staged.

Even today at the conventions people ask me about it and some bring the article from the magazine for me to autograph.

It was 1973, and Stan "The Man" Stasiak was destroying his opponents night after night. I got the idea to call his manager, Ernie "The Grand Wizard" Roth, to ask if I could somehow be a victim of the heart punch to tell readers what the experience felt like firsthand. Ernie loved the idea and suggested that he, Stasiak and I show up at Madison Square Garden at 4 p.m. on the day of the next show.

Two weeks later, there we were. Ernie was in his wizard gimmick, and Stasiak had his wrestling garb on and his right fist taped. That was the hand that administered the all-too deadly heart punch.

With a photographer (my father) in position in the bathroom area of the locker room, we did this photo session in four shots. In the first shot, Stasiak held my left hand and elbow just slightly up near my head as he took aim at my heart. Shot two showed him "hitting" me with the big taped fist and a look on my face like I was about to pass out. In shot three he held me while I collapsed to the floor. The final photo was me on a stretcher with Wizard gleefully standing over me showing the world what had happened.

I was "taken to a nearby hospital for observation" of course. Wizard commented that Stasiak did not hit me with the force he would have hit someone like Pedro Morales.

I was over with the magazine readers.

Hundreds of letters poured into the magazine office. They commentated on either how brave I was—or how stupid.

* * *

Other "quick" attacks:

When I was the "Commish" at WXW in Allentown during the early '80s, manager Supremely Great slapped me during a setup skit and I literally saw stars. It was as hard a slap as the heart punch may have been from Stasiak. At Georgia Championship Wrestling, manager Gary Hart had Don "The Spoiler" Jardine put the clawhold on my face in a story similar to the "wanting to see how a punch feels" Stasiak story. At the urging of manager Fred Blassie, in the early '70s, Willie "The Wolfman" Farkas lifted me up like a baby and tore my pants. That took place backstage at Madison Square Garden. In mid-2012, Matt "Doink" Borne threw a playful punch at my mouth as he was "kidding around" backstage at a New Jersey independent show. The "playful punch" went right into my mouth and loosened some bridgework!

Was all of this a bit terrifying? It certainly was. But I wouldn't have traded this "terrifying fun" for any other job in the world.

PUBLISHED

THREE

One day in 1959 changed my entire life. I was 14 years old and a rabid wrestling fan. It was a Tuesday night in late summer when my dad and I went to a show at Sunnyside Garden in Queens, New York. After buying two general admission tickets and a program for 25 cents, I saw the same vendor, Joe DeLall, hawking a box of wrestling magazines. It was the debut issue of *Wrestling Revue*. To me, this was a must-have, and I begged my father for 50 cents to purchase it. Dad reached into his pocket, no questions asked, and moments later I had the Fall 1959 issue in my hands.

Between matches, I was either reading the magazine or running up to the ring to try to get some wrestlers to autograph it. At home later that night, I recall reading it cover to cover. It had such a great feel. The magazine was printed on slick, glossy paper and most of the photos were in stunning color. It fully captured my imagination. Little did I know that I was holding my future.

Somehow, I had a sense that I wanted to be involved in a wrestling magazine. Not knowing how to pursue this, I decided to put out my own "fanzine." I called it *Wrestling Stars*. I typed the news from wrestling shows I saw on TV, and then re-typed 10 copies that I would hand out to my friends in school. For photos, I went to a thrift shop that had a machine with pro wrestling postcard-sized pictures for five cents each. You didn't know which one you would get, but I bought 10. There were Bruno Sammartino, Primo Carnera, Pampero Firpo, Sweet Daddy Siki and a few others. The 10 magazines all had the same stories, but the cover photo was different—the luck of the draw from the machine.

I put out *Wrestling Stars* for a few weeks, but the rigors of school made it too difficult for me to keep it going. However, I didn't stop buying *Wrestling Revue*. Most times I bought two copies so I could cut one up and put some of the photos on my wall at home. *Wrestling Revue* also had great two-page pinups in the centerfold, all of which made their way to my wall. My room was all about wrestling.

As the years progressed, *Wrestling Revue* changed its look and feel. It was because the original publisher, Stanley Weston, was no longer the owner. The "flavor" of the package changed under the new ownership of publishers Lew Eskin and Burt Randolph Sugar (yes, the famed boxing journalist-broadcaster-publisher). In later years, Norman Kietzer joined the team.

After the ownership changed, I purchased the magazine only a few times a year. I was still a passionate wrestling fan, but the magazine didn't thrill me enough to collect them. I just thumbed through it when it came to the local store. Then in late 1970, I made my first move to get published by a real wrestling magazine. At that time in my life, I was buying time on New York radio station WHBI and doing celebrity interviews. I called the promoter, Mike Rosenberg, at Sunnyside Garden and asked if I could get dressing-room access to an upcoming show. In exchange I would promote upcoming events on my radio show. Mike put me in touch with the local WWWF contact, Oscar Conill, who approved my request. This would be my second venture to the Sunnyside facility as a journalist, the first being roughly eight years prior when I cohosted a comedic talk-radio show called *Billy's Place* with a friend named Jim Keogh. We were allowed to interview Bruno Sammartino back then. Oscar remembered how respectful we were and that helped get me in this time.

With my tape recorder and camera, I climbed down the small staircase from the arena floor into the dressing room, one that I would visit dozens of times in the following years. My dad accompanied me, since I needed someone to work the camera while I was interviewing the wrestlers.

All the wrestlers were very receptive to me, as Mr. Conill had told them I was okay. I interviewed Victor Rivera, Arnold Skaaland, Tony Marino, the Black Demon, Mike Pappas, Bill White and Tony Angelo, manager of Bepo (who would become Nikolai Volkoff years later) and Geeto, known at that time as the Mongols.

The interviews were aired on my show as well as on the plugs for the Sunnyside shows (I still own these tapes and have run some of them on 1Wrestling.com). The relationship

Ray Candy (left) and "Bad, Bad" Leroy Brown flank my father, Nat, at the West Palm Beach Auditorium. The duo known as "The Zambuie Express" were monsters in the ring, but they didn't scare my dad!

grew, and Oscar asked if I could help write press releases that they mailed out to the people who signed up to get the "What's Happening at Sunnyside" newsletters and flyers. I was now writing for a real company, but the pay was nonexistent—I did it for free. It kept me in Conill's good graces, and it helped put me over with the wrestlers.

I decided to transcribe my interview with Tony Angelo and send it to *Wrestling Revue*. Along with the story, I sent a photo of my father posed with the Mongols in the dressing room (the one of me didn't come out for some reason).

A few days later, I received a call from Lew Eskin who told me they loved the interview and would publish it in their January 1971 issue with Jack Brisco on the cover. I would be paid $35 after the magazine was on sale. My magazine career had officially been kick-started.

When the issue came out, there were a few problems. First of all, the interview with Tony Angelo had, as the main photo, the image of my dad with Bepo and Geeto. The caption read, "Tony Angelo and his team, the Mongols."

I don't know who the proofreader was, but not knowing there was a country called "Croatia," I typed "Crow Asia." That's the way it read in the magazine. To this day, there are people (especially *Pro Wrestling Illustrated*'s editor Stu Saks) who still rib me about that.

Weeks later, no check had arrived. I called Mr. Eskin, and he told me many times, "The check is on the way." I didn't like that. It wasn't the money, but the principle of doing business. *Wrestling Revue* looked like a major heel in my eyes now.

I was proud of getting published, and I showed people the story at every opportunity. The local magazine-soda-sandwich shop had me sign a few copies for them. One night, while going to see if that issue was selling well, I noticed a new magazine right next to *Wrestling Revue*. It was called *The Wrestler*. I thumbed through it. It was more like a tabloid—not my style. But when I looked at the staff box, I noticed the publisher was Stanley Weston—the man who invented *Wrestling Revue*. Perhaps I would take the rest of my interviews to him. Maybe this would be a better business model for me.

A few days later, another transcription was in the mail along with a letter explaining who I was. I received a letter from Mr. Weston two weeks later—he wanted to see me face-to-face.

We would meet for the first time a few weeks later.

JALART HOUSE INCORPORATED

P. O. Box 58 • Rockville Centre, New York 11571 • Phone: 516-678-4959

PUBLISHERS:
INTERNATIONAL BOXING
WORLD BOXING
BOXING ANNUAL
THE WRESTLER
INSIDE WRESTLING
WRESTLING ANNUAL
BIG BOOK OF WRESTLING

PUBLISHER: STANLEY WESTON
EDITORIAL DIRECTOR: BOB WATERS
MANAGING EDITOR: ROBERT J. THORNTON

October 17, 1970

Mr. William S. Apter
Aptko Media Productions
62-19 53rd Ave. (Suite 5M)
Maspeth, Queens, NY 11378

Dear Mr. Apter:

Thank you for your letter of October 1, and for the series of wrestling photographs you sent along. Some of them were quite good and there is a good possibility that we can use them in the near future.

I am interested in the transcripts of the wrestler interviews you've done and would like to have a list of all the transcripts you have available. I am sure we can make a satisfactory financial arrangement if they contain the kind of information that meets our requirements.

However I am thinking about other things we can possibly do together. Wres___ ___agazines are a small part of our publishing operations. Perhaps we can have lunch together in New York City someday in the near future. At that time we can discuss everything.

Give me a call at the number shown above and we'll set up the luncheon. I usually have these kind of meetings at the Men's Grill at either the Roosevelt or Vanderbilt Hotels. I assume getting to that part of town (just opposite Grand Central Station) would be convenient for you.

Sincerely,

Stanley Weston
Publisher

SW/bt

The reply to a letter I sent to Mr. Stanley Weston that put the key in the ignition and got my life in the wrestling business on the road.

MR. WESTON AND ME

FOUR

T he luxurious Biltmore Hotel on Madison Avenue and 42nd Street was where I first met Mr. Stanley Weston. We got together over lunch at one of his favorite spots in the building, The Men's Grill. After a few minutes of discussing what to order, he quickly got down to business.

"How do you get those interviews and backstage pictures?" he asked.

I told him that I was buying time on a local FM radio station and got my press tickets that way. He was surprised and explained that most promoters didn't like press, because most of it was negative. I explained that I told the local promoters that I wasn't looking to do any exposés, I just wanted to cover the matches like any reporter would cover any sport, and that seemed to be the key. At that point, he went over his history from working an as office boy for *The Ring* magazine to his creation of magazines *Wrestling Revue, Boxing Illustrated-Wrestling News* and *Wrestling Illustrated*. He explained that his offices were once in New York City but were now housed in his home in the Long Island town of Rockville Centre. He needed someone to work in the office to file wrestling and boxing photos, do some writing, and help the art and layout department. I told him I was interested, and he offered to give me a trial run. I would work for three days at the rate of $25 per day. The workday would commence at 9 a.m. and end as late as I could stay. Under the company name G.C. London Publishing, the magazines he was publishing were *The Wrestler, Inside Wrestling, Wrestling Yearbook, Wrestling Annual, World Boxing* and *Boxing International*. He also published two Western magazines that dealt with life in the Old West.

After I accepted, we shook hands and he gave me two sets of instructions. They were, "You will see things in the files and hear confidential things that you must agree to keep that way. I do not let many people into my home and business. Also, do yourself a favor and stop being so polite to waiters. They are

> I wasn't looking to do any exposés.

here to serve you, not enjoy your company. All they want is a big tip, and I took care of that." Then, another handshake, a bit of confusion on my part regarding that last piece of advice and we parted company.

I went home and told my parents about this, and they were thrilled. My dad asked if he could meet Mr. Weston one day to thank him for this opportunity. I told him to let me get my feet wet first, but that after a few weeks I would see if I could arrange it. I was very close to my parents, and I knew that my father wanted to check Mr. Weston out to make sure this was on the level.

One week later, I was on the Long Island Rail Road headed to the Rockville Centre train station. After Mr. Weston picked me up, we stopped at the post office where I helped him gather the huge bags of mail that his magazines had received—both editorial comments and subscriptions.

We arrived at his home a few minutes later. It was a small, modest house. As we went into the front door, we were greeted by his sheepdog and wife, Hope. Mrs. Weston had a lovely, welcoming smile and shortly introduced me to their daughter, Toby; later, I would also meet their other daughter, Barbara.

We put the mail down on a green table in the kitchen, and Mr. Weston explained that this was where all the magazines he created were brought to fruition.

"From the days of us being poor, living on cans of tuna, to today, this table is where it all happened," he said. We then headed to the "editorial department." Cutting through his living room, he introduced me to his mother-in-law, Mrs. Patrick, who was in a wheelchair due to an accident.

We climbed a short set of steps and arrived at Mr. Weston's desk. There was a Royal typewriter and dozens of photos and layout boards awaiting approval. He also had a small collection of pipes and tobacco. I soon found out that his love for smoking created a tobacco-smelling workplace at times. But he was the boss.

To my right, working at another desk, was editor Steve Ende. I introduced myself. "This is our wrestling expert," Mr. Weston told Ende. "He might also be after your job, so you'd better watch him." Ende smiled, told me to ignore Mr. Weston's "unusual sense of humor" and assured me I would get used to it after some time. I had

a flashback to the first day I met Mr. Weston and his crack about waiters.

Next it was into another room down the hallway, a bedroom converted into the art department. There were Charlie Sargent, Karl Hlavac and Charlie Foster hard at work creating layouts for the magazines. In the following days, I met Weston's copublisher and writer Robert Thornton and writer Jeff Super, who had dropped in to pick up assignments.

After a few minutes, Mr. Weston took me down to the basement, where most of my work took place. He showed me the filing cabinets, dozens of them, and the thousands of photos waiting to be filed—both wrestling and boxing. There was also a photo darkroom the size of a small closet. I told Mr. Weston I knew how to process and print black-and-white pictures and that I would be glad to add that to my duties.

"The photos we get from our freelancers are the lifeblood of the magazines," he pointed out. "When I feel I can trust you, maybe I'll let you do it." I was not ready for the cold honesty of a reply like that. If this was the romance period of the job, I was becoming concerned about what would present itself in the next few days.

I shot a lot of great fights for the boxing magazines Mr. Weston published. Here I am on my way to knocking out one of my favorite people, former world champion Larry Holmes.

The routine stayed the same: picked up from the station, then to the post office, then to the house to work. One afternoon as he was driving me back to the station, I asked if my father could come to meet him. He didn't hesitate to say yes. My dad drove out to meet him toward the end of my next workday. It was such a nice meeting. My dad thanked him for giving me my break, and Mr. Weston told him what a nice kid I was. My dad drove me back home, and we were both very happy. Mr. Weston's sarcastic sense of humor was nowhere to be found.

The next morning, I was in the basement and Mr. Weston called on the intercom requesting I come up to editorial. It was just he and I, and he asked me to sit.

"You brought your father in here to check me out, didn't you?" he asked, apparently irritated.

I assured him that was not the case. I told him how close my family was and that they were part of

27

everything I do.

"Your father has a horrible hairpiece!" I could not believe he said that. I was stunned. Then his face softened like I had never seen before, as did his mood. "Tell him he'd look better without it," he said. "I just want to tell you that you showed what type of person you are by the way you talk about your parents. I can tell you are good in character, and I'm glad to have met you. If you want to start working here more hours a week, I would be glad to have you. Go home, think about it, tell your father to get rid of that horrible wig and let's move on!" I smiled, gave a salute (he was a former air force major) and a "Yes sir, I will see you tomorrow" and walked to the train station. It was more than a mile away. I didn't think to ask him for my usual ride back that day. It was beautiful and sunny out, and I was on a roll.

Things progressed in the weeks that followed. He and his wife left for a cruise. While he was away, I used his darkroom to process all the black-and-white rolls of film from the freelancers (he hadn't given me permission to do that) and left prints of the best shots waiting for him on his desk. When he returned, he was both surprised and grateful. From this tiny darkroom

to the one in our eventual office in Rockville Centre, those stinking chemicals would be a sweet smell that would take me further in my chosen career.

* * *

A few days after I began in the office, Mr. Weston let me take over the gossip column, "Here's What's Happening, Baby!" He was well aware that I knew what was going on, since I watched hours of wrestling on TV every week. In order to get the dirt from places outside of the New York area, he called various correspondents throughout the United States and told them that I was "the wrestling guy" now. He put me over!

There were no computers. Whenever I made an error, I had to take the paper out of the typewriter, rip it up and start all over again. If I were halfway through, I kept going and then Steve Ende edited the copy by hand. Next it was typeset and sent to the art department. After I pulled the photos from the master files, my column was finished. I also picked photos for most of the stories in the magazines and keyed where I thought they would work best in the layout. If the artist had another idea, he would consult with the editor or

Mr. Weston, and sometimes it went in his direction.

As the years progressed, some editors, artists and writers moved on to other companies or other careers. The only constant for me was Mr. Weston. As my boss, I felt he was very demanding, but that helped make me better at my job. He gave me all the tools I needed. He replaced my little $49 Minolta camera (which I had used to photograph Bruno Sammartino lose the WWWF title to Ivan Koloff and so many other matches prior to that) with my first Nikon F. If I came back to the office after photographing a show and a photo exposure was a bit too dark or a bit too light it went right in the garbage. With 36 exposures available on a roll of film, Mr. Weston expected 20–25 of them to be near perfect! When I brought the processed film to him (color slides), I used to sweat as he inspected them and tossed the ones that didn't meet his standards. In the first few months that meant a lot of my photos went straight to the garbage bin. That number decreased as I learned out in the field.

As far as the writing goes, I had no formal training. The boss liked my columns, but he tore up my feature stories after reading a few lines. He would sit me down and very sternly tell me, "Your problem is you're trying to write like a writer. It's not good, because you're not a writer and I can see that. What I want you to do is write the way you talk. I listen to you talk on your radio show and that's what I want in our magazines. I want the readers to hear your voice."

He was a lot more patient as time went on, but I was made for columns. I would write a few obits (he really liked those), because I knew the particular wrestler's history—but other than that, it was, "Here's What's Happening, Baby!" and eventually "Names Makin' News" (that one I coined).

Our talks became a daily occurrence. He would ask me what's going on in wrestling, we'd talk about "MacMann" (that is how he pronounced it), Sam Muchnick, Jim Barnett and other promoters. One day he received a call during our meeting from his old friend "Kangaroo" Al Costello. Al told Mr. Weston that he and Don Kent were going to win the United States Tag Team belts in Detroit and wondered if he could send someone to cover it. Al suggested "That nice boy, Billy" that he had met at Madison Square Garden a few weeks ago. What Mr. Weston didn't know was that Al had told me that he was going to call Stanley and ask me to come down.

He knew Stanley would not refuse. They were that close.

Mr. Weston offered to send me on a flight to Detroit. Instead, I told him that at the matches I had made a friend who told me he was planning to go to Detroit soon—and maybe Toronto on the same trip. He had also become friends with Costello that same night at Madison Square Garden. That new friend was George Napolitano. I didn't tell Mr. Weston that George was working for *Ring Wrestling*; I knew Mr. Weston wanted me to get exclusive coverage. A few weeks later, I went on my first road trip.

My career continued to progress. Eventually, I didn't have to ask Mr. Weston if I could go on a trip. He gave me an open option to call the travel agent and go where I needed to if I thought it was important to the magazines. It lasted through most of my years with him. I never abused the privilege and he never offered that to anyone else.

* * *

Through years of work-related criticism and praise, I felt like I was the son Mr. Weston never had. When I went through a divorce (from my first wife) he told me to take some time off—at his expense—to get my mind back on my work. He knew how close I was to my parents and suggested I book some time in West Palm Beach, Florida, where they lived. He suggested I call Eddie Graham at the Florida office and "travel with the boys for a week or two." He knew I would love that, as well as have time to see my parents.

When my current wife and I wanted to buy our first condo on Long Island, not far from the office in Freeport, he gifted us $10,000. When the company was sold to a new publisher in Pennsylvania, he gifted us another $10,000 toward a new home. Who could ask for more? I had a boss who looked after the needs of me and my family. It was a great job.

It would take another entire book to write everything that happened in both my personal and professional relationship with Mr. Weston and his family.

I do need to deal with two painful issues here, however. The first was his decision to sell the magazines in 1993. I knew Mr. Weston was shopping around for a buyer and finally settled on Mr. Nick Karabots from Pennsylvania, a wealthy man who owns publishing, printing, farming and real-estate businesses, among others.

When the staff on Long Island

first met Mr. Karabots, we were impressed—he's a charming and savvy businessman. He did indicate that the entire staff was welcome to move to Pennsylvania and continue their jobs. He spoke of changes to some of the magazines that he felt would make them more profitable. Those changes were not necessarily editorial, but were things like reducing the dimensions of the product to make it more cost-effective. I felt like the wrestling magazines were my babies and I didn't want anything to change, but there was nothing I could do about it.

Craig Peters, Stu Saks, a few of the artists and I all moved our families and headed to Ft. Washington, Pennsylvania. With the new owner came some changes that I had to get used to, including a major change to the magazine's budget. Gone were the days of traveling whenever I wanted to if I thought a trip was "worth it." But I do know this was done for the good of the company: profits just weren't as high as the peak years with Mr. Weston.

> **The wrestling magazines were my babies.**

However, I did like some of the other changes. I was put partially in charge of *Country Music Magazine* (Craig Peters was the editor along with Ms. Camille Pomaco), overseeing photography and some interviews. The best thing though is that I still had a steady income, and Mr. Karabots made sure of that until I finally resigned to go to *World of Wrestling Magazine*.

The other painful issue was Mr. Weston's health. Even though we were living in Pennsylvania, I called him regularly and visited him on occasion. On one of those trips, around February 2002, I went to see him at the old office in Rockville Centre. He had lost a lot of weight and told me he had cancer. He died in April of that year.

At his funeral, after his family spoke, the clergy person asked if anyone wanted to come up and say a few words. I didn't hesitate, and these words came out naturally . . .

"My parents were responsible for my birth. Mr. Weston was responsible for giving me life."

HOW APARTMENT WRESTLING NEARLY COST ME MY CAREER

FIVE

I remember it just like it was yesterday. Sometime during 1973, publisher Stanley Weston called me into his office to show me some pictures sent in by Theo Ehret. Based in Los Angeles, Theo was our photographer at the weekly NWA Wrestling shows at the Olympic Auditorium and was one of our best. The quality of his work was magnificent. I always loved being handed a package that came from Theo, so I could see all the shots, action and posed, before they were even considered for publication. Part of my job was to identify the wrestlers in the photos and put a sticker with that information on the back.

One of the most memorable shots Theo took was of "Maniac" John Tolos tossing a medicated powder into the eyes of Fred Blassie on the set of an NWA show. It blinded Blassie and was the catalyst behind their classic feud. Then there were the shots of competitors like Mil Máscaras, Victor Rivera, Black Gordman, Goliath and Ernie Ladd, among others. Theo was also our shutterbug whenever a big boxing event was in Los Angeles or Las Vegas. He shot at the training camps of fighters like Muhammad Ali and George Foreman.

However, on this particular day in 1973, the photos Mr. Weston gave me to include for possible publishing were not wrestling or boxing. They were 8" x 10" prints of incredibly sexy bikini-clad ladies in wrestling poses. My question was, "What are we going to do with these—what magazine are they for?"

"They're going into one of our wrestling magazines," he said. "Probably *Sports Review*. Put sticker tags on them to read 'Apartment Wrestling.' I want to see how this sells."

Sports Review was not a hot-selling title. Weston wanted to find a way to increase the sales, and this was his plan.

I didn't express my feelings that I felt these salacious images did not belong in a wrestling magazine. Kids who were wrestling fans bought the magazine, so this seemed wrong to me. A few months later I realized I wasn't alone in my thoughts.

I made it a regular practice to bring copies of *The Wrestler* and *Inside Wrestling* magazines to the shows I covered, mainly in the New York area. On one 1973 trip, I also brought two copies of *Sports Review*. I really didn't want the wrestlers to see this magazine with an Apartment Wrestling photo on the cover. However, I had promised Chief Jay Strongbow that whenever he was featured in one of our magazines I would make sure to bring him a copy.

It's 1970 and I'm ready to interview Joe "Chief Jay Strongbow" Scarpa at Sunnyside. We became good friends through the years, but "Apartment Wrestling" always remained a very touchy subject!

IS WRESTLING FIXED?

I was backstage at Sunnyside Garden in Queens, New York, handing out *The Wrestler* and *Inside Wrestling* when Bill White, a journeyman wrestler, came from behind me and slipped a magazine out of my camera bag.

"Whoa, what is this?" he said. "When did you start taking photos of naked women wrestling?"

Oh my God. What I thought would be bad was now turning into something horrible. Sunnyside had a little hole-in-the-wall dressing room, and White's gawking brought everyone right to us. I tried to explain to White that I was going to slip this to Strongbow very quietly, but that wasn't going to happen now. Of course, Strongbow saw the cover and immediately asked, "What is this crap doing in a wrestling magazine? Why is my picture next to them?" In the meantime, Baron Scicluna, Dominic DeNucci and a few others asked if they could come with me the next time I took the photos. I assured them I was not the photographer, but they all laughed it off as, "Bullshit, Bill!" DeNucci was trying to be nice about it when he said, "Billy, don't put my picture in a magazine with naked girls. I

> What is this crap doing in a wrestling magazine?

don't like that. It doesn't go in a wrestling magazine, that stuff." Strongbow passed the magazine back to me saying, "I can't take this home. Thanks for putting me on the cover, but, please, no more sharing the cover with the girls. If you keep doing this just don't bring me a copy. I don't want to see it." The nail went into the coffin when Gorilla Monsoon, who was the agent for the show, picked it up, tossed it across the room and said, "You can tell Weston this doesn't fly!"

The next day, I went right to Mr. Weston and told him what had transpired.

"That's too bad," he said. "We got more photos from Theo. We're going to continue this feature and see how the sales go." I hated his decision, but he was the boss, and after only three years with him I was still walking on eggshells.

The interaction with the wrestlers was terrible, but worse news came a few months later when sales figures for two issues of *Sports Review* with Apartment Wrestling features came in. Weston was right; sales had soared. I was called into his office and was told, "They love it and we're going to make

34

Apartment Wrestling a regular feature!" It devastated me. I was the one in the field who had to deal with the wrath of the wrestlers. So I made the decision to not bring copies of *Sports Review* with me to any shows. That backfired too, as wrestlers still picked up the magazine at the airport to see if their photo was in it. They always questioned me, and I gave them the real answer. "It's not me, it's the publisher. The magazine is selling really well so he's not going to stop." Eventually, some of the wrestlers got used to it and would ask me to bring a copy to the next show.

Vince McMahon Sr. and promoter Willie Gilzenberg hurried over to me one night while backstage at Madison Square Garden. Willie had a copy of *Sports Review* in his hand. He always liked Mr. Weston. Vince, on the other hand, was not a Weston fan (I'll explain more about this later).

"I want you to tell Stanley we don't like this," McMahon said as he took the magazine from Willie and pointed to the Apartment Wrestling photo on the cover. I explained that he knew it wasn't popular with most wrestlers, but it was with readers. "Well, I don't know how long you'll be welcome around here if this keeps up," McMahon exclaimed and he

stormed away. Willie, in a calmer state, suggested, "Talk to Stanley. See what you can do."

My pleas to Mr. Weston fell on deaf ears. He told me I could assure Willie that he got the message, but Apartment Wrestling would not stop.

Apartment Wrestling didn't go away until nearly 10 years later. I don't know if it was because of declining sales figures or Mr. Weston finally tiring of hearing complaints from everyone in the business or a combination of both, but the feature finally ended.

Apartment Wrestling's best team was writer Dan Shocket and photographer Theo Ehret. Dan created most of the storylines, and his alter ego was "Millionaire playboy Apartment Wrestling impresario" Dave Moll.

Although there were Apartment Wrestling writers before Dan, the Shocket-Ehret era was indeed the golden days of the "sport."

Young Dan Shocket died from cancer in 1985. To the persons who doubt that Dan existed, I can assure you that he was a very real living, breathing and wonderful human being. Theo lived to the ripe old age of 92, dying in May 2012. He even published a photo book called *Exquisite Mayhem*, which was a photographic collection of many of his best Apartment Wrestling photos.

At this point I have to come clean. Whenever the wrestlers asked if I had photographed Apartment Wrestling and said "No," I told a little white lie. In the mid-'80s, when Randy Gordon was one of our editors, he had convinced two model friends to pose for an Apartment Wrestling photoshoot. His apartment was just five blocks from our office in Freeport, New York. He needed a photographer and Mr. Weston told him to use me. Did I enjoy that photo session?

On a personal note, to my dear friend Missy Hyatt: I know you think that I did all the photography and even dated the Apartment Wrestling gals, but alas, you now know the true story . . .

I miss Theo Ehret.

And I miss Dan Shocket.

But I'm glad Apartment Wrestling is dead.

A DAY AT THE OFFICE

SIX

Most people think my career is a whirlwind of glamor, travel and wrestling shows, night after night, but that's not true. Although I've traveled quite a bit, I spent most of my time in the publishing-company office as part of a team who put the magazine out. A lot of what I did was, well, office work. A while ago, I wrote down what a usual day at the office consisted of during my days as a full-time magazine guy. Here's what my day was like at the Long Island office of *PWI* circa 1980:

I'd leave home around eight, and a half hour later I'd go into the file room to begin filing the hundreds of wrestling and boxing photos that were used in the most current issues (that was until I was allowed to hire an assistant to do this as well). If any photo was not properly identified with the name of the subjects, as well as the date and place it was shot, I was responsible for labeling the photo too.

Next, I'd go to the current magazine plan-sheet to see what stories were in a particular issue and where the photos were coming from. If I saw, let's say, pages 20 through 24 had a feature on Dusty Rhodes, I would get the type for the story, read it and decide what photos I thought would complement that piece. Sometimes I would go to the photo logbook and find a proof sheet with certain images that I had in mind, and then I'd pull the negatives, go into the darkroom and develop the photo. This was true with most every layout. Next the photo and the type would go to one of the editors (let's say Stu Saks), and he would accept or reject the photo choice. Once it was approved, it was up the stairs to the art department to talk with one of the layout people (let's say Ken Morgan) to discuss the lead shot and which other photos were most important. The artist could also reject the order of the photos if he didn't think it would complement the layout.

After doing this for several layouts, I would call various wrestling offices, wrestlers and promoters to gather news and find out if they were running shows we should send a photographer to (if it was newsworthy, of course). From there, I would call the various photographers and assign them to cover an event.

Once a week, usually Fridays, all the editors would sit around Saks's desk for an editorial meeting about what would be in the upcoming issues. My job was to have a list of the new photosets that had come in and pass it around so ideas for story angles could be formed. Most of the time, the angles were tied to whatever angle that particular wrestling office was doing. Sometimes we would go off on our own and create what we thought would be a better-selling magazine story. It would be my job to let the promoters and wrestlers know what was coming, and if they didn't agree—well most of the time we went with it anyway . . .

I used to sit for 15 minutes or so in Mr. Weston's office to chat about the business. I did most of the talking, as he wanted to hear what was going on and I had my finger on the pulse of the sport back then. I could see in his face that he fed off my enthusiasm and it invigorated him. I miss those sessions. Besides wrestling, we would also talk about the boxing trips I went on—I got to photograph some great fights. I met many of

My entrance into the boxing community at a press conference in 1971. I'm "sparring" with former World Middleweight champion Rocky Graziano (left) as famed boxing and wrestling ring announcer Johnny Addie (right) hams it up with us.

his old boxing friends, like corner-man Al Braverman, fighter Rocky Graziano and many others.

And when there was a lag in a day's work, there was always some photo filing and photo processing to do.

One of my other daily routines would be to visit the local photo store where we had the freelance and in-house color photos pro-cessed. It was there—at least when it came to my photographs—that I was able to toss out what wasn't good before Mr. Weston could see it. He was very demanding and wanted to see everything after it was processed (especially my work, as I was a house guy on salary).

I would also write my columns, of course, some stories, and log incoming photos and negatives into the master file book.

That was a typical day at the office.

Throughout the years, I asked a lot of wrestlers what they thought I did for the magazines. Most of them thought I owned the company. Many figured I got paid for shooting photos at the shows. The truth is most of them didn't have a clue. They thought I was the *sole* person at the magazine—that I wrote every story and published the magazines and was a millionaire. Sorry, wrong on all counts.

My job was just that—a job. I never got paid per photo. I was hired by Mr. Weston in 1970 and put on a salary. It didn't matter how many photos I took, how many columns I wrote or how many miles I logged, I was a salaried employee. That held true from Mr. Weston to the man who purchased the company, Nick Karabots, to *WOW Magazine* and to the U.K.'s *Total Wrestling* magazine as well. It was never a freelance gig for me, thank goodness.

APTER'S ONE NIGHT STAND WITH MADUSA

SEVEN

I t was a cold winter day in 1986, when I flew into Minneapolis-Saint Paul to report on and photograph a few of Verne Gagne's AWA shows. I was supposed to be picked up at the airport by AWA producer and referee Al DeRusha, but for some reason Al couldn't come. Instead he sent one of his newest TV wrestling stars, the lovely Madusa Miceli (who, as the character Alundra Blayze, was inducted into the 2015 WWE Hall of Fame). I had never met Madusa before. The drive from the airport to the AWA TV studio took about 25 minutes and we quickly became acquainted. We mainly talked about wrestling politics, her goals and our mutual friends in the business. She was attractive, sarcastic, witty, funny and intelligent. We went on to become dear friends and we're still in touch a few times a year.

Madusa worked one or two matches that

night. Afterwards, Verne Gagne suggested that she take me out to dinner and a club since she was my ride. He gave her some money to treat me. I had heard that Verne was pretty "tight with the dollar," but he was very giving this time. Madusa was glad to do this. We would go for some Japanese food and then to a place with a live band and dancing.

We went to a small eatery, stayed about 90 minutes and then drove about 40 minutes to the club. As we neared the parking lot she told me, "I feel safe here. There are a lot of clubs where the guys are all over me. They know me from TV, and it's really annoying to have guys hit on you when you're trying to enjoy a place. It's different here. I really like it, and I come quite a lot."

As soon as we walked through the door it took only an instant to understand why no guy in this place would hit on her. It was clear many of the guys here knew her, as greetings of "Hey, Duce" and "Madusa ba-by" could be heard as she pulled me through the crowded dance floor to the bar. A few couples waved to us and tossed hand kisses.

As we planted ourselves at the bar, a few guys came over, pointed to me and asked, "Who's this?" They were eyeing me up and down—remember this was 1986, and I had a lot of jet-black hair and was dressed in a dark shirt and tight jeans. *She* wasn't being hit on, I was! The couples I watched dance were guys.

After five minutes of chatting with her friends, she put her arm around me and whispered in my ear, "I've got to find the little girls' room, Billy-Boy. Keep my friends company, I'll be back in a few!"

So here I was, a straight guy in a very non-straight situation. After a couple of minutes, I also felt the urge to visit the men's room. Everyone was very polite and said I should hurry back so we could talk. They were curious about what I did and how I knew "Duce."

As I exited the bathroom, I saw Madusa back at the bar with the same small group we were with a few minutes ago. She had already clued them in about what I did. I had offers to dance from some and was even asked for my business card for possible freelance photography opportunities. I eventually relaxed and handed out my cards, and I even gave in to dance—with Madusa!

An hour or so later, we left the venue and got back into her car. I never heard anyone laugh as hard as Madusa as she put her arms around me and thanked me for being "such a good sport!" I laughed along with her. The joke was on me, but it had all been in fun. It was finally over—or at least I thought it was.

Early the next afternoon, Al DeRusha picked me up at my hotel to drive me to the next town for a sport show. As I got in the car, he didn't wait a split second to quip, "I heard you had quite a fun time last night!"

It didn't end there. That night in the dressing room, most of the guys on the card made like they were "hitting" on me! Madusa came in laughing and made sure everyone could hear her say, "Hey, Billy-Boy, all the guys said you were great last night!" I stared her right in the face and yelled, "I told you not to tell anyone about my personal business!" A roar of laughter rocked the locker room and we all went back to business as usual.

When I recently saw Madusa in Philadelphia, we spent a few hours at a pub. There was karaoke that night, and where there is karaoke there is me, singing. As I got up to do John Michael Montgomcry's version of "I Swear," I dedicated it to Madusa and "the boys."

I swear she knew what I meant.

HOW APTER FOUND OUT BRUNO WAS GOING TO LOSE

EIGHT

On January 18, 1971, I felt like a secret agent. For the first time in my life I was given some important information and vowed never to tell anyone. Although it was an incredible burden to bear, I somehow got through it, and I can now reveal the secret told to me in the highest confidence all those years ago.

This story begins in publisher Stanley Weston's home in the suburban town of Rockville Centre, New York, where dozens of filing cabinets containing many thousands of wrestling and boxing photos were stored in his basement. There were also dozens of drawers containing historical newspaper clippings and magazine articles collected by Mr. Weston throughout the years. Many of them had rare press-credentials and handwritten letters from wrestlers and boxers.

On January 18, 1971, around mid-afternoon,

Mr. Weston summoned me to his office. He instructed me to sit down near him and not say a word—just listen. He informed me he had something of a very highly confidential nature to tell me. "You cannot tell anyone what I am going to tell you," he stressed. "Not even your parents!"

Oh my God, I thought. If he doesn't want me to tell my parents, this really has to be earth-shattering. Was he plotting some kind of illegal activity and wanted my assistance? I had only known the man a few weeks at this time. Living with my parents, Weston knew I always discussed what went on at the office when I arrived home each day. He was also very well aware that my father regularly accompanied me to the matches. He sat next to me when I photographed the action at ringside.

> You cannot tell anyone what I am going to tell you.

I assured him I would keep his secret. I could not even fathom what bombshell he was about to drop.

He took a few moments to get his thoughts together by puffing several times on a pipe he enjoyed smoking. Finally taking the pipe out of his mouth and putting it on an ashtray he spoke.

"Tonight when you go to [Madison Square Garden], something major is going to happen."

I was totally spellbound.

"I'm going to tell you about it but keep in mind that this conversation never took place. If I find you repeated this to anyone I will deny I told you, and you will never be welcome in my home again. Get it?"

I nodded and he continued.

"I just got a call from Willie Gilzenberg, the WWWF promoter, that Sammartino is going to lose the title to Ivan Koloff tonight. He wanted to make sure I was sending you with a camera. I don't know what the finish is going to be, so make sure you have plenty of film and keep shooting. This is the biggest thing to ever happen in the business, and I am counting on you to bring back the best photos! Again, we never had this conversation. I'll see you tomorrow."

I had just been tipped off about what would become one of the biggest stories in the history of pro wrestling. Bruno had held the WWWF belt since May 17, 1963, beating "Nature Boy" Buddy Rogers. Tonight that incredible reign would come to an end and I knew about it hours before it was going to happen. It was my first "I have to kayfabe this" moment of my career.

I took the train home to Maspeth, Queens, packed my camera and about 15 rolls of black-and-white film to shoot the entire card. I was not experienced enough at this point to try to shoot on color film. Black-and-white had a lot of exposure latitude. With color you had to be totally accurate. We needed images for sure, so no experimentation tonight. As backup

my father had another camera and he was going to shoot right next to me in a press seat, as he had been doing for many shows. He drove us to the subway and we took the train to 34th Street. We talked about the matches and when he brought up Bruno versus Koloff I almost broke kayfabe.

"Dad, I gave my word to Mr. Weston that I would not talk about the Sammartino match," I said. "Please don't be mad but I don't want to break my promise to him." He didn't pursue the issue, but I think he knew what was

Here I am sitting between two greats—Bruno Sammartino (left) and Larry Holmes (right)—at a dinner in Atlantic City honoring athletes who appeared on the TV show *Greatest Sports Legends*.

going to happen when I said, "Just make sure you shoot a lot of pictures of that match so we don't miss anything."

Looking back, I have to laugh. We were about to photograph one of the most historic matches in history, yet neither Dad nor I had a "real" camera. He had a cheap Kodak "Instamatic" drop-in-load-film camera. It was totally amateur. Mine wasn't much better. I had a $49 35mm Minolta AL-F model camera. History was about to be made and the two photographers shooting for the wrestling magazines had subpar equipment.

When we arrived one hour before showtime, the hallway backstage at the Garden was extremely hectic. There was Vince McMahon Sr., wrestlers, promoters, people just hanging around and my father and me. We both shook hands with everyone, even people we didn't know. Then we came face-to-face with Willie Gilzenberg. He knew I worked for Mr. Weston, but I didn't know if he knew that I knew about the upcoming title change. The secret was safe with me. He greeted us warmly and after exchanging a few pleasantries he questioned, "Did you bring your camera?" I pulled the trusty Minolta out of my camera bag and he smiled. "Have fun and take lots of shots. And tell

Stanley I said hello," he said. Dad and I headed to the ring.

We shot the prelims and then it was time for Sammartino against Koloff. As soon as the bell rang we clicked picture after picture. About 18 minutes into the match Koloff caught Sammartino with a kick that floored him. Ivan began to climb the ropes. At that precise moment, I could sense this was probably the end. I told my dad, "I think something's going to happen here, take a lot of shots!"

Koloff perched on the top of the corner post and came down with a knee-drop on Bruno. It was "the finish." A three-count later and the world was stunned as "The Russian Bear" had done the impossible. We rewound the film in the cameras, tossed them in my bag and headed home. I felt like such a heel not telling my father I knew what was going to happen.

The next day, I brought the film to Mr. Weston for processing. Days later I was filing photos, and that unmistakable click of the intercom sounded. It was Mr. Weston asking me to come up to his office. He had the Sammartino-Koloff photos back from the lab. I was a nervous wreck. I didn't know if any of the photos were useable.

"Your father's pictures are too grainy, but he got the finish," he explained. "Your photos are grainy too. I'll have to look into getting you a good camera. Maybe a Leica or a Nikon. By the way, your shot of the finish came out good. We're going to use it in the story about Sammartino losing the title." I was thrilled! Then Mr. Weston added,

"Willie Gilzenberg called and said you were very respectful to everyone and if you knew about the title change you hid it really well. If you keep this up, you'll go a long way in this business. Good job, kid! Now get back to work."

Just another day at the office . . .

REVEALED: SOME OF MY SECRET CONTACTS AND HOW RATINGS WERE DONE

NINE

One of the most popular features in the magazines was the wrestling ratings. These were the Top 10 listings of wrestlers in several key categories ranked from one to 10 with the number one spot being the "Best in the World" of a particular federation. (CM Punk would have hated that system.) We regularly ranked the Big Three—the National Wrestling Alliance, the World Wide Wrestling Federation (which became WWF and then WWE) and the American Wrestling Association—when I first began my tenure with the magazines. Tag teams had their own space, as did Women, Most Hated and Most Popular. There was also an overall Top 10. Keep in mind that the ratings changed in layout and design, and additional wrestling companies were often added to or subtracted from the mix.

Most fans took these ratings very seriously,

as did the promoters and wrestlers. Sometimes the ratings were taken much too seriously, and that could make my job out in the field quite uncomfortable.

First let me explain how the "Official Wrestling Ratings" in *Pro Wrestling Illustrated*, *Inside Wrestling*, *The Wrestler* and *Inside Wrestling* magazines were compiled.

Once or twice a week I would spend many hours on the telephone calling most of the wrestling offices around the United States to gather information. I always had an established point of contact in each company. If my contact wasn't available, there was always someone else willing to talk to me, as they usually understood the value of the publicity derived from the ratings.

When I first started in 1970, I knew a lot about my home territory—WWWF—as I lived in a suburb of New York City and watched their TV shows. As for the rest of the wrestling world, I knew about them from what I read in the magazines, so I had a handle on what was happening almost everywhere. One of the first jobs my mentor, Stanley Weston, assigned to me was creating the ratings. If I was unsure about a certain territory he would assist me or call one of

the offices and put me over to the person in charge, explaining that I was smart and it was safe to give me information.

Even though I worked under three different editor-in-chief administrations at the publishing company, the routine of how the ratings were done never really changed. The only fine-tuning that occurred was during the Stu Saks era. Previous editor-in-chiefs Steve Ende and Peter King were not avid wrestling fans. Although they were well-educated journalists, they left the decisions about the rankings to me. I was never second-guessed. On the other hand, Stu was a huge wrestling fan. He had even published his own newsletter during his teenage years. So there were times that my ratings copy was questioned. This even happened when he was just an editor under the reign of Peter King. I had no issue with that, and it felt good to know that there was a second pair of eyes making sure the list was as accurate as possible. Sometimes we butted heads and sometimes I won. No matter, it was all to benefit the educated wrestling reader.

When the magazine's deadline approached, I went into ratings mode and made my calls. It would take a day or two—remember there was no email, this was all by telephone. I was at the mercy of catching people at their office or at home. I always loved this part of my job.

I would usually start by calling Willie Gilzenberg (who was one of the main promoters of WWWF). Willie's life was always in the wrestling and boxing business, and he was always receptive to talking to "Stanley Weston's boy," as he called me, even though he knew I wasn't Mr. Weston's son. I would run through a list of WWWF ratings that I had already prepared from the TV shows, and he usually said, "It's fine, run with it." A few times a year he would suggest I talk to Vince McMahon Sr. to see if he had any new talent coming in that he wanted planted in the ratings. Vince never ordered me to do anything but sometimes he suggested something like, "You might want to put Billy Graham in there if this doesn't come out for a few months." Gorilla Monsoon was another office person I talked to if Willie or Vince weren't available. Like Vince, he would make suggestions that would help the magazine's ratings match what was happening on TV.

Going down my list, I would next call Verne Gagne's American Wrestling Association office. My contacts there were promoter

Wally Karbo, Verne's son Greg or program producer and referee Al DeRusha. I rarely talked to Verne about ratings or angles, as he was in his kayfabe mode at all times. The few times I had asked a pointed question, he made like he didn't know what I was asking. It was hard to get any real information from him. He knew I spoke with the other three regularly, but he didn't want to funnel any info to me directly. When all else failed and I couldn't get anyone in the office, my next call would be to either Bobby Heenan or Nick Bockwinkel. I had struck up a really close business and personal relationship with both of them and had their trust. I usually listened to 10 minutes of Bobby's great jokes before he would get to the matter at hand. Wally Karbo was the most candid, but he made sure I knew to never mention to anyone in his office that he leaked anything to me (even though they all knew). I assured him I wouldn't and like all my other wrestling contacts, I never broke anyone's confidence.

I had a good working knowledge of the Florida territory as the shows were aired on a New York Spanish-language TV station. Even though I used the television shows to create the ratings, I always called just to be sure nothing had changed between airings. Gordon Solie was my go-to guy there. He had a wealth of information and he really understood the true value of the magazines. He would talk business to me from the office but most times asked me to call him at home later in the evening. There he felt he could chat a bit more freely about office politics and where he thought various angles were going. I had to be very careful about the information Gordon fed to me, as he sometimes embellished a bit too much after a drink or two.

Gordon always promoted the magazines on Florida TV and we appreciated it. As a matter of fact he became the very first broadcaster to have his photo on the cover of one of the magazines. When Gordon wasn't in and it was deadline time, Dusty Rhodes would get on the phone in a flash, and say, "Willie, you know what's right to do by us. I'm busy, just do it—I trust

The *Pro Wrestling Illustrated* achievement awards ensured both the magazine and I got face time on TV. Here, Florida Championship Wrestling's broadcaster Barbara Clary and I present James J. Dillon with the 1982 Manager of the Year honor. [Photo courtesy of Bill Otten]

you!" Perhaps besides Gordon, J.J. Dillon spent the most amount of time talking to me. He was very eloquent and remembered storylines perfectly. Through the years J.J. and I became close friends. When he left Florida for other territories, we maintained our relationship, which still holds steadfastly today. I also sometimes talked with Mike Graham and Buddy Colt when Gordon wasn't there.

Perhaps the longest time I spent on the phone was when I called Bill Watts's Mid-South promotion. The key man there was "Good *young* J.R.," Jim Ross. Jim was the only contact who gave me too much information—but that was a good thing. When I would call and ask for the ratings, he would give me the rundown of the most recent TV taping in complete detail and then suggest who to put where in the listings. Remember, we were on a deadline, and sometimes a call would last 30 minutes. Eventually, one of the main editors would hustle over to my desk and whisper to me, "You've got to get off the phone already." But when I tried to rush Jim, it never worked. Regardless, I am so grateful to him for taking so much time to make sure I was totally clued in. I did talk to Bill Watts at times when Jim couldn't get to the phone and

Bill would usually give me his version of who he thought should be in the Top 10 and what placement position they deserved. He was all business and not very social on these calls.

In the Kansas City NWA office, I had the choice of Bob Geigel, Harley Race, Terry Garvin or Pat O'Connor. I actually requested a different one each week. This was so I could get to know each of them equally—good politics, in my opinion!

Bob Geigel always greeted me with a: "Hello, William!" Harley's raspy voice wanted to know: "Bill Apter, what are you up to today?" And Pat O'Connor's greeting was: "Billy Boy, how are you and my old friend Stanley Weston?" I didn't speak with Garvin as often as the other three, but he was a pleasant person to talk to when I did.

It was fun to call Georgia Championship Wrestling and speak with Ole Anderson. Yes, you read that right! I enjoyed talking with and dealing with Ole Anderson. Most people have written how they hated to talk to Ole. What they didn't realize is that if you treated Ole in the same manner as he treated you, he was a great guy. I'd call and he would blurt out, "What the hell do you want? I'm busy, Apter!" My retort was, "What the hell do you think I want?" We'd exchange some other barbs and get down to business. I recall getting a big laugh out of him one time when I suggested that he must have graduated with top honors from the Don Rickles Charm School (Rickles is the most brilliant insult comedian in history). I would also want to know what time he would have to be home to walk his pet rat! Ole gave me all the information I needed, and I found a side of him that many were never able to get from him.

Beside Ole, I would get information from others in the office, including agent and referee Ron West or broadcaster Freddie Miller. Freddie was always a bit gun-shy to talk. He exuded a paranoia that was shared by most people who worked in a wrestling office. He did not want to be accused and fired if information was leaked. Freddie would tell me a bit and then ask me to call back when Ole was there.

Two lovely ladies, Louise and Janie were always there to help me as well. They knew it was okay to talk to me, so if the guys were on the road and it was deadline day I could get my listings from them.

Although we didn't cover Puerto Rican wrestling in a big way, once a month I would call the people that ran the World Wrestling Council. They were Carlos Colon and Victor Jovica. During those calls, both of them would rally to get more coverage. We did try to give them more when their TV show ran in the New York area, but the story and rankings never became a regular part of the listings.

World Class Championship Wrestling was a hotbed of wrestling and one of the key territories. The man responsible for almost all of the excellent information I received was booker Gary Hart. Gary was so very precise with everything he told me. Gary also picked my brain about certain angles and how I thought they would go over. He was a pleasure to deal with, and I looked forward to calling him. Sometimes I would talk to company-owner Fritz Von Erich. It was always a very business-like discussion with Fritz, unlike the casual and candid times with Gary. At times, the phone would be answered by legendary Bronco Lubich. He was pleasant but did not want to give me details about anything. He would quickly say, "Hold on, I'll get Gary for you."

Jim Crockett Promotions' contact was usually Mr. Crockett. He was very casual and candid with me, and I became accustomed to calling him, like everyone else who knew him, "Jimmy." He was glad to go over ratings with me, and any other questions I had about his promotion were mine for the asking. He had a lot to do with the magazines and was a big help in getting me national TV exposure, but that's explained in another chapter. I became a close confidant and friend to him, and for many years we talked on a daily basis. We talked wrestling gossip, news and office politics nearly every morning around 9:30 a.m. If I didn't call him, he'd call me. We had a great bond.

Calgary was a different story. I would talk to Stu Hart. Anyone who knew Stu knew that he never told you what you needed to know until he told you some stories first. He'd tell long stories about his days as a wrestler or how he trained this one or that one. He equaled Jim Ross in time on the phone but not quite for the quality of information. Stu was a great character. At times his lovely wife Helen would answer the phone and scream out to him, "Stu, it's Bill from New York! Hurry up, it's a long distance call!" Just a few years before they both died, I visited them while they were in New York to see their son Bret in a match at Madison Square Garden. Stu pulled out a Hart baseball cap from his bag and

both he and Helen autographed it for me. I still hold that hat dear to my heart, and it resides in "Apter's Alley" with all my memorabilia.

Stu was actually a pleasure compared to another information source. Every month, Austria's Otto Wanz would send me audio cassettes with news, results and rankings. His voice was deep and he spoke very slowly with a very thick accent. He filled an entire one-hour tape. I usually listened to most of it. They all started off the same, "Hello, Bill, dis esss Otto. Here is vat happened dis month." I appreciated the tapes but dreaded listening to them—it was quite a task.

We move on to Portland, Oregon. Similar to Puerto Rico, we didn't do a lot of coverage of this area. The main reason was that we didn't have a regular correspondent or photographer there. I talked directly to promoter Don Owen. No matter how many times I spoke with him, he always said, "Who is this and waddaya want?" I explained the same reason each time and he would tell me to call back later and talk to his son Barry.

The lovely Lia Maivia was a pleasure to call. She was the grandmother of Dwayne "The Rock" Johnson and part owner of Polynesian Pro Wrestling, another "sometimes covered" promotion. She was one of the easiest people to get rankings from. I wish she were alive today to see what an incredible megastar her grandson Dwayne has become.

The Pensacola, Florida, territory was owned by the Fullers. They were brothers, Ron and Robert, and father, Buddy. Ron West, who I mentioned was in the Georgia office, was my key guy here.

I will never forget the calls with Texas Southwest Sports promoter Joe Blanchard and Houston Wrestling's Paul Boesch. They both owned their own very successful promotions in different areas of the state. Both were total gentlemen and always happy to help.

The St. Louis Wrestling Club was run by legendary promoter Sam Muchnick and was the heart of the National Wrestling Alliance. I never called Sam directly for information, as he had his own in-office staffer for that job: Larry Matysik. Just like Jim Ross, Larry could stay on the phone for hours talking about what was happening in St. Louis. Larry was so thorough when he explained the happenings in his area. He loved the business. He was a true student and credit to the game of pro wrestling. In recent years, Larry has been dealing with some health issues, but he still has that glow in his eye when he talks about pro wrestling.

When I finished making the calls, I then transferred all my handwritten notes to the typewriter or the computer (actually a word processor). It took a long time. I look back now and wonder how I ever survived my early office days without my trusty Toshiba. The next step was for the art department to typeset the rankings. After that, I picked photos from the archives to use on the ratings page.

Due to the magazine publishing-lag, it took a few months from the time we all submitted our respective parts to when the magazine appeared on the newsstands. Therefore, the rankings represented the last day we put the magazine to bed and sent it off to the printers.

With the issue published on the newsstands, we always received ratings feedback via snail mail. The fan mail ranged from, "Who makes this crap up?" to "It's about time you recognized that my favorite wrestler is better than the bum you ranked ahead of him in the Top 10." The letters were fairly easy to deal with: either an editorial response in the next issue or a one-way trip to the garbage can. What was tough to comprehend though, was that some of the wrestlers and promoters didn't get it. This was a

One of the boxing editors having fun as I chat for hours with my wrestling news contacts.

"work." Most of it was completely supported by the wrestling companies I had called.

Once, I had received a call from a high-ranking member of the National Wrestling Alliance (I don't remember who it was now, 30 years later). He was pissed that we had the former World champion still listed as the current World champion. I had to explain about the publishing lag time to newsstands, but that still didn't appease him. "Make sure it's changed in the next issue," he said very sternly. "If not, we could take your photo credential privileges away!" Click and he was gone, and I shook my head in amazement as I told the rest of the staff what had just happened.

A lot of wrestlers also complained. Nearly every time I was backstage, a wrestler would call me over and ask, "Hey, can we talk about something?" Here's an example from the WWWF days. I liked Ivan Putski a lot, but he was always making an issue about his ranking being one spot lower than someone else, like Chief Jay Strongbow. "Hey, Vince [McMahon Sr.] didn't like that either," he would tell me. My reply would be, "Ivan we rate people based on how they are being used." He didn't like the answer, but it was true. My relationship with him always stayed very friendly despite his complaints on the issue. Keep in mind, he was just one of dozens who bitched about the ratings.

The Most Popular and Most Hated rankings mixed the federations. Wrestlers' egos ran wild if a placement was not what they expected.

When Dusty Rhodes ruled the Most Popular ratings, jealous babyfaces accosted me at the shows and called me on the phone, saying they were more popular than "that no-talent whale." (Yes, some of them actually said that.) The truth is, Dusty was red-hot and selling magazines. The sales figures and the amount of pro-Dusty mail we received supported that. He was never in our pocket, as some wrestlers accused him of being. He was just the most popular—that was the fact. We also had headaches when Bruno Sammartino was on the top of the lists. Wrestlers would complain that he was only based in the East Coast, so how could he be at the top? Again, it was the mail and sales that dictated what happened in the magazines.

I recall when the AWA and WWWF were upset that the NWA got the primary layout spot in the rankings (this was shortly after I started in 1970). I dealt with many telephone calls from AWA's Greg Gagne and the WWWF's Willie Gilzenberg, who both wanted to be where the NWA was placed!

The overall Top 10 category was also a complaint fiasco. Each of the major federation world champions took offense if he wasn't the number one guy. Wrestlers who I considered very levelheaded showed their best non-levelheaded judgment many times.

It was unreal—really.

> **Egos ran wild.**

FINALLY REVEALED: "MY CONFESSION TO A DECEASED WRESTLER!"

TEN

I enjoy marriage so much I've done it twice.

This story revolves around Tony Parisi (also known at Tony Pugliese), and it takes place during my first marriage. As a matter of fact, it was while my first wife and I were on our honeymoon.

My new bride nicely asked me to try to keep the wrestling business totally off my mind during what is supposed to be the most blissful, personal time newlyweds can share. I didn't know how I was going to actually accomplish that, but I gave her a "Yes, dear," as any other guy would have done under the same circumstances.

On a bright Saturday morning in April, we left Long Island and began our week-long vacation in Niagara Falls and Toronto.

We checked into the hotel late and grabbed a quick bite to eat. The next morning we started sightseeing. All was serene for the newlyweds, or so I thought. As we were coming out of an attraction, I noticed someone who looked like a wrestler. Through the crowd I saw his eyes meet mine and he called out, "Bill Apter, it's me, Tony Parisi!"

As he began walking toward me, my wife asked who he was and of course I said, "A wrestler." This was exactly what she hoped wouldn't happen. Tony playfully grabbed me and gave me a hug.

"How come you didn't tell me you were coming here?" he wondered out loud. "You know I own a hotel and a restaurant—I would have taken good care of you, my friend."

I introduced him to my wife, and she was very cordial to him. He was thrilled to learn about our marriage. The three of us chatted for a few minutes, and then he dropped the bombshell.

"I want you to take a picture of me with some of my friends tomorrow right by the Falls. You can use the pictures in the magazine. I'll take you guys to lunch afterward. You'll be my guests. Meet us here around nine!" More hugs and he turned and left.

My wife knew I was in a jam and she rose to the occasion and took it in stride. So much for not thinking about wrestling during the honeymoon. We were stuck— we had to do this.

About 20 minutes before the photo meeting, I went into my camera bag to put film in my trusty Nikon FM. I had used that camera the previous day to take what I hoped would be masterpiece images of the Falls. I was so anxious to get the film developed, I considered taking the rolls to a local Niagara Falls camera shop instead of waiting until I got home.

I found 10 rolls of film in my camera case, but they were all used. I started sweating as my hands moved faster and faster trying to find a fresh roll of film, but there wasn't one to be found. I had shot them all the day before.

In a near panic, I went to the hotel front desk to ask if there was a store open where I could buy film. The desk clerk informed me that the one store that had film didn't open until 10 a.m.

What was I going to do now?

Meeting time was quickly approaching. My wife and I headed to where we were scheduled to meet Tony. He was there, right on time, with a whole group of friends. To make matters worse, he insisted, "I need this shot on the cover of the magazine!"—A promise I could not make, since I wasn't the person

It's the calm before the storm as I check the photo equipment.

who chose the cover shots. Even if I was, I knew that a photo of Tony Parisi and his pals in front of Niagara Falls would not have been a big seller on the newsstands. I'm sure it would have done well in Niagara Falls and other areas he worked regularly but not on a national magazine cover at that time of his career.

Tony and his buddies lined up. I took out my camera and posed them at various angles for five minutes. No one, not even my wife, knew that I had no film in the camera. I had to make like everything was perfect.

With the photo shoot over, we declined Tony's lunch treat as we wanted to continue sightseeing. He understood, and as we parted he reminded me again, "I would like one of those shots on the cover."

The heat was off. I told no one

what I did. When we returned from our honeymoon I brought all the rolls of film, perhaps 20 of them, to a local chain called Fotomat for processing. A few days later when I went to pick up the film, the girl in the Fotomat booth told me they'd been misplaced, sent to some other Fotomat in some other location.

I guess somehow, it was payback for the Parisi incident. Not only did I not have the photos he wanted to see in the magazine, but I had no honeymoon photos either. Eventually they found three of the rolls, but the rest were gone.

A few months later I was covering some matches in Upstate New York, and Tony was on the card. Of course he approached me and asked what happened to the photos taken at Niagara Falls. He said his friends wondered when it would be on the cover. I had only one answer: "Fotomat lost all the film, including my honeymoon pictures. I'm so sorry."

During the next few years, I occasionally saw Tony while I was photographing shows in Upstate New York and Canada. In a kidding way he always brought up that photo shoot. He never let it go. There were more than a dozen opportunities where I could have told him, but I just couldn't do it.

Tony died on August 19, 2000.

I'm sorry I never got to tell him.

DID THE GHOST OF CURT HENNIG LEAD APTER TO GEORGE STRAIT?

ELEVEN

Curt Hennig was a fun-loving guy and I thoroughly enjoyed being around him. I first met Curt in 1979, when he was honing his craft in Verne Gagne's American Wrestling Association. I traveled much of the Midwest area with him, photographing his matches as well as the other bouts on the AWA card. Postshow, we would go out and discuss the business at whatever local Denny's Restaurant was nearby. After filling up on great, greasy culinary delights, we would find a bar to enjoy some entertainment—both musical and liquid. Let me state for the record, I am not a connoisseur of alcoholic beverages. I've never liked the taste of beer. Take me to a bar, and if Sprite, 7-Up or Sierra Mist is on tap, I am truly satisfied. If there is a cold bottle of orange soda, then it's drink ecstasy for me—I'm a cheap date. Although he knew I didn't drink, Curt always insisted on buying me a beer. He hoped I'd break down and give in, but I never did. Instead I would offer to buy him a Coke, which would elicit a hearty laugh.

Most of the bars we went to, as per Curt's choice, were country music establishments. He was a huge country music enthusiast.

At that time in my life, I was accepting of most musical genres. I tolerated everything, but I loved crooners. This will make some of you cringe, but I was a huge Barry Manilow fan and I still follow him. Country music was okay, but the real "twangy" stuff did not sit well with me.

In the '90s, I began to listen to more and more country, as it seemed all the easy-listening crooner tunes I loved were beginning to fade. Singers like Neal McCoy, Collin Raye and George Strait were recording some excellent ballads, and I was becoming a true fan.

Curt moved to the World Wrestling Federation in 1982. I saw him whenever he was in the New York area, but we rarely got to go out after the matches, due to his grueling schedule. It was a "Do the show, get in the car, drive a few hundred miles with some of the other talent to the next town, get a few beers, go to sleep, get up

and do the same thing" routine. It's one that all the wrestlers had to get accustomed to if they wanted to last in the business. He did that in WWF for two years before returning to the AWA.

Curt really blossomed as a wrestler when he went back to WWF in 1988 and became "Mr. Perfect." It defined his entire career. Even today he's remembered best for that role. Curt loved playing Mr. Perfect, and he really was great at it. The other role he had fun with was with World Championship Wrestling in 1999. It was there, along with Barry Windham, Kendall Windham and Bobby Duncum Jr., where he became the leader of "The West Texas Rednecks."

"It was great," Curt told me in an interview. "I didn't have to act. We were all about being rednecks and singing country music. We preached and sang about that horrible music that was dominating the airwaves. We called the song 'Rap Is Crap!'" The WCW fans loved it.

I saw Curt many times during his WCW run and we did get to hang out and talk wrestling and country a few times. At this point both of us had something in common: George Strait was our favorite performer. One night when we were driving and playing George Strait, Curt told me, "I know George's people. If you ever need a hookup for concert tickets let me know. You can even meet him." I thanked him but forgot about this very quickly. I was trained to do that. You see, I learned throughout the years that when a wrestler promises you something you really want, it's probably not going to happen. They forget what they told you and they probably told that same thing to 100 other people. They figure no one will call in the favor. I've had that happen dozens of times with wrestlers, so Curt's kind thought really went in one ear and out the other. It was nice of him to offer, though.

It was now 2003—almost two years since I had spoken to Curt. I was still a fanatical George Strait fan and I was thrilled to learn that his current tour was going to bring him to the First Union Center in Philadelphia, on February 7. Since I was living near Philly at the time, I had to get tickets—I had the fever. I went to the Ticketmaster website on February 1, but I was too late. The concert was totally sold out.

Around this same time, William Moody (Paul Bearer) instant messaged me on AOL. He was just checking in to say hello. I remembered he was also a big country

music buff and that George Jones was his idol. I decided to mention my George Strait dilemma to him, and he quickly chimed back with, "Call Curt Hennig. He's in Vegas with George and his managers."

I instantly remembered Curt's offer, and I was on the phone with him within five minutes.

"How many tickets do you need, Bill? I told you years ago I could hook you up." His words were beautiful music to my ears. I told him one ticket would be fine, I just wanted to go to the show. "I'll get you two," he insisted. "They will be at the box office will-call window. Call me the day after the show and let me know how you liked it."

I did ask if there was any way to get backstage to meet George and he told me, "Not this time, but we'll do it sometime down the road. Maybe when he's back on tour next year. I'll make it happen, Bill. I assure you of that!"

On Friday, February 7, 2003, along with my former *PWI* co-worker Brandi Mankiewicz, I witnessed an amazing show. George performed all his hits and some new songs. To this day, it's still one of the best concerts I have ever seen. To add to the pleasure of the night, we also had the best seats in the house. We were in the fifth row, dead center, just slightly above the stage. I would have never been able to score those seats on my own!

On Saturday, February 8, I called Curt to express how grateful I was for the tickets.

"You have done so much for me through the years, Bill. You don't need to thank me," he said. "It was my pleasure. What I would like you to do though is call one of George's management people, Steve Ford. He owns a club in Nashville called the Trap. He's the one who was able to juggle some things and get the tickets." He told me to wait until Monday, as Steve was away for a few days and wouldn't be back in Nashville until then. Curt also told me that he would be going to Florida for a few days, but I could always reach him on his mobile phone.

On Monday, February 10, around 2 p.m. Nashville time, I called the Trap and asked for Steve. I was told by the bartender that Steve would not be in, and he wasn't sure when he would come to the club. I struck up a conversation with the bartender, Andrew, who recognized my name. He said he would deliver my personal thank you to Mr. Ford. Andrew also mentioned that this place was Curt's favorite hangout in Nashville and had been there just a few weeks ago. It was a pleasant conversation and Andrew told me I should come on by the next time I was in Nashville and he'd buy me a drink or two.

After I hung up I called Curt but he didn't answer. I left a message on his answering machine.

In a moment that I will never forget, all the joy I felt over the past few days disappeared instantly. Just after leaving the message for Curt, I signed onto the internet and read an email from someone, telling me that Curt Hennig had been found dead in his hotel room in Florida.

I searched some wrestling sites and they all had the same horrible story. I called William Moody to see if he had heard about it, as I was hoping it was just not true. Unfortunately he had confirmed it with someone close to the Hennig family. It was just devastating.

I felt it was my duty now to inform Steve Ford. I called the Trap and bartender Andrew answered once again. He was near tears when I broke the news to him. Steve was not there but I was promised he would return my call. About one hour later, Steve, who had already heard the bad news from Andrew, needed to hear it directly from me. I felt sick. It was so hard talking about this.

That night I thought of Curt and how one of the last things he did in his life was make me—his friend—happy. He was a true and caring friend.

* * *

February 2004 was, I thought, just going to be a run-of-the-mill month. I had a few trips planned and one of them was to go to Nashville to photograph a TNA show.

I was shooting the matches at ringside, and while changing film I leaned on the guardrail that separated the fans from the ring. Someone came over, tapped me on the shoulder and said, "Mr. Apter, I don't know if you remember me. I'm Andrew. I'm the bartender at the Trap." I greeted him with a hearty handshake and a hug and told him to wait around after the show so we could talk. I was so glad to meet him. It had been just a few days short of one year since I made the call telling him of Curt's death.

The matches were over and Andrew and I chatted briefly about the events last year. He asked me how long I would be in town, and I told him I was leaving in two days. He explained to me there would be a private get-together for a few friends at the Trap the next night and he was sure that Steve Ford

would love to have me there. Sold. There would be nothing to keep me away.

I arrived at the Trap sometime around 8 p.m. Andrew greeted me at the door and walked me past the bar and down a long hallway to a dining room. There, seated at a high-riser table were five men and a blonde woman. Andrew pointed to the center of the group and introduced me to Steve Ford.

"It's been a year since Curt died," he recalled as he shook my hand. "I still remember your call." He introduced me to the people at the table, and the last person I met was a guy in a baseball cap named George. Yes, you guessed it. It was George Strait.

"Mr. Strait, do you remember me?" He smiled and seemed a bit confused. I cured his confusion with a joke, "You were singing your song 'Write This Down' at the First Union Center last year. I was in the mezzanine, section 327, and you waved to me!" A hearty laugh and he said, "Oh yes, I remember you very well!" We eased into conversation, and I told him and the rest of the group how Curt Hennig and Steve Ford got me tickets for the concert in Philadelphia. But my most important point was forthcoming.

"Before Curt died he promised

Was it fate, coincidence or the ghost of Curt Hennig that made this a "perfect" chance meeting with country music legend George Strait?

of them since Curt's passing, but I really wanted to share some time with them and tell them how much I loved their son.

I was sitting in the kitchen area of the museum when Mr. and Mrs. Hennig walked in. Larry remembered me and I asked him if I could tape a video interview for 1Wrestling.com. As we spoke, his wife listened, smiling. "He loves to talk," she commented after I stopped recording. It was at that moment I felt I had my opening and just blurted out, "I have a story to tell you about your son." It was uncomfortable for a few moments and in a whisper Larry said, "I don't think my wife can handle a Curt story." I should have not pursued it any further, but I did. "It's a really good story; please, I need to tell this to you." They both nodded okay.

As I slowly unraveled the entire George Strait tale, you could see a misty look in both their eyes. Yes, it was hard for them, but it was also heartwarming. When it was over, we all hugged and both of them agreed they were glad to know about the wonderful gift their son gave to me.

I guess you could say it was just *perfect*.

me that I would get to meet you," I explained. "Now about one year later here I am talking to you." A solemn moment of quiet cast upon our small gathering as we all felt that this meeting was indeed special. It was not just a George-Strait-meets-a-fan moment. Someone else certainly had a hand in this.

In July 2012, I was honored with the Jim Melby Award for Journalism at the National Wrestling Hall of Fame Dan Gable Museum. Curt's mother and father were in attendance. I had not spoken with either

THE "SUPERFLY" VOW I MADE TO VINCE McMAHON SR.

TWELVE

"Superfly" Jimmy Snuka is one of the most easygoing people I have ever met. Soft-spoken and always gracious, this is the Snuka you want to spend a lot of time with, because it's always a great experience.

The first time I ever saw Snuka was in a photograph. Around 1977, he was wrestling in Houston for promoter Paul Boesch. Freelance photographer Jim Caldwell was our guy at ringside, and he regularly sent photos from Boesch's promotion.

On one occasion, after opening a package from Caldwell and looking at the photos, I was awestruck. There were amazing images of a very muscular athlete performing some incredibly high-risk aerial moves. It was Snuka.

As if watching a film, I viewed the images through a magnifying glass (known as a lupe) on a proof sheet (about 36 photos printed on an

8" x 10" photo paper). As my eyes slowly scanned from left to right, Superfly Snuka climbed to the top turnbuckle. When he reached his perch it was as though he had arrived to the peak of Mt. Everest. He slowly raised his arms and targeted opponent Mike "The Alaskan" York who was laying prone mid-ring. He glanced left and right, looking into the audience as if to ask for their approval.

As my eyes continued to scan the pictures, Snuka gracefully spring-boarded high into the air. He flew perhaps 10 feet, until finally crashing down on top of York. Three seconds later he was declared the winner. The final shot had the glistening warrior down on one knee with his arms raised in victory. It was awesome. I hoped that one day I would make his acquaintance.

It wouldn't be long, just a few months actually, until I finally met him. He had begun working for the Charlotte, North Carolina–based Jim Crockett Promotions. When I introduced myself, I was called, "Bruddah Bill" for the first time. That would be his moniker for me in the years to come.

Snuka had seen the coverage of some of his Houston matches in the magazines, so he was already somewhat familiar with me. I was over with him very quickly. He was always willing to pose for me and do interviews. Although his interviews were not his strongest asset, I would get the basics on tape and then after a playback in the editorial office, the editors would "translate" and put it into some sort of cohesive form. We didn't make him sound like Einstein, but he didn't sound like the Snuka I had heard on tape either. We knew who he was feuding with and where it was going, so the tape was an excellent guide.

We became good friends and traveling companions throughout the Carolinas and also when he worked for Georgia Championship Wrestling. Then his major break happened in 1982, when he was booked in WWF. He became an instant star. While wrestling there he was also allowed to honor tours he had already booked with All Japan Pro Wrestling. The WWF's Vince McMahon Sr. was an honorable man. Nineteen eighty-two also marked my first trip to Japan. Through United States bookers Dory and Terry Funk, All Japan's head man, "Giant" Shohei Baba, invited me to cover all the action and show U.S. magazine readers what a hot product he had on the "Island Nation." His top competitor, New Japan

Pro Wrestling's Antonio Inoki, had already brought wrestling magazine photographer-writer George Napolitano to cover his shows (George worked for a different publisher than I did). I guess I was Baba's "equalizer." This was fine with me, as I had always wanted to travel to Japan. Now, not only was I going, but I was going to get to photograph and report on the matches and travel with Bruiser Brody, Stan Hansen, Harley Race, Snuka, Lou Thesz, Ted DiBiase, Archie "The Mongolian Stomper" Gouldie, Buck Robley, Haku and more.

In late June, a few days before leaving, I received a call from Vince McMahon Sr. After exchanging a few pleasantries, he got to the point.

"Are you going on the same tour in Japan as Snuka?" he asked. I told him I was, and he continued. "I've got a large investment in this guy. You know that he's my headliner next week at [Madison Square Garden] against Bob Backlund in the steel cage. Listen, Snuka likes to drink and go out, and I need someone to make sure that no matter what happens, he gets on the airplane home and gets to the Garden. I am depending on you to make sure he gets there. Keep an eye on him—especially the last day. Get him to the airport. I really need

you to help him get there."

Although I didn't work for Mr. McMahon, I knew that to maintain my good relationship with him I needed to pacify his worries. I would certainly make sure Superfly did not miss that main event. It was something I knew I could do—I mean, how difficult could it be?

I flew to Japan out of Los Angeles along with the Funks, Thesz, Haku, Buck Robley and a few others. Snuka traveled another route, so I didn't see him until the first night of the tour.

Each night after the matches, several people would go out to various bars, Japanese bathhouses or the busy Roppongi district where there was entertainment and hookers galore. I went out a few times with Haku, Ted DiBiase and Terry Funk. I never went out with Snuka. I had no idea where he went or who he was going with either.

The tour was wonderful. From the enthusiasm of the wrestlers and fans at the shows to the sightseeing and entertainment, it was the trip of a lifetime.

Since we were both flying back to New York, Baba made sure that Snuka and I were on the same flight. He understood that Jimmy had to be back in time for the Garden shot, now just a few days away. Unfortunately, we didn't get a direct flight and had to spend two days in Hawaii. I had never been there before and was actually looking forward to this leg of the trip. Snuka, of course, had roots on the Island and promised me that he would show me around and make sure we were entertained. I told Snuka about my conversation with Vince Sr. and he assured me there was no way he would miss the flight to New York.

We checked into the waterfront Waikiki Circle Hotel in the early morning. We both had rooms on the highest floor at the hotel. The room views were magnificent. After resting for a few minutes, I wanted to go sightseeing. Snuka, who I found at the hotel bar, declined, saying he was a bit tired and just wanted to stay at the hotel. The odor of beer followed his words, and I could tell by his red eyes that this was not his first beer since we arrived at the hotel.

I spent the next few hours walking the strip. I went back to the hotel and there was Snuka—still in the bar. He got up to hug me and he was clearly tipsy.

"Bruddah Bill, tonight I am taking you to a luau," he said. "Meet me in the lobby at 7 p.m." He slapped me on the back and went back to the bar.

I was in the lobby at 7 p.m. Snuka was not. I called his room, and there was no answer. So I took the elevator up and knocked on his door. One, two, three knocks and finally he opened the door. He was wrapped from the waist down with a towel and looked confused to see me.

"The luau," I reminded him. "Right, Bruddah, give me a minute and we'll go!" I waited in the hallway and he came out about five minutes later. Although he was in a great mood, I did notice quite a few empty beer cans on the desk.

We hailed a taxi and went to the luau, where Snuka introduced me to this magnificently beautiful Polynesian woman named Sharon. The way they gazed at each other and the initial hug let me know immediately she was obviously "his girl" in this port. She sat with us at the beginning until the "Traditional Tourist Show" commenced. Sharon was one of the many entertainers in the show that performed in front of a few thousand tourists, myself included.

About 20 minutes into the show, Sharon came over to us, took my hand and led me onto the stage. She put a Hawaiian grass skirt on me and motioned for me to do whatever she did. It was a hula dance. The audience, especially Snuka, was hysterical.

After the show, we waited for Sharon and she accompanied us back to the hotel. We all sat at the bar for a few minutes. They had some mixed drinks and I had my usual Sprite. After a short time, they excused themselves and went to Snuka's room. On the way to the elevator I reminded him that we would have to leave for the airport in about six hours. He had drinks at the show and more at the bar. I could see how smashed has was as he said, "Okay, Bruddah. Meet you down here at 8 a.m."

I went to my room to get a few hours of shut-eye before the flight. About one hour into my sleep I was awakened by loud banging in the hallway. It sounded like someone was pounding on everyone's door. I got out of bed and looked through the peephole, but I couldn't see any-thing. Out of curiosity I opened my door and, to my horror, there was Snuka, with barely a towel draped on his naked body, pounding on doors looking for me.

"Jimmy, I'm here," I said. In a drunken stupor he staggered down the hallway, pushed me out of my doorway and stormed into my room.

"Sharon!" he screamed. He looked at me and asked, "Where is Sharon?"

"I have no idea, Jimmy. You've got to go back to sleep. We have to get to the airport in three hours." My words meant nothing to him. The towel slid off his waist. Here I was staring a naked madman in the face as he asked me again, "Where is Sharon?"

"Go back to your room, Jimmy. Sleep it off," I said. He looked at me and then turned toward the balcony doors. He slid the glass open and was now stark naked on the balcony, screaming, "Sharon, where are you?" over and over again. He started to move closer to the railing. All I could envision was him mounting that railing and doing his signature "Superfly" leap from 14 stories aboveground.

> **I was staring a naked madman in the face.**

Somehow, I convinced him to come back into my room. I was able to hold up his body and act as a crutch as we walked back to his room. Once there, he col-lapsed face-first on the bed, and I slammed his door and left. All I could hear in my head now was Vince McMahon's words, "No matter what happens, he gets on the airplane home and gets to the

Garden. I am depending on you to make sure he gets there." How was I going to accomplish this now?

A few minutes before 8 a.m., I knocked on Snuka's door repeatedly. There was no answer. I went down to the lobby and saw one of the other wrestlers who was also staying at the hotel. He told me that I should just let Snuka sleep it off and that he would be okay. I don't recall who that wrestler was, but he did convince the hotel management to let him into Snuka's room to see if he was okay. I didn't want to go with him. A few minutes later, he came down and told me that he couldn't wake him up fully. Again he said Jimmy needed to sleep it off. This was not the first time he had seen him in this condition.

I was a dead man. Over 19,000 tickets had been sold, and the man who was half of this highly anticipated main event at Madison Square Garden was lying drunk in a bed at the Waikiki Circle Hotel.

I had to get back to New York, so I took a taxi to the airport. With just minutes before boarding, I sat in the waiting area trying to figure out what I was going to tell McMahon.

As I sat in a window seat near the front of the airplane, just moments before they closed the aircraft's door, I heard a very familiar, charming voice greet the stewardess. "Hello, sistah, how are you today!" It was Snuka. I was in a state of shock. He put his carry-on bag in the overhead bin and sat next to me. He grabbed my wrist with his thumb and index finger, squeezed it a bit and asked, "Did you have fun dancing at the show last night?"

The weight of the world melted off my shoulders. We arrived at JFK and took a taxi to the Garden, making it there with plenty of time to spare. Vince asked us how the trip went and thanked me for "looking out for Snuka."

If only he knew what I went through to get him there.

Aloha!

To this day I have no idea how Snuka arrived in time for that flight. I have told him this story many times, and though he always enjoys hearing it, he can't remember how he got there either.

CALL THE COPS— APTER'S BLEEDING

THIRTEEN

Although there were deadline pressures, there was also a strange but fun side of the magazine publishing office.

One of my favorite periods was when the office was based in Freeport, New York, in the early '70s. Randy Gordon began working for Stanley Weston's boxing magazines in 1974. He also wrote a column for *Inside Wrestling* magazine. The boxing department and the wrestling department had desks in the same room. We were separated by an aisle.

I'm not sure when this actually happened, but one day early in his tenure Randy and I passed each other in the aisle and I threw a fake wrestling-punch at his chin. I am here to tell you that I have never seen anyone sell a punch so well. Other editors, concerned, got out of their seats and rushed over to him thinking I really connected. That is how good Randy sold.

Things escalated over the next few months to where we would actually do a quick match in between the desks. I had been doing this since I was a kid with friends and family. So had Randy. We were perfect opponents.

I'll use the term rambunctious for Randy, but even that is a bit too mild. Together we were like two grade-school kids. After one double date, our wives refused to go out as a group again. We were great at embarrassing them with our juvenile ways (we are both divorced from those ladies and who knows if that started it all). We did things just to stir up emotions so we could say, "Did you see how they bought that?"

One floor below us was the local motor vehicle office. On the last day of the month there were probably 100 people waiting in line outside for the office to open at 8 a.m. One day, just for the hell of it, Randy and I decided to take our act from the office out to the public. The motor vehicle line was the target. Our most recent office match had received rave reviews from the editors. We "finished" the match behind the filing cabinets where I had my head "smashed" into the steel drawers. Then I showed my face to the editors and fell to the floor, bloodied (Halloween vampire blood) with several teeth spilling from my mouth (white-colored Tic Tacs). We'd adapted our show for the unsuspecting public.

We met around 7 a.m. at a local bagel joint. In my pocket was a tube of the blood and a full pack of Tic Tacs. Through the window of the restaurant we could monitor the length of the line, waiting for its peak, just before opening. When we left the eatery, it was showtime.

As we walked to the building I put some blood on my face and inserted the Tic Tacs into my mouth. My head was down so no one in the long line could see the crimson covering my forehead. I was in front of Randy. He grabbed the handle of the front door that led both to our office on the second floor and the motor vehicle office that was on the ground floor. He smiled to the first few people in line and said, "I hope they don't open late like they did yesterday." This got their attention. The setup was made. I stood about six inches from the door, and as he spoke he pulled the door open for me. I stopped it with my foot and at the same time "bashed" my head into the door. I screamed out in pain as I turned toward Randy and yelled, "What did you do?" I showed my face, forehead covered with blood, and spit out a few of the Tic Tacs. I started to fall down and Randy caught me. Trying not to laugh, he said, "Someone call an ambulance."

"No, take me to the office, I need first aid," I said.

Remember, there were no cell phones back then, so people were scrambling to find a pay phone—but there weren't any around. My wife worked at a hospital a few blocks away, and Randy told a few of the concerned, "His wife works for Lydia Hall Hospital. I'll get him up to the office and call her to send an ambulance."

He put my arm on his shoulder and dragged me up to our office. We walked in and a few of the editors were already there. Randy dropped me to the floor. There was no sympathy from anyone. Everyone just went about their work. The "immature jerks" were up to it again.

Slapstick has always been my favorite kind of entertainment fun. If we go out for a meal and I order pie, this is how I like it served!

Randy and I relished that morning.

More madness ensued when a new employee began work in the editorial department. Now that Randy and I were "office wrestlers," we decided to put our talents to work on whoever the "new guy" was.

In 1978, a young Steve Farhood became the newest boxing writer and editor. Around this time, Randy and I were having nearly daily office matches as soon as Mr. Weston, the big boss, left for the day. This was a strange occurrence for Farhood, the rookie, to witness. Randy and I sensed Farhood's "I just want to do my job" work ethic and parlayed that into an angle, and we turned up the heat a bit. We started ranking on each other's wives. The back and forth became brutal after a few days and I took exception to one of the wisecracks and threw a fist to Randy's jaw. He sold so well, even the editors that "knew" came to look to make sure he wasn't hurt.

This incident drove Randy's part of the angle—and he became "horribly enraged!" For our match the next afternoon, ranking on the wives continued and led us behind the filing cabinets. We could not be seen, but you could hear us shoving each other into the cabinets. At one point I yelled something about his wife and he tossed me to the floor. Next Randy ran, in full view of everyone, to his desk and got a razor blade from one of his drawers (we all had them to cut open magazine boxes when the new issues arrived). He looked like a madman and, with his face contorted in anger, yelled to Farhood, "I've had it with that bastard. He's never going to say those things about my wife again!"

We had crossed the line. Farhood was beyond uncomfortable. The "fake wrestling" looked like it had taken a turn to the real. As Randy got the blade from his desk, I took another tube of Halloween vampire blood and drenched my forehead with it and even put some on my mouth. Randy came back behind the filing cabinets and I shrieked as he "cut me!" He emerged into the editorial pool looking like a madman and then I staggered to the same area, finally falling to the ground. Randy was going to do more damage, but Farhood ran in to stop him. Mission accomplished. He knew at this point he had been had.

I spoke to Randy a few days after writing this and he recalls, "We ranked on the wives for an entire week for this setup. It is one of my favorite times of my career at G.C.

London Publishing."

It is one of mine as well.

The matches continued and when another editor joined the staff (his name is not being revealed by request) a new storyline was concocted by Randy and me. One day, I brought in some baseball photos I had taken at a Yankees Old Timer's Day a few years earlier. One of the editors (I am pretty sure it was Gary Morgenstein) was a big fan. I had a photo of baseball legend Satchel Paige that "Morgy" really liked. As the new editor admired the photo, I made it a point to explain how the photo was a gift to my dad, because he admired Paige so much. The new editor smiled, so I knew the photo was on his radar. I had the negatives to these photos, so if one was damaged it was no issue to print another one. Little did anyone know the photo was about to be the center point of the next Apter-Gordon blowup.

The next day I brought in the identical photo, but this time it had an autograph on it. It was "autographed" to my late father. It read, "Dear Nat, thanks for being a fan! Your friend Satchel Paige." Of course the autograph was fake. It was even signed in blue crayon. But I made it a point to gloat about it.

I also made sure to show everyone it was in the top right-hand drawer of my desk in case anyone wanted to admire it at any time, and I stressed the emotional value it had because of my father (he would have loved this shtick).

When I went out to lunch that day, Randy went into the drawer, scissor in hand, sliced a piece of it off and then Scotch taped it back together. Everyone in the office played along except the new guy, who was really upset. I came back from lunch and was just about to open the drawer, but I knew this was too early to do the finish.

The buildup continued for an entire week. I was about to leave on vacation and asked Randy and a few of the other editors, including the newbie, to make sure the photo was safe.

Each day I was away, Randy cut another piece of the picture. By the time I returned, Randy had made it look like a taped together jigsaw puzzle.

For a day or two after my return, I didn't go into the drawer. It was all part of the plan. One day, Randy started talking about the Yankees and that prompted me to open the drawer. I stared down at the "valuable" photo—the one dedicated to my father—now held together by tape.

"Who the hell did this?" I said. Everyone kept typing. Gordon's head was down and he was almost laughing. Again I asked, "Who ruined my father's photo?" Randy turned to me and pointed to the new guy, but I refused to believe him. I slammed the drawer closed and stormed out of the office. This gave me the opportunity to put blood on my face. I already had scissors in my pocket.

I returned to the office and called Gordon over to the filing cabinets, asking for his help to find a boxing photo. As soon as Randy turned the corner to the cabinets, I "attacked." The crashing, banging, screaming from that area must have seemed so real to the new editor. Finally I emerged from the filing cabinet area with bloody scissors and a bloody Gordon behind me.

Shocked, the new editor ran to a nearby telephone in the art department and started to dial the police. Luckily, we stopped him before he could finish dialing. The initiation ended right here. And through the years, Mr. Weston never knew any of this had gone on after he left for the day.

By the way, nine years later, the "immature" Gordon became chairman of the New York State Athletic Commission—the body of authority that keeps all the wrestling and boxing events in the state under a very careful watch. Randy was a boxing guy, but I will never forget my "office wrestling" days with him. It was the start of what would become a very cultlike wrestling genre known as COW— Championship Office Wrestling.

As for Steve Farhood, he rose to become editor-in-chief of *The Ring* and *KO Magazine*, and he has been an award-winning on-air analyst for Showtime Boxing, ESPN, CNN, SportsChannel and USA Network's *Tuesday Night Fights*.

Gary Morgenstein is the current director of communications at the SyFy Network. He's also a playwright and has had several shows produced off-Broadway in New York City. It's amazing that Gary was not a fan of pro wrestling when he joined the magazine team—and never became a fan. Today he deals with WWE on a semiregular basis as SyFy is the home of *SmackDown*!

"THE DEAD WRESTLER—WHO WAS ALIVE!"

FOURTEEN

When I was a kid, one of my favorite wrestlers was Bearcat Wright. A lanky 6'6" at 250 pounds, the agile Wright mesmerized me as I watched him in single matches against "Nature Boy" Buddy Rogers, Bob Orton Sr. and other main-event wrestlers. Often he would team with other "goodguys" like Sweet Daddy Siki or Cowboy Bob Ellis to take on the evil Eddie and Jerry Graham combo or the Fabulous Kangaroos— Roy Heffernan and Al Costello.

It was summer 1973, and I had been working at the magazine for a little over two years and had already got to meet many of the wrestlers I admired. At this point Bearcat was wrestling overseas and in Canada on a very reduced schedule.

One morning I received a telephone call from a man who had by now become one of my most valuable contacts and friends, WWWF President Willie Gilzenberg. After a few pleasantries he asked, "Do you remember Bearcat Wright?" I went on to tell Willie what a fan I was of Bearcat and my sentence was cut short with his words, "He's dead. I just got the word and wanted to let you know so you could do a story on the guy." I thanked Willie, hung up the phone and immediately went into Mr. Weston's office.

"If Willie called you then it's got to be real," Weston said. "I'd call McMahon [Sr.] just to double-check." Senior confirmed Willie's story. "We heard it from a few sources," he added. "Yes, it's true."

Within the next few hours, I received calls from many wrestlers asking me if I had heard about Bearcat's demise. I told them I did and who my source was as well. Most of them said they heard it from other wrestlers and some, including Bruno Sammartino, pointed directly to Willie.

I went to my typewriter and began writing my memories of Bearcat. I had a sincere affection for the heroes of my youth and he was definitely one of them. The words poured out from my mind, to my fingers and onto the keyboard. Editor Steve Ende told me

it was one of the finest tributes he had ever read. It was my first (though far too many would follow in the ensuing years). Bearcat was dead. Part of my past died along with him.

A few months later, the magazine hit the newsstands. To be specific it was the October 1973 edition of *Inside Wrestling*. I received a lot of praise from fans who sent letters to our editorial office. However, one letter made me stop in my tracks. It was postmarked from Toronto, Ontario. I will never forget the wording:

Dear Mr. Apter,
It appears you have made a grave *error. Just a few days ago I went to a show in Toronto at Maple Leaf Gardens and saw a ghost wrestle. Sweet Daddy Siki teamed with the dead Bearcat Wright.*

There was even a photo included. How could it be? I went right into Mr. Weston's office and showed him the letter and picture. He was stunned. The obvious thing to do was call Gilzenberg.

"Yeah, I found out a few days ago," Willie said. "I'm glad the guy is still alive." He was happy, but we had thousands of magazines distributed all around the world telling everyone that Bearcat was dead. Our only remedy was to print a retraction—and we did of course.

As the weeks and months went by I always wondered how this even happened, and also why we never heard directly from Bearcat. Many wrestlers told me that Bearcat put the story out on his own to generate publicity when he was "resurrected." Although I was happy Bearcat was alive, I felt a bit of the credibility I was trying to build might be compromised. Instead, when I went back into the field, wrestlers and I chatted about it and most of them believed that it was Bearcat who had actually started it all, not knowing how far it would reach. Two years later, I was in Florida covering the matches and Bearcat Wright was on the roster, managing the Mongolian Stomper. Here was my opportunity to finally meet him.

I walked into the dressing room and shook hands with everyone, and among them, standing tall, wearing an traditional African dashiki was Bearcat Wright. He was right in front of me—and very much alive.

I extended my hand in friendship and reminisced about the good old days I used to see him at Sunnyside Garden in Queens, New York, and what a huge fan I was of his work. Now that I knew we had become quick friends, it was time to drop the bomb.

"Do you remember the story about you being dead?" I asked. "How couldn't I?" he replied. "That story was the biggest help of my career."

"I'm the one who wrote it." I said. He stood back for a moment and said, "I was going to sue you guys over that, but I decided against it." I didn't question why. I asked him how the rumor got started and he told me that he believed Gilzenberg, McMahon and some other promoters back east, who didn't like him for one reason or another, had planted it.

During the rest of that week, each time I saw Bearcat he was friendly and cordial and always asked if I needed any photos of him or the Mongolian Stomper. I posed them, ran a story or two, and all was good.

I heard and read that Bearcat did actually die in 1982. However, until I see written proof—in the form of an official death certificate—I won't ever be sure.

BUDDY ROGERS —
I KNEW THEM
BOTH

FIFTEEN

As a teen, I admired many wrestlers and was fortunate to meet many of them in the twilight of their careers. Perhaps the two that had the largest impact on my life back then were "Nature Boy" Buddy Rogers and Antonino Rocca. Like most rabid wrestling fans, not only did I watch TV hoping Rogers and Rocca would wrestle, but I also watched so I could emulate their moves. I remember standing in front of the mirror in my jockey shorts—they were my wrestling trunks of course—and posing like I'd seen them pose on TV and in the photos I saw in the first wrestling magazine I bought, *Wrestling Revue* (created, owned and operated by Mr. Stanley Weston, the man I would start working for nearly 10 years later).

Rocca's mantra was that if you took care of your body and mind, you would be successful.

For those of you who are not familiar with him, here is all you really need to know—he was the first flying wrestler I ever saw. A bit apelike in appearance, the man from Argentina was very agile; he introduced the flying dropkick to the world. He wrestled barefoot and he was lightning fast. With just one short leap, he would mount his opponent's shoulders, kind of drive him around by turning the hapless adversary's head in whatever direction he wanted, and then flip down, keeping thc opponent's head tightly between his legs, and roll him up for the pin. His other signature finisher was three tremendous dropkicks followed by an over the shoulders backbreaker, which usually garnered a submission.

My pillow was the victim of all my dropkicks, rollovers and backbreakers. I did this high up on the bed so I could see the match in the mirror. One time Rocca announced that he was going to have his legs insured by Lloyd's of London. Since I was on my Rocca kick (not a pun) I requested to my parents that this might be a good idea for me as well as I had become the "Pillowweight" champion of the house—wrestling barefoot, of course—and I was now "Bouncy Billy Apter!" They were impressed that I was the champion—but I

was not getting the insurance policy. Damn. As a youngster I got to meet Rocca a few times at various arenas around the New York City area. That he would take a city bus or train rather than a car or a limo to the buildings so he could be with his legions of fans impressed me. Even in the days when he was making large money at Madison Square Garden, he usually took public transportation. As an autograph hunter, I did get him to

The National Wrestling Alliance gold belt was one of the most prestigious championships in the world. Here is what it would have looked like with "Wonderful Willie" as the title holder. Not bad, right? [Photo courtesy of Buddy Myers]

sign something on several different occasions and briefly chatted with him. As busy as he was, and no matter how many fans surrounded him, he always found time to talk to his admirers. I never got to meet him once my career began. I wish I would have had the opportunity, but we never crossed paths.

As a voice mimic, I would regularly conduct interviews in the Apter Arena (my bedroom). I would be the broadcaster and ask "Rocca" a question, and then I would imitate his voice to answer, using a large spoon as my microphone.

With Rogers it was on an entirely different level.

Rogers was being managed by the loudmouth Bobby Davis. Although Davis spoke and generated so much heat, Rogers was also a good interview. Davis was loud and talked fast. Rogers had a gravel-like voice and spoke very slowly. (I can still do these voices today.) His entire look, the bronze body, the blond hair—man he was the original Total Package.

Unfortunately, pretending to be Rogers got me beaten up on an almost nightly basis. I grew up in Maspeth, Queens (about 45 minutes by bus and subway from Midtown Manhattan). There was a luncheonette called The Hilltop

across the street from the six-story building where I lived with my parents, sister and brother. Every evening a gang of older teens gathered on the corner—perhaps seven or eight of them—and caused a bit of havoc. They called themselves "the Hilltop Stompers." They would intimidate people and "rank out" nearly everyone who came near the corner. Most of them dressed in black leather jackets, had a mouthful of chewing gum and smoked.

I was close friends with Lon and Edith Zane and their family, who owned The Hilltop. Around 7 p.m. each night, I did some work for them. Lon and Edith knew about my passion for wrestling and made sure that I was home by 9 p.m. on Wednesday and Thursday nights to watch. If we were running late, they would turn on the TV in the store so I could watch there. One night a few of the Hilltop Stompers were seated at the counter having sodas when the TV was turned to wrestling. They laughed through most of it and ranked on me for being a wrestling fan. Lon warned them to watch their manners.

One night—I don't know what drove me to do this—when I was coming out of the store, they glared at me and one of them made some remark about me being a "dumb wrestling geek." Instead of just going across the street to the apartment, I launched into a Buddy Rogers impersonation. I started to strut in a big circle and pointed to the side of my temple with my index finger, just as Buddy would. Next Buddy's words came right out of my mouth. "Ya know something, you guys think you're tough. Well you may be, but you don't have it up here in the head." That didn't sit well as one of them said, "Hey, let's stomp out 'Nature Boy!'"

My imitation must have been too good they started coming at me. I ran like there was no tomorrow, and they laughed so hard you could probably have heard them all the way in Brooklyn.

This same scenario played out night after night, and they caught me after a few days. When they did, they beat me down to the ground (I purposely fell quickly). Then these street ruffians began stomping me. It became a regular thing.

After a minute or two, Lon would run out of the store and tell them to leave me alone. At that point they backed off and I would get up, put my index finger to my temple and strut away, just like Rogers would have done. What I didn't tell Lon was that they weren't really hurting me. Their stomps were—well—almost good-natured. Eventually, we started having fun.

A month or so later, the Hilltop Stompers would stand on the corner, I would strut in and out of the store, and we would all talk about wrestling. They tried to convince me that wrestling was fixed, but I never broke kayfabe. I was proud of the sport I loved and never agreed with them. It didn't really matter. I was one of the guys now. It was sort of my initiation to the Hilltop Stompers' corner.

I always wanted to meet Rogers, but I didn't think I would ever get the opportunity. He was retired and living somewhere in Cherry Hill, New Jersey. No one knew where. He had dropped out of the business and was not on anyone's radar.

One day, I was sitting in the magazine office pulling some photos for a story, and one of those pictures was of Rogers. That inspired me to try to find him. It was around 1975. I remembered that he lived in Cherry Hill and figured that if I called the police department there, perhaps they could track him down.

It took just one call to the head of the police department. Not long after I hung up I received a call.

"Hey, Billy," a slow-speaking but unmistakable gravelly voice said on the other end of the line. "How yah doin', pally? It's the

Nature Boy!" A sense of euphoria overcame me. He sounded exactly as I remembered. He called me Billy as if he had known me forever.

"I know who you are," he continued. "I sneak a look at the wrestling magazines sometimes. You're making quite a name for yourself!"

I thanked Buddy and told him, "This is the greatest moment of my short career!"

We talked about the business and he asked how his old friend—my boss—Stanley Weston was doing. Then he said he was pretty keen on this guy "Superstar" Billy Graham, who he had seen on TV a few times. We talked for almost one hour and he promised to keep in touch.

After I got off the phone, I called Ernie "The Grand Wizard" Roth, who was Graham's manager, and told him how Buddy praised Graham. Roth was ecstatic and wondered if I could use that in a story. I thought it would make a fabulous cover story.

I called Buddy and he quickly agreed. I went to the editor to pitch the story and it was thumbs-up from everyone. Both Ernie and Graham were thrilled.

With everything in place, we were ready to put a story together when I received another call from Rogers. However, his mood

was different. Instead of the slow, grandfather-like tone, this time he was a very emotional, fast-talking Rogers. He wanted to change the rules.

"Yah know what, pally, I thought about this Graham thing and you can forget it!" I was stunned as this new version of Buddy Rogers continued. "I'm not going to lend my name to get anyone over. How dare they ask me to do something like that. No way!" Click. That was the end of the call.

I called Ernie and told him what happened. He said, "Yes, that is the Buddy Rogers we all know, Bill. No problem, it was just an idea."

Buddy's call really rattled me. He called me back the next day in that slow, calm tone again and never alluded to the situation that had come and gone so quickly. I talked to Weston and he said he loved Buddy, but you never knew what his personality would be like at any given time. It was never a constant.

I lost touch with Rogers for a long time and then on New Year's Day 1979, I received a stunning call from my father who was at the matches in West Palm Beach, Florida.

"You will never guess who just wrestled here tonight," my father said. "Buddy Rogers! I even got to talk to him! He wrestled and beat Jim Garvin." I told my dad he must have seen a Rogers imposter. Rogers was retired and living in New Jersey. I quickly got on the phone and called Eddie Graham's Florida Wrestling office and spoke to Gordon Solie, who confirmed it. My hero was back!

I called Buddy a few days later and this time it was the sweet Rogers, who told me he had met my dad. Buddy also said he was being booked soon to work in the Carolinas for Jim Crockett Promotions. This was great news for me, as I traveled to that territory pretty regularly.

Finally my big day came. It was in Norfolk, Virginia, in mid-1979. Rogers had been in the territory, and I called to let him know I would be there for a week. I checked into a motel in Hampton, Virginia, and as soon as I headed to my room I saw him sitting outside basking in the sun, keeping that bronzed body perfectly colored.

He sat up as I approached him, not knowing it was me. As I got within a few feet of him I dropped my bags and began strutting toward him, index finger to the temple, and then Buddy's voice came out of my mouth, "Hey, Rogers, how are you gonna beat this, pally!" I said. He got up quickly, hugged me, gave me

a kiss on the cheek and said, "Billy Boy, it's a pleasure!" My hero and I were one! It was fabulous. He even let me put the figure-four on him on the grass outside the hotel and taught me how to "work it" the best way. Many wrestlers do a spinning toe-hold into the figure-four, but he told me that leaves too much chance for the opponent to get away. Instead he showed me how to grab the legs and go right into the hold. Little did he know that this was the way I learned by watching him on TV when I was a kid.

We sat and talked for hours, and later that night I did a life story interview on cassette tape with him (I still have it, of course). I traveled with Buddy, his lovely wife, Debbie, and his son David for the whole week. On this tour he wrestled the younger "Nature Boy" Ric Flair. It was incredible—there I was on the ring apron photographing my wrestling idol against the man who would carry on his legacy.

For the most part, I got the "sweet" Rogers on this trip. Only once did things change. After a match, we went to eat dinner at a local Howard Johnson's with Debbie and David. Also seated with us was Japanese magazine photographer Kiyotaka "Jimmy" Suzuki.

During dinner Rogers was very cordial to the fans who came to the table, even though he was trying to eat. After about 10 fans cleared out, a man in his late 20s, who was sitting with his girlfriend in a booth just opposite our table, made a comment.

"Mr. Rogers, I really love what you wrestlers do," he said. "You all make it look so real!"

Rogers, who was in a very placid mood, looked at me and threw his fork down onto his plate. Everyone in the restaurant turned toward our table. His face went from a tan to a bright red, and his eyes had a look of the devil. Indeed, this was the man who called me to rescind the Superstar Graham story before it ever got to a typewriter. It was a real life Dr. Jekyll becoming Mr. Hyde right in front of us. Debbie, who had probably seen this transformation many times, put her hand on his arm, but he just pushed it aside as he slowly rose to stand over the man in the booth.

Then the enraged Rogers spoke, "Come on, you, let's go outside and I'll show you how real it looks! Come on, you piece of crap! Let's go, big shot," Rogers said as he pointed his hand to the door. The man looked at Rogers and said, "Hey, I didn't mean to say anything bad, I'm sorry." That didn't calm Rogers one bit. He wanted to take him outside. Finally, Buddy came back to our table, pushed his plate into ours, grabbed his car keys, stormed out of the eatery and drove away. Debbie, who was still at the table with their son David, went over to the customer and told him she was sorry and that Buddy must have had a long day. The patron accepted the apology.

When we got back to the motel, Buddy was in a horrible mood. He didn't want to talk to anyone, including me. For the next day or two, this personality of Rogers dominated. On my last day, we said a few nice things to each other and promised to keep in touch, but it was not the Rogers of the first few days, the one I really enjoyed being around.

Weeks later, I called his house and he was back to—I guess—normal. He was the Buddy I wanted him to be.

We stayed in touch for years. In the 1980s Buddy worked as a greeter for the Playboy Club in Atlantic City, and I went to visit him there many times. You couldn't miss him in the casino. A gold suit, puffing on a huge cigar and his signature strut. Yes, it was "Nature Boy" Buddy Rogers—the nice one—for sure!

APTER SUFFERS BRUISED RIBS WRESTLING SHAWN MICHAELS

SIXTEEN

In December 1999, while working as editor of *WOW Magazine*, I called Shawn Michaels to see if I could visit his new wrestling school and the Texas Wrestling Academy shows he promoted. I thought it would make a great cover story and inside feature. Although Shawn and I were very good friends, he didn't want to say okay until he talked to Vince McMahon. WWF did not particularly like *WOW* (for reasons I will go into when I write about my years at *WOW*), and Shawn has always been a "If Vince says 'No,' I don't do it" guy. I totally understood this. Shawn was the current WWF commissioner, so it was totally up to Vince.

Within a day, Shawn returned my call. He said that Vince was okay with the project. Instead of just shooting photos at the Academy and the TWA show, he suggested I come to his home and do an entire "HBK—The Private Life of the WWF's Commish" feature. This was better than I could have imagined.

Armed with my Nikon-FM2, about 30 rolls of film and my trusty cassette recorder, I headed to San Antonio. Shawn picked me up at the airport and drove me to his spacious new house on the outskirts of town. The 5,500-square-foot house was custom built with a Mediterranean decor. It was the exact opposite of the dingy hotel rooms he stayed in when he was on the road. This house was very open with high ceilings, so even giantlike friends like Kevin Nash could hang out with no issue.

His wife, Rebecca, and I had already been acquainted. She was a former *Nitro* Girl, working under the name of Whisper. I met her while covering the WCW events. Rebecca was now pregnant, their baby was due in a few months, and her and Shawn were still completely in love—you could see it in their eyes and in their every move.

After catching up in their spacious kitchen over lunch, Shawn took me to the gym in his house for his daily workout. I unpacked my camera and shot three rolls of 36-exposure film. Next we drove to the Academy where he introduced me to his business partner and one of the school's trainers

Rudy Gonzalez. Paul Diamond and Jose Lothario were also a large part of the Academy. Shawn conducted a class as I photographed away. Students Lance Cade, Bryan Danielson (Daniel Bryan), Brian Kendrick, Paul London and others did calisthenics and other exercises. After an hour or so they got into the ring to do some falls and learn a few holds.

Shawn told me that the next day there would be an intense workout in the ring. We headed to the arena where Shawn's Texas Wrestling Academy show was taking place. It was there that I got to see his parents—whom I met back in 1984. The show was well-done, mainly featuring Shawn's students.

Back at the house, Shawn and Rebecca had a nice bedroom waiting for me. They made me feel totally at home.

The next day was my last in town. I spent the morning taking photos of Shawn and Rebecca around their home and also spent a couple of hours interviewing Shawn. Since my flight was scheduled for later in the evening, I said goodbye to Rebecca, and Shawn drove me to the Academy so I could take pictures of him working with Danielson, Cade and others in the ring. Gonzalez also worked with the students.

I was shooting at ringside at one point and motioned to Shawn, pointing to my watch, that I needed to get to the airport. "I'll get you there in time, Apter, don't you worry," he assured me. "I'll tell you what, why don't you put down that camera, come into the ring and show my students how to really do this stuff right."

Without hesitation I put down my gear and climbed through the ropes. All of the students were on the ring apron. Here I was in the ring, face-to-face with Shawn Michaels, and he asked me, "What do you want to do?" My mouth spewed words faster than I could think, as I whispered so the students wouldn't hear, "Shoot me into the ropes. When I come back on the rebound I will give you a flying dropkick and then put you in the figure-four leglock for the win." Like I was a real student, Shawn said, "Okay then, let's do it." He shot me into the ropes as planned, and when I came back, he was mid-ring and I flew up in the air as high as I could and my sneakers caught him around his navel. He sold it and fell to the mat with a thud. He played groggy, and now it was "time to go to school!" I grabbed his legs and slipped into the figure-four. He cried out in pain! I screamed for someone to get my camera and snap a photo of the moment. I just beat Shawn Michaels in front of all his students. As I got up and raised my arms, they applauded. Shawn sprung up to his feet and said, "I'd like to see you do that again." I told him I'd rather not—I didn't want to hurt him.

We had some laughs at his expense, but now it was time to get me to the airport. Seeing how tied up Shawn was, Rudy Gonzalez was nice enough to drive me.

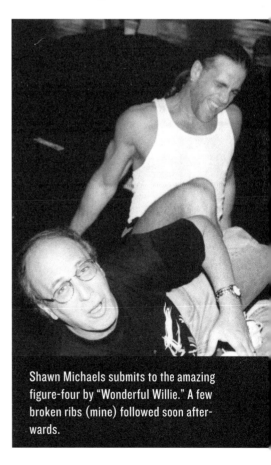

Shawn Michaels submits to the amazing figure-four by "Wonderful Willie." A few broken ribs (mine) followed soon afterwards.

IS WRESTLING FIXED?

As I got out of Rudy's car, I felt a slight pain in my left side. I said nothing, figuring I must have strained something. I waved good-bye. As I went through airport security, the pain worsened. I didn't know what to do. All I knew was that I wanted to get back home to Pennsylvania. Soon I was near tears and almost doubled over in pain, but I persisted and got on the aircraft.

An elderly lady sat next to me. I was slouched over and she could see the pain etched in my face. She asked, "Are you okay, young man?" I tried to smile and said, "Yes ma'am, I just have some pain over here," pointing to my left side. "Maybe I should call the stewardess," she said. "Perhaps you're having a heart attack." I cut her off just as she was about to make the call and told her that this happens sometimes. She did convince me to take two Advils that she had in her pocketbook.

Nearly three hours later, I arrived in Philly and drove myself to a local hospital. The results came quickly. I had damaged a few ribs. I could not believe it. For years I had dropkicked in backyard matches when I was a kid and on hard floors in Championship Office Wrestling matches. And now, in a real ring, I screwed up and fell wrong and was paying for it. (Literally: it was a $100 emergency room bill.)

Later that afternoon, I called Shawn to tell him what happened. He still insisted that we have a rematch. Someone get Vince on the phone. I think I'm ready to do it. All I want is a $100 payoff so I can recoup that money . . .

STALKED

SEVENTEEN

I n 1989, my family and I were living in a condo in Massapequa Park, New York. After
leaving the *PWI* offices for the day I'd pick
up dinner. Let me digress here for a moment: my
wife and I didn't do a lot of cooking. We both
had fast-paced lives and, as the old joke goes,
when friends would ask, "What do you make for
dinner?" my reply was always "Reservations!"
Don't worry, we didn't raise the kids on fast
food (although those Nathan's French fries were
incredible). When we did decide to cook I would
usually go to the Grand Union Supermarket
right near our condo and get the ingredients to
burn to a crisp the next night.

The Grand Union was open 24/7 and I did
most of my shopping there late—like midnight
or 1 a.m. Sometimes I went nightly just to pick
up a Hershey bar or an orange soda. I vividly recall one week when there was another customer

who seemed to be keeping the same shopping hours and frequenting the same aisles as me. If I switched aisles, he would not be far behind. After a few days, this seemed a bit odd. Finally I wondered if I was being followed. It just seemed to be happening a bit too often to be sheer coincidence.

One night, I decided that if he was there I'd find out if he was indeed following me. Let me stress that he didn't seem like an intimidating person—no one would look at him and think *this guy is out to hurt me*. So I decided to walk up to whatever food he was looking at and start a conversation.

I can't recall what the item was, but I do remember asking him, "Hey, are those good?" He looked me directly in the eyes and said, "Yeah, I think so." Then the real reason he was there came out.

"Hey, you're Bill Aptah, right?" That's how he pronounced my name (and so many still do today). I asked, "Where do I know you from?" He told me, "I'm a big mark for the magazines, I seen your picture, seen you on TV. I thought it was you."

We had a good laugh when he mentioned that he had seen me in here and wanted to talk to me but didn't want to disturb me. He was very polite. He told me his name was Pete. We shook hands and chatted a bit, and I found out we lived about one mile away from each other. He told me he was a wrestler and had been trained by Johnny Rodz, who is a dear friend of mine, and had even worked in Puerto Rico in bookings arranged by Johnny. I liked Pete and we exchanged telephone numbers. I suggested he come over to my house one night and talk wrestling. You should have seen the glimmer in his eyes. It was blinding. He asked me, "Do you have any kids?" He mentioned that his father is a distributor for a vending machine company and gets a lot of sodas and candy for free. Yes, I had two little kids, but this was a gold mine for me. I was (and still am) a sodaholic and candy freak. He told me he'd bring some refreshments when he came over.

We walked out to the parking lot together and went our separate ways. The next morning I called Rodz, who told me, "Pete's a great guy. He's worked as Kid Krush for me. Nice kid. Anything you can do to help him, go do it."

Pete called me a few days later just to thank me for speaking to him. I asked him if he wanted to come over to my home one night and we arranged a date. I remember when he pulled up to the house and my daughter Hailey, who was three years old at the time, looked through the blinds and called out in her cute, high-pitched voice, "Daddy, some man with a lot of soda is here!" I opened the door, and Pete had six cases of canned sodas in various flavors and a few boxes of teeth-cracking candies and potato chips. For months to come, Hailey would announce, "Pete's here with more sodas, Daddy."

After some pleasantries with my family, he and I went down to my dungeon—the basement. Pete brought some videotapes and a photo of him in a new gimmick he had designed. It was a character he called the Tasmaniac. At first glance I said to him, "You need professional photos. If this is what you're ready to show promoters you won't get one job." I suggested that he come to my office one day and I would take some good photos. Don't ask me why I jumped right onto his bandwagon, but I did. I'm known to be a nice guy, and I guess that part of me was in full bloom.

I remember his frustration at not being able to get anyone from WWF to call him back, despite many calls to various people. He was looking for a break. I was quick to tell him that WWF was "the land of the giants" and at

his 5'8" or so and 240 pounds, he might not be someone they were looking to put on their roster. In their world of Hulk Hogan, Andre the Giant, Don Muraco and Bam Bam Bigelow, I could not see where the Tasmaniac fit. Instead, I suggested he get new photos and then I would call some of the indy promoters I knew well, and maybe they could find a home for this Tasmaniac. Perhaps after making a name for himself, and a reputation, WWF might be interested. It was worth a shot.

Pete took me up on my offer and we shot a ton of photos in the studio. He was a willing subject and I was able to fool around with the studio lights and do some "horror" lighting, back lighting and some straightforward pictures.

The weeks went on, the soda cases piled higher in my basement, and one night I decided to move things a step further. At this time I was doing some on-air broadcast segments for Mario Savoldi's International World Championship Wrestling promotion. Mario was always willing to listen to any angle I pitched for interviews on his syndicated shows, as well as any other ideas I had. I told him about the Tasmaniac and offered to send some photos, and he could let me know if he liked the gimmick. Mario said, "If you think this guy has what it takes to make it here, have him call me." Although I had only seen Pete in some subpar quality videos, I felt he had the drive to succeed. He also had the expertise of Rodz's training under his belt. Pete called Mario and within a few weeks was working on their roster. I helped guide him to the first step of what would become a fabulous career.

Pete kept visiting, and one night he asked if he could bring a friend over who had been working hard to get into the business. That man was named Tommy Laughlin, and he came over for many of our wrestling chat "summits." Pete, who had become successful with Savoldi, suggested Tommy, who became TD Madison in ICW. He would go on to become a hardcore legend—Tommy Dreamer.

All of this took place in my little basement.

Through the years I did many more photo sets with both Tazz and Tommy. They even did a job for me in a COW belt match (a "Backroom File Cabinet Death Match!").

I was not looking for payback, but when Tazz became a major star in ECW, he made a very interesting call to me in March 1999.

"Bill, me and Paul [Heyman] just met with the owners of *WOW Magazine*," he said. "They do the *ECW* magazine. Anyways, I was tellin' them that to make *WOW* successful they gotta have you. So here's the name of the main guy and his number. Paul and me put you over big and they're interested. I think you need to really look at this, Bill. You helped me a long time ago, now I wanna help you!"

The full story of my tenure with *WOW* is elsewhere in this book, but it was Tazz and Paul E. who got the ball rolling. Thank you.

Some guys thank me with an autographed photo, some with a phone call, some with nothing at all. In my collection, I have an autographed singlet that Tazz wore for most of his matches in ECW to go along with an autographed picture. You don't want to see what it looks like on me!

The real finish to this story is that Tazz did make it to WWE after so many frustrating years. After competing for a short time, he went on to become one of their broadcasters, and now he is one of the signature voices on TNA's weekly *Impact* shows. Yes, the "little man" did it!

BISCHOFF DISSES APTER—CALLS HIM A "PARASITE"

EIGHTEEN

May 31, 1996, was a very long a day for Eric Bischoff. He had just flown from Atlanta to Los Angeles. As the taxi shuttled him from the airport to the hotel, he tried to get a few minutes of sleep, but he was too exhausted and annoyed. Flight delays had caused his precious time to be greatly compromised. To amplify his aggravation, his baggage was misplaced by the airline and would not arrive until the next day.

As he entered the lobby he was greeted by wrestling fans, wrestlers and photographers, all there to work at or witness the first Antonio Inoki–organized World Wrestling Peace Festival the following day. Bischoff, at this point of his storied career, was an executive with Atlanta-based World Championship Wrestling. He was there representing the company along with several WCW wrestlers who would compete at this highly anticipated event.

As I watched him try to be as cordial as possible to well-wishers, I saw an opening to approach as he got close to the hotel's check-in desk. I smiled and put out my hand, looking for a handshake, but it was hardly forthcoming. Instead he gazed at me for a moment. His face contorted a bit and froze at a look of total disgust. It was then he spoke.

"I've had a real shit day and now that I see you here, it's just gotten much worse. Do me a favor—leave me the hell alone. Go away." His words thoroughly stunned me. I didn't know what to think. Finally, I was about to open my mouth to say something—although I have no idea what that might have been—when he raised his hand in front of my face and continued. "Oh, by the way, I assume you are here to take photos at the show. Do not take any photos of my WCW guys. You are not permitted to do so. There are plenty of other wrestlers from all over the world here. I don't care what you do with them. My guys are off-limits. Now get the hell out of my way and let me check in you . . . you . . . parasite!"

Shocked, I backed off. If I hadn't,

> **Do me a favor—leave me the hell alone.**

he might have just shoved me out of the way. There were people in the lobby who had witnessed this entire exchange. As I looked at them they gazed at me, and you could see they were totally uncomfortable. No one had any idea why Bischoff was so rude to me. Of course I had no idea either. I was shocked and infuriated that someone who I had always treated with respect showed such deep disgust for me.

After signing in, he turned to go to the elevators. He stopped short to further address me.

"Oh, by the way, I've got a message for you from Randy Savage. He wants to kill you. Goodnight, Bill." He walked to the elevator and went to his room. No one in the lobby knew what to say to me. They all heard Bischoff's rant and were speechless.

A few minutes later, as everyone tried to figure out why I had been treated this way, Mike Lano, a photographer I have known for years, tried to console me.

"He's probably tired and miserable and will forget about this in the morning," he tried to assure me. "Don't worry about it."

Knowing I felt sick about this

verbal assault, many of the people who heard the exchange came over, hoping to ease my pain. It didn't help. All I could think about was what could I have done to him to be treated like a subpar human being. Not only that, why did he say that Randy Savage wanted to kill me?

I went to my room and immediately telephoned my editor, Stu Saks. I was so anxious to tell him what had just transpired. I didn't even give him a chance to get a full "Hello" out before I said, "Stu, I've got a big problem here. We've got to talk." I went on to tell him the story, and as I went on my tone escalated from a concerned calm to very pissed off. My pride was seriously hurt. Worse, Bischoff embarrassed me in front of a lot of people who knew me. I was the face of the world's most prestigious wrestling magazine, *Pro Wrestling Illustrated*. I should not have been talked to that way.

"Bischoff cannot and should not treat you like that, no matter what the issue," Saks said. "Don't let him bully you like this, Bill! You're better than him. Do not let him get away with it. You've got to find out why he did this." When I told Stu about the "Randy Savage wants to kill you" comment, he was as dumfounded as me.

Stu's support from a few thousand miles away was very reassuring. It changed my frame of mind. After we finished our call I looked in the mirror and thought, *You know, I'm Bill Apter. I've been in this business much longer than that bastard, and unlike him, I'm respected and liked by almost everyone in wrestling. How dare he talk to me like that?* My mental state was totally renewed. I would confront him at the show tomorrow.

It was now about 9 p.m., and I resolved to try to put this Bischoff incident out of my mind for the night. I decided to go downstairs and see if I could get someone to go with me to a nearby eatery. I left my room and waited for the elevator. As the door opened I heard an, "Oh no." There I was staring face-to-face with its lone passenger— Eric Bischoff. With my renewed attitude, my words came quickly as I stepped onto the elevator.

"Whatever your problem is with me, Eric, you have no right to treat me like this," I said. "I have never treated you with anything but respect. I want to know what this is all about."

He lowered his head, getting his thoughts together, when the elevator door opened in the lobby. As we walked out of the lift I added, "Oh, by the way, I am not a parasite."

Photographer Lano was about to walk over to us but thought better and changed his direction. At this point Bischoff and I stopped walking and the discussion began. He spoke first:

"Okay, I didn't mean to call you a parasite. I'm not upset at you personally. It's the magazines. You guys are always writing about how Turner's *Nitro* is kicking McMahon's ass. Why don't you print the real story? Ted Turner isn't at war with Vince McMahon—I'm the one who's waging the war on the front lines. But I never see that. It's always Ted Turner versus Vince McMahon, when it's really Eric Bischoff against Vince McMahon! You have no idea how much it irritates me to read that in every one of your magazines!"

I told him he had a valid point and I'd bring that information back to the magazine office for discussion. Even though I understood, it didn't really justify how I was treated. However, I was glad it was out of the way. Again he said he didn't mean to come across the way he did and proved it later on at a welcome dinner for everyone involved with the show. I was sitting at a table with a few other people from the media. Dave Meltzer, the man behind *The Wrestling Observer* newsletter, and I were conversing when Bischoff came up behind us and gave us both a pleasant greeting. He looked at me and said, "You're fine to take photos of my guys tomorrow, Bill." As Bischoff moved on to another table, Meltzer asked me why Bischoff made that remark. I don't know what I told Dave, but I didn't tell him what had transpired in the past few hours. In the years to follow, Eric Bischoff was nothing but sarcastically blunt, friendly and respectful to me.

All was serene again—except now I had to find out why Randy Savage wanted to *kill* me. Ohhhh noooo!

HOW OHHHH YEAHHHH BECAME A TERRIFYING OHHHH NOOOO!

NINETEEN

This is one of the toughest, most emotional stories I will tell. I want to preface it, though. The incidents I relate here are all true, but I beg of you: don't let your memories of "Macho Man" Randy Savage be tarnished by what I write—I am thrilled that he is finally in the WWE Hall of Fame. The entire series of events was isolated—it was between Savage and a few other parties—and should not take away from his legend or all the wonderful, charitable things he did during his life, which was cut way too short.

On January 22, 1996, Randy Savage became a two-time WCW World Heavyweight champion. It was a fabulous time in his career. I had recently posed Randy in our portable studio, so we had some great photos to choose from for a cover of the *PWI* issue that was cover-dated February 1996 and on-sale in early April.

Although this was a big story, it was still run-of-the-mill—just a title-change piece, angled around his feud with Ric Flair. At our weekly editorial meeting to discuss how we were going to present the stories, I brought up the fact that a lot of fans consider Savage old—perhaps "over-the-hill." On more than one occasion, I heard fans call him "old man." It wasn't limited to Savage though. Hulk Hogan was getting it, as well as many of the other veterans in WCW.

"What if we went with that angle?" I asked. One of the other editors chimed in with, "Wouldn't that be negative and hurt Savage's image?" Finally Stu Saks (if I recall correctly) came up with the suggestion that some fan called Savage an old man, Savage heard it on his way to the ring and then amped up his performance to show he is ageless and still very much at the top of his game.

To err on the side of caution, I told Stu that I'd feel more comfortable if I called Savage and ran this angle past him.

I called Randy and laid out the entire angle. He told me, "I trust you guys. You've always done good by me. If you think it's good then go with it." So that's what we did. The final headline for the cover read "'Give It Up Old Man!' The Insult That Made Randy SAVAGE Again!"

There was no further contact with Randy. He never telephoned me with a change of heart. All appeared fine.

In May, just a few weeks after the magazine hit the newsstands, word got back to me from Eric Bischoff and a few others: "Randy Savage wants to kill you." Eric was not totally specific but did mention it was regarding some story in *PWI*.

I called Savage several times and left many messages on his answering machine, asking if he was angry with me. I never got a call. I tried to forget about it, but it really bothered me. Savage was known to be a loose cannon at times, and to hear that I might be directly on that radar was quite concerning.

I wanted to face Savage head-on, so if there were any fences to mend I could take care of it immediately. I checked the upcoming WCW road schedule and saw they would be in Philadelphia the next week. The main event was Savage against Flair.

I got to the building a few hours early and had the *PWI* 1995 "Comeback of the Year" plaque to give to Savage. I had not seen him since the plaque was made and figured he would love this gem of an award.

Soon wrestlers began coming into the backstage area. Kevin Sullivan, who was one of WCW's bookers and was helping run the show, saw me and said, "Hey, Randy Savage is coming in soon. You'd better be careful."

My nerves were on edge, but I was optimistic that, whatever the problem, my smile and the plaque would fix it all.

Savage was quickly walking down the corridor with Miss Elizabeth, heading toward me. I smiled, held the plaque in the air and looked him right in the eye and said, "I've been waiting weeks to present this to you, my friend." He took the plaque from my hand, glanced at it and slammed it into the concrete wall repeatedly—smashing it. Then he tossed it a few feet and looked me in the eyes, saying nothing. He was seething and looked like he was going to do to me what he had just done to the plaque.

Sullivan stood between us now, and Savage looked at him, pointing his finger in Sullivan's chest and then in mine, and bellowed, "The two of you, come with me!" The other wrestlers in the corridor and Miss Elizabeth were dead silent. It appeared that I was perhaps headed to my execution as Savage led me and Sullivan to a dark, dingy backstage closet. There was barely enough room for the three of us. Sullivan was positioned between us.

Looking totally irrational, his eyes a fiery red and the smell of beer on his breath, he said to me, "You piece of crap. You mean nothing to me. Your award means crap to me. I came to your house last year and met your little kids and your wife. They mean crap to me too. You have possibly ruined my contract with the Slim Jim people, you asshole."

I cannot tell you how terrified I was at this point. I mustered up enough courage to ask, "What the hell are you talking about?"

He shot back with, "You don't know what you did, you scumbag?" I shook my head no—I had no idea. He continued. "That bullshit headline about me being an old man—the Slim Jim company are thinking about canceling my endorsement contract, because they don't want an old-man image representing them. *Get it?*"

I shot back, "Randy, I called you about that angle and . . ." I was cut off as he bellowed, "Yeah,

> **You don't know what you did, you scum-bag?**

you called me, yeah, you called me. Stay the hell away from me you bastard, and if I lose my Slim Jim contract, I'll come and get you!"

With that, he stormed off. Sullivan looked at me and tried to put some words together. All he could say was, "It'll pass, Billy. He's under a lot of pressure in his personal life, in the company. Try not to sweat it."

I was shaking in my shoes, but I figured I was there and I would

not show my fear. Stupidly, I decided to stick around and shoot the matches. This would only make things worse.

With the main event coming—Flair versus Savage—I approached the ring to shoot on the mat as I had always done. Flair made his entrance, accompanied by the lovely "Woman," Nancy Sullivan. Next came Savage. I could see him looking toward me as he came to the ring, and I backed away to be safe.

In character as "Woman," Nancy Benoit flirts with me as she always found time to do. Her death remains one of the most horrid tragedies of my lifetime.

About 10 minutes into the match, Nancy walked toward me and started playing with my hair (or lack of) as I took photos. "Hey, Mister Bill, take my picture," she said in a seductive tone. At this exact moment, Savage and Flair were getting ready to lock up again, and I saw Savage drop his arms, look at the referee and give a time-out sign. He walked over to where I was, put his head over the ropes and made a motion with his mouth. A moment later, all the spit he could pack into his cheeks came out in a large puddle right onto my face. Yes, he stopped the match to spit on me. Nancy looked puzzled, Flair waved him back and the match resumed. I left ringside as confused fans asked, "Hey, Bill, what did you do to Savage?"

I quickly went to the bathroom to wash off the spit. The match ended, and as I came out of the bathroom, Savage passed by me, saying, "You're a piece of shit. Stay away from me, asshole!"

I remember calling Stu Saks late that night. He was very calming, but now I was more angry than scared.

That same day I called Hulk Hogan, who was a confidant of mine in many ways, and I knew he had a handle on Savage's erratic actions. I needed to hear that Savage would not proceed in his quest to harm me. Hulk assured me, "The guy really wouldn't hurt a fly."

In the weeks to come, I did cover another show with Savage in it but totally kept away from him.

I had an interview with Hogan in July. He told me to fly into Tampa, and he would pick me up and we'd go to his house for dinner. As I got into Hogan's car, he told me he wanted to stop at the gym, because a friend of his wanted to talk to me. He did not tell me who the friend was when I asked.

We entered the gym. It was totally deserted except for a shirtless man, sitting on a bench with his back to us. "Hey, big man, we're here," Hogan said.

The man slowly rose to his feet and turned toward us, looking very calm. It was Savage. Hogan pushed me toward him and Randy quickly embraced me.

"Hey, man, I'm really sorry," he said in a very low, respectful tone. "I was in a bad place back then. A really bad place. The demons really got to me. I am so sorry and hope you can forget all that."

> **He stopped the match to spit on me.**

"No problem, Randy," I said. "It's water under the bridge."

* * *

Years later, I found out from Randy's brother Lanny Poffo that age was a highly sensitive topic for the "Macho Man."

"Randy had wanted to do a series of matches with Shawn Michaels in WWF," Lanny told me. "Rather than agree, the powers that be decided that Randy was too old to be a wrestler and should remain as part of the broadcast team. This made him highly bitter and caused him to seriously consider leaving."

Not soon after he was denied a match against Michaels, Savage went to WCW and convinced the Slim Jim company to go along with him—and WWF lost all that revenue.

The "Old Man" story came out right after his move to WCW, which was why Randy Savage exploded the way he did. It was a double-barrel age matter right in his face. So much seemed to be going wrong and it was all pointing to the issue that irked him so much—age.

I'm glad to have found this out and I totally forgive his actions. Lanny and I were always friends, but our bond has become even stronger after discussing this story multiple times. He told me, "No matter what happened, Randy really loved you, Bill. It was a bad time for him and I'm glad you were able to make peace with him."

WATCHA GONNA DO, BILL APTER, WHEN SYLVESTER STALLONE CALLS YOU

TWENTY

July 2014

APTER DISCLAIMER: I did not get Hulk Hogan the part of Thunderlips in *Rocky III*. He landed the part on his own merits. This is the story of how I helped to get the ball rolling that ultimately led to Sylvester Stallone casting him.

t was 1981 and I was sitting at my desk in the *PWI* offices when my telephone rang. Natalie, our switchboard operator, who was really great at screening our calls, said, "Someone says they are from Sylvester Stallone's office and wants to talk to you." Had my big day arrived? Did they want to cast me in a film? I couldn't wait to find out . . .

Unfortunately, it wasn't me they wanted. The nasal-voiced woman on the other end told me that Mr. Stallone had picked up a recent issue

Here I am posed with (left to right) Angelo Savoldi, ring announcer Johnny Addie and Arnold Skaaland. I was working on my wrestling radio show on WHBI-FM in New York.

and was looking for a wrestler with a specific look—well built and blond—for a role in an upcoming movie. It would be the third in the *Rocky* series, aptly titled *Rocky III*. All suggestions would be appreciated. She gave me the mailing address of the production company and their FedEx number, so I would be able to send the photos overnight.

Two wrestlers who fit that profile immediately came to mind—

"Superstar" Billy Graham and Hulk Hogan. I went to the photo files and picked the five most flattering images of both and sent them to her.

It took only one afternoon for them to call me back and ask for more photos of Hogan, to which I obliged. A few days later I was asked to contact Hogan on their behalf.

Keep in mind there were no cell phones back in those days. After several tries and a few messages on Hogan's answering machine, I decided to call his mother, Ruth. Years prior to this, through Hulk, his mother and I became telephone friends. He always told me if I couldn't reach him, his mother would always be able to find him.

I also reached out to my contact at WWWF, Arnold Skaaland, who was one of Vince McMahon Sr.'s closest confidants. Arnie (as everyone called him) told me that he would get the message to Hulk. I also telephoned contacts at Verne Gagne's AWA offices, as I knew they were in and out of contact with him.

Not long afterward, I lost track of this entire situation, as it accelerated very quickly, and I had to move on to whatever deadlines I needed to satisfy. I hooked the right people up with each other and the rest was history. I wasn't really looking for anything more than a thanks. Weeks later, I got that from Hulk's mother—but I hadn't heard from Hulk. I was told by someone that Skaaland gave him the message, and even though Hogan thought it was a rib, he went ahead and called Stallone. It would be the biggest break of his life.

Months after filming started, Ruth called to say that Hulk wanted to thank me and had contacted the production company to make sure our magazines get exclusive color images of the film. She was so thankful that I sent Stallone the most flattering photos of her son, helping him secure the part.

I always wondered why I had never heard from Hulk directly. It would be years later when he was in WCW that I brought it up, and he seemed totally confused. He thought it was Arnold Skaaland! I told him to check with his mother and she would set the story straight. To this day I'm not sure if he ever did that, but the letter she sent along with the photos told the true story.

* * *

Hulk and I became good friends, and even in the days when the magazines were banned from WWF, we kept in touch regularly through his mother. He was a loyal WWF employee—even though there were a few side-incidents.

The first incident took place the night he won the WWF title from Iron Sheik in front of 19,000 or so rabid "Hulkamaniacs" at Madison Square Garden. To document the match, our company had a photographer with a 400mm lens in the balcony (we had to buy that ticket and he had to sneak the lens and camera into MSG—not an easy task). Getting great shots from that distance was almost impossible. We wanted to give Hogan's win a huge cover story, but couldn't do it without the highest-quality photos.

I watched the title change from another seat at the Garden. I wish I was allowed at ringside with my camera, but we were not permitted. It was very frustrating.

After the show, I went to the local New York hotel where a lot of the wrestlers were gathered at the bar. This was the usual routine after matches. Hogan wasn't there, and another wrestler, I don't remember who it was, told me where Hulk was staying. I excused myself and went to call him from a pay phone. I was connected to his room but only got his answering machine. No matter, I left a message explaining to him that I needed a cover shot of him with the belt. When I arrived home hours later, I was thrilled when I checked my answering machine and had a voicemail from Hulk, asking me to call him no matter what time I got in.

This time I got him. His wife Linda answered and told me he was waiting for my call.

"Willie Apter," was his greeting. "Wassup, brother? Were you there tonight?" I told him my story and when I was done he asked, "How early can you be here

tomorrow morning, so we can do the pictures?"

We agreed on 9:30. As promised, I was in their room at that time. He was fully dressed and suggested we take the photos in the clothes he was wearing. I told him it would look best with his shirt off and I'd only shoot from the waist up, so it wouldn't look like he was wearing jeans.

He wondered where my studio equipment was to properly light him. I told him I would use flash-on-camera, as I didn't want Vince McMahon to be upset if the shots looked too good and take it out on Hogan! Hulk thanked me for "thinking in the right direction" as I mounted my trusty Vivatar 283 flash onto my Nikon FM. Now we were under way. I took about 35 photos, and then Linda took one of Hulk and me together that I have never used in any magazine. I promised him it would be a personal photo. There we were, with "shit-eating grins" on our faces as we broke the WWF rules. He assured me that if Vince gets hot, he'd personally take care of it.

During the height of his championship reign I had less and less personal contact with Hulk, but his mother and I kept the lines of communication open.

It's the morning after Hulk Hogan won the WWF title from The Iron Sheik. I'm in Hulk Hogan's hotel room proud to be the first person to formally photograph him with the belt.

***

After his WWF(E) days, Hulk began to call me every few weeks just to chat. A lot of people told me, "He'll only call when he wants something," but that was okay with me. In the year 2000, he told me that the A&E channel was going to do a biography about him and wanted a list of "approved talkers" for the show. He requested that I be one of them. That was pretty cool. I was part of an elite few he actually trusted with keeping his image shiny.

That show ran a few times that year and it's still shown on the Biography Channel pretty regularly. As much as I enjoyed being included in the biography, I did get a bit of heat. Apparently, Vince McMahon took exception to something I said.

When you watch the show, my final on-camera take has me saying, "If it wasn't for Hulk Hogan, wrestling would not be as big as it is today." After I said that, I asked the producer to do a second take. On that one I proclaimed, "If it wasn't for Hulk Hogan and Vince McMahon, wrestling would not be as big as it is today." They assured me that they would use the second take. But when I saw the show on A&E, I was pretty rattled to see that they used take one! Years later, I saw McMahon in a St. Louis hotel lobby and explained the situation to him, but he shrugged it off as "No big thing, Bill." He was already a multimillionaire and at this point, that show meant little to him, if anything at all.

***

In the early days of his WWF reign, Hogan was the main event at a show in Atlantic City (this was not a *WrestleMania* show). Although WWF banned the magazines from photographing, I thought I would just pop in and say hello.

I was able to talk my way backstage, and whenever a wrestler saw me they had the "what are you doing back here" look on their face. Gorilla Monsoon, who was the agent for the show, came over to me and was very pleasant, but he told me that I shouldn't be back there and if Vince found out, there would be trouble. At the same time, Hogan came over, put his huge arms around me and told Monsoon, "He's cool, Gino. He's my guest." Monsoon accepted that, and Hogan asked me, "Do you have your camera?" I told him

I just came to say hello and my camera was in my car, since I wasn't allowed to shoot. He told me to get my camera and make sure I was at ringside for his match.

A short time later, after watching the prelim matches from a back row, Hogan's music hit and I headed to the ring with my camera. I told the ringside guards that I was cleared to shoot this match and they just let me go (actually one of them recognized me). As Hogan got into the ring, he posed and hammed for me. During the match, he made sure I got all the best shots. After he won, he asked me to get up on the ring apron, where he took the microphone and blasted, "*Pro Wrestling Illustrated* is number one!" I kept shooting away. He came over, shook my hand and left through the thousands of cheering fans. I heard through the grapevine that Monsoon took a lot of heat for that, and Hogan just brushed it off with McMahon.

***

I did a lot of exclusive interviews with Hogan through the years, mainly during his WCW days. I used to visit his home in Clearwater, Florida. I witnessed both the good and the bad times with his ex-wife, Linda. I watched his son, Nicolas, play soccer and was charmed by his lovely teenage daughter, Brooke. From an early age she exuded so much class. No matter how busy he might have been, he truly cared for his children. I sat for many hours, waiting to conduct an interview or photography session, while he worked with his kids on homework or other projects. He was Hulk Hogan, one of the most recognizable people in the world, but here at home, he was just dad.

Hogan has always been very cordial and has opened up his

Hulk Hogan made sure I was always in the "cool nWo loop." Here I am with two of the New World Order's coolest—Kevin Nash (left) and Dennis Rodman (right).

home to me. As a matter of fact, when my son, Brandon, was celebrating his Bar Mitzvah, Hogan recorded a promo for him (as did several other wrestlers, including Dwayne Johnson)—we called it a "Brawl Mitzvah." We did other shtick videos throughout the years and he never said no.

No matter what negative things "the boys" may say about Hogan, he was once the biggest superstar in the business, and he allowed me to be a part of Hulkamania in both his business and personal life.

When Hogan, Kevin Nash and Scott Hall were the coolest group in town—the New World Order—hanging out with Dennis Rodman and so many other celebrities, Hogan made sure I was included whenever I was in town, and he made me feel part of that faction. He always put me over to everyone.

Many times throughout the years, when WWF Magazine was going through changes, I would receive calls from several WWF office personnel telling me that "Hogan suggested you again for the editor position when he was talking to Vince about the magazine." I don't think he ever knew that I knew, so if you're reading this, Hulk, thanks for putting me over. Again.

SHOOTING *PWI* COVER #1—A MASK TASK AND AN IMPOSSIBLE "DREAM"

TWENTY-ONE

(The very first *PWI: Pro Wrestling Illustrated*, Issue No.1—September 1979)

To make *PWI* extra special and different from sister publications *Inside Wrestling* and *The Wrestler*, we had to find something different and compelling. What would make the consumer want to buy a new magazine?

Sometimes you need to shoot a new photo and sometimes the archive you spent years building is the answer. I have a great memory for the photos I shot, and I recalled a photograph of "The American Dream" Dusty Rhodes with Mil Máscaras. It was taken in mid-1978 and was never used. When it was time to choose the cover of the first issue of *PWI*, my memory bank went right to that shot. Two megastars and a photo that had never been seen—it was perfect.

The photo session almost never took place. I was at the Westchester County Center in White Plains, New York. The WWF card was loaded with top talent, and I thought two in particular would make a great joint cover-image: Rhodes and Máscaras.

The building had a huge stage that hosted many concerts. For wrestling and boxing, the curtains to the stage were drawn and the

One of my first face-to-face interviews was in the mid-'60s with Professor Toru Tanaka.

ring was in the center of the building. This allowed for the wrestling and boxing talents to peek through the curtains and watch the other matches. It also allowed them to socialize and do media interviews and photos.

With Dusty already backstage, I approached him and asked if I could take him to Máscaras's dressing room to pose them for a photo. He said, "Willie, I'll be in my dressing room. You bring him to me if you want that shot." Okay. Strike one.

Dusty left the stage area and Mil showed up moments later. "I will gladly take the picture," he smiled through the mask.

I went to Dusty's dressing room to let him know Mil was on the stage, but when I waved him over he said, "Willie, not now. I gotta go over my match." I went back to find Mil, but he had already struck up a conversation with someone and I didn't want to interrupt. Bad timing. I figured it wasn't going to happen.

Up until this time, I thought that Dusty and Mil were in single matches. But a quick glance at a lineup sheet pasted on one of the dressing-room doors spelled out that they were teaming against Professor Tanaka and Mr. Fuji.

Just moments before the match, they were both on stage. This was my chance.

"Dusty, let me get the shot," I insisted. He looked over at me and said, "Okay, Willie, let's do it." Máscaras came over and I discussed how they would pose. "Willie, just take your dang picture, we gotta go to the ring." I suggested that Dusty go down on one knee and Mil stand right behind him. "I ain't goin' down on one knee, Willie. Shoot the picture or I'm done." Mil looked at me and winked. He knew the shot I wanted. He quickly knelt down and I shot the photo. "Hold on, let me get a few," I suggested, but Dusty said, "Enough, Willie."

If you want to see that cover go to the *Pro Wrestling Illustrated* website and click on cover history, year 1979. Note how "thrilled" Dusty is to be in this picture!

That photo would not be seen for over a year, but I'm proud to say I got it done!

THE STUNNING TRUTH ABOUT DAN SHOCKET AND EDDIE ELLNER

TWENTY-TWO

When I make appearances at conventions, I'm often asked about this headline. Sometimes fans will blurt out, "Hey, Bill, how did you end your feud with Shocket or Ellner?" And then giggle or wink to let me know they're in on it—meaning they know that Dan and Eddie were just made up characters in the magazine. They're wrong.

Yes, I was always the babyface columnist. Non-opinionated, just writing the news, taking photos and conducting interviews. Most of the mail I received was favorable. In the case of Dan Shocket and Eddie Ellner, it was the total opposite. Most fans disliked them because they wrote about their hatred of the good guys and their admiration for the bad guys.

I never wrote a heel column. I never wrote a Dan Shocket column. I never wrote an Eddie Ellner column. I know this will shock many of you. Both guys were real. Eddie Ellner is still alive. Sadly, we lost Danny in 1985, after a bout with cancer. He was in his mid-thirties.

Much of Danny's heel persona was actually culled from his true personality. Dan was one of the most sarcastic people I had ever known. He had a natural ability to rile you up if he thought you were at all vulnerable.

Daniel Shocket actually went to high school with Mr. Weston's daughter, Toby. "Dan and I grew up together, but he was pretty insular," she said. "I didn't know him well, but he did bring his boa constrictor on the school bus one day and scared us all. He was in the Lens Club (literary creativity), the United Nations Club and was a technician in a school play of *Ten Little Indians*. He did not show up for any of the group photos." (Strangely enough, I couldn't find Dan in any of my personal group photos from our days together either.)

Although small in stature—I estimate Danny was about 5'4"—he liked to portray an image of a man who liked the finer things in life. He loved cigars (and puffing the smoke in people's faces), wine, great-looking "wenches" and good food. He liked to think he exuded the playboy image. That led him to

two very enjoyable stanzas of his journalism career.

When the Apartment Wrestling series was born in *Sports Review Wrestling*, it was the creative-writing genius of Shocket along with the expert photography of Theo Ehret that turned this genre into a magazine sensation. Dan's words and the creation of the promoter of the erotic sport, Dave Moll—a playboy-like character—were all that thousands of male readers needed to keep the "sport" alive for years to come. It was true Dan all the way.

Aside from writing for the wrestling magazines, Dan branched out and also became a regular writer for Al Goldstein's *Screw* magazine, as well as other male-oriented periodicals.

My job became much harder when I was out in the field due to Dan—and subsequently Ellner as well.

Keep in mind that the people in the business—the wrestlers and the promoters—didn't really grasp that these guys were heel writers. Too many people took what they wrote personally, and I became the target. I cannot tell you how many wrestlers—good guys, of course—would bitch and moan to me at shows, because Shocket called them "wormslime" or "has-beens" or "losers" in a column. It didn't matter that I told them he was a heel columnist. Many of the nicest good guys I ever met told me, "If this keeps up, you had better watch where you go." Really. It is all true.

Many promoters also reacted negatively. One Georgia promoter told me that our magazines would be banned from shooting photos at their arenas if we continued to say nasty things about Tommy Rich and Mr. Wrestling II. Tommy was pretty furious as well, but II got it.

When I would get back to the office after a wrestling trip, I would tell the staff what happened and would get good laugh from Danny or Ellner. The other editors would say, "They need to get what we do. It's good publicity for them." It made me very uncomfortable.

I usually brought a couple dozen issues of the magazine to pass around to the talent, but sometimes I'd choose not to bring a particular issue, in fear for my well being. I examined every column and story before I put myself in the same dressing room as the wrestlers and that magazine!

Ellner was a lot like Dan in real life and, of course, in the magazine. More than Dan, Ellner picked on me in his columns, and fans still talk to me about that. Eddie can be found these days at yogasoup.com.

I enjoyed both Danny and Eddie. I became good friends with Shocket, and my ex-wife and I were always trying to set him up with women—but he didn't have any issues doing that on his own. Eddie was also a great guy, and I always sensed his respect for me no matter what he wrote in the magazines.

> **Too many people took what they wrote personally, and I became the target.**

"I'LL KICK YOUR ASS IF I'M NOT ON THE COVER NEXT MONTH!"

TWENTY-THREE

The headline came directly from the mouth of Scott "Razor Ramon" Hall. It happened in 1993, during the height of his days as the "bad guy." Hall was not the only wrestler to threaten me with bodily harm. His story is just a prime example of the grief I put up with on the road. It might surprise you to know that a lot of "good guys" were equally pissed about not appearing on covers. Although they were not as graphic in their verbal assaults, I knew they felt shafted when they weren't chosen to be a cover boy. It didn't matter if there was a six-page spread about them. If it wasn't a cover shot, it meant zero.

There was always a line of wrestlers waiting for me to hand out free copies of the current issue. There were very few compliments. They complained about their placement in the rankings, or a photo they didn't think was flattering, or simply about not being in an issue. But the cover was always the main focus.

"What is this son of a bitch Mil Máscaras doing on the cover?" one babyface asked, pointing to a full-face photo of the Mexican icon on the cover of *Inside Wrestling* magazine from November 1975. (I still talk to him regularly so rather than risk our friendship he will remain unnamed . . . but I will talk about him in Q&A sessions tied to this book if you ask.) "Jesus, Bill, how docs this geek get a full cover shot when I can't even get a small one? None of us like him; he's a damn prima donna. I just don't get it. He can't work. He does the same damn thing every time he's in the ring. This is bullcrap. What docs he pay you guys to get on the cover?" He tossed the magazine back at me and walked away in a state of disbelief.

> He's a damn prima donna.

Paying to get on the cover . . .

That's an interesting idea. I never thought of that angle. Perhaps I could have cashed in and made a fortune from guys who wanted to be all over the newsstands—but it didn't work that way.

Many of the veteran wrestlers told me stories . . . They said "Cowboy" Bob Ellis, Ricki Starr and the Fabulous Kangaroos (Al Costello and Roy Heffernan) regularly paid my boss, Mr. Weston, to get on the covers. I never confronted him with those rumors, and I do not believe it happened. I wrote it off as jealousy.

The bottom line about getting on the cover was, and is, very simple: the photos on the cover, whether it is one, two or three different images, are put there to sell magazines. I always compare it to a wrestling card at a major arena. Would you publicize the prelim or mid-card guys to sell tickets? No. With the magazines it is the same mentality. The hottest guys get the cover. The rest, if they're newsworthy, wind up in a feature story or a column inside. I'm here to say they should be happy they get any publicity. So many were more upset than grateful through the years. I had to learn that complaining was a major part of the business, and I had to learn to live with it and find ways to deflect it. Many times, it took the fun out of my job.

Going back to the subject of paying to be on a cover, here is a question I often get:

"Hey, Bill, how much did Dusty Rhodes and Jim Crockett pay you guys to put Dusty on the cover almost every month? Or did you just work for them since you were on their TV shows so much?"

The truth is that we put Dusty on a cover once, and it sold so well

we continued to put him in the spotlight. He was red hot on national TV. The television exposure and the magazines were a natural marketing tool for each other. As long as Dusty was being pushed hard and was on TV, we'd put him on a cover. At least until sales

Road Warrior Hawk, Road Warrior Willie and our manager "Precious" Paul Ellering.

figures began to decline.

In the 1970s, there was a formula in place for the covers. Because our offices were close to New York City, we knew that the monthly cards at Madison Square Garden, drawing 18,000-plus fans nearly every time, would be a good source of cover material. I photographed the shows, mainly headlined by Bruno Sammartino, nearly every month. We felt secure that we would get a good cover shot of Bruno or one of the other main-event people (Chief Jay Strongbow, "Superstar" Billy Graham and many others). Sales proved that the Garden covers did well for us, and that process continued until cable TV came along, spotlighting other territories and giving people like Dusty, Tommy Rich and the Road Warriors the opportunity to get on the covers.

One of the ways to get on a cover was to agree to pose for me in the portable studio or simply stand against a wall and let me take a few poses. What used to make me laugh was when wrestlers who refused to pose also bitched about not being on the cover.

Throughout my years in the magazine business, there was only one person who actively dodged being on the cover. He was a young impresario working as a broadcaster at his father's wrestling company. This was around 1977. His name is Vince McMahon Jr.

"While I appreciate the offer, the magazines are something for the wrestlers as far as I am concerned," he told me. "I really don't want to be on the cover or inside the magazines, and I would appreciate it if you would respect my wishes."

That Vince guy did okay . . .

VON ERICH'S FURY CAUSES ANXIOUS DAYS AND SLEEPLESS NIGHTS

My relationship with the Von Erich family spans many years. There were good times and, of course, far too many sad times. There is one story in particular I have to share. The telephone rang at 3 a.m., rocking me out of bed. Of course at that hour the first thought that comes to mind is, "Who died?" When I picked up in the very dark hours of February 10, 1984, the answer came quickly:

"David Von Erich died a few minutes ago," Jimmy Suzuki, a photographer friend, said. "No one knows how. I will call you back when I know more." He was calling from Japan.

I hung up the phone and sat on the corner of my bed, trying to make some sense of how a really nice 25-year-old kid could be dead. I liked David very much. In the past few years I had photographed him and visited him and his wife, Trish, at their home in Dallas, and we had become friends. At least once a month, David and I would talk on the telephone about the business and our families. Whenever David wrestled in West Palm Beach, Florida, he always made sure to give a special hello to my father, who sat at the timekeeper's desk every Monday night.

In the hours that followed, I put in a call to David's parents, Fritz and Doris, to send my condolences. I remember Fritz telling me, "David loved you, Bill. You were part of the family to him and that makes you part of the family to me too. Thanks for the call and I'll see you soon."

A few days later, on February 14, I was on a flight to Dallas. The funeral would take place the next day. I was picked up at the airport by wrestler Brian Adias who drove me to the Von Erich ranch in Denton. There were a lot of mourners there and as soon as I entered the premises, Trish walked right over to me, greeted me with a warm hug and said, "I wondered when you would get here. We're really happy you came, Bill." Next, Fritz and Doris came with hugs as well. Indeed I felt like a close member of the family.

The next day thousands of people paid tribute to David at the funeral. If they could not get into the church, they waited outside to catch a glimpse of the family and pay their respects. I was driven to the church by Gary Hart. Gary and I were close friends, and he was Fritz's right-hand man in the Dallas World Class Championship Wrestling office, which Fritz owned.

Entering the church and gazing at the huge group of mourners, I spotted Vince McMahon Sr., promoter Jim Barnett and wrestlers from all over the globe. It was quite a tribute to the young star.

After the service and burial, I went to the house. The other Von Erich brothers, Kerry, Kevin, Chris and Michael, and I reminisced about David and how we covered his career in the magazines. Kerry told me, "You were one of David's favorite people, Bill. He really respected you." Again, it felt like I was just naturally part of the family.

A few hours later, I was back on an airplane and headed to the magazine office to write my "Remembering David Von Erich" story. I poured my heart and soul out and the story garnered me a Writer of the Year award. The story was all too real and so were my feelings.

The outpouring of love for the

Von Erich family after David's death did not diminish. The family decided to pay tribute to David's memory by arranging the David Von Erich Memorial Parade of Champions on May 6, 1984, at Texas Stadium. It was a star-studded outdoor event, and the main event had Kerry Von Erich getting his shot at Ric Flair's National Wrestling Alliance World Heavyweight championship. Without question, I would be headed to Texas again to cover this historic card. As a matter of fact, it was so huge that the magazine boss Stanley Weston approved two of us to go on the trip. Editor-photographer Craig Peters would accompany me and we would get full team coverage. I couldn't wait. I had the fever—until a few days before the show. That's when my relationship with the Von Erichs took a terrible turn.

I was sitting at my desk and received a phone call from Gary Hart. I assumed he was calling to see when I would arrive in Dallas and allow me to treat him to dinner (we had a running joke about that for years). Instead of being the lighthearted Gary Hart I knew so well, this time he seemed troubled.

"Mah man," he said. "Fritz is furious with you about that story in the magazine that just came out. He said he thought you were part of the family, but after reading this story he doesn't even want you here." I had no idea what he was talking about. He explained.

"One of the names you write under—Dan Shocket—wrote a story comparing David, Kerry and Kevin to Moe, Larry and Curly, The Three Stooges. How could you do that, mah man?"

The words shot out of my mouth quickly: "Gary, I am not Dan Shocket! Dan is one of our editors. Let me take a look at the story and I'll call you back."

We had a quick meeting in the office and I saw Dan's column—the one Gary was talking about. Although it was written before David's death, because of the publishing lag it hit the newsstands at the worst possible time. I called Gary back and explained it all.

"Gary, you've got to tell Fritz that, first of all, this is such an unfortunate situation—the story was written before David died," I said. "Also Dan is our heel columnist. It's an angle. He always writes about hating the good guys and supporting the heels. You can look back at previous issues and you'll see."

Hart told me he would talk to Fritz and try to iron things out.

The next few hours, actually the

next few days, were hell. I called Fritz and left messages for him, but he did not return my calls. Gary told me that Fritz got my messages and he just "doesn't get it" and he is too upset to call me back. He also wanted to know that even if it was written before David passed, how could I let this get published. I told Gary (and he knew this) I was not the boss and I did not see everything that we published. However, in Fritz's mind this was my doing. Gary suggested I stop calling Fritz and he would try to arrange an early meeting on the day of the Parade of Champions.

How could I let this get published?

I didn't listen. I called Fritz again. This time his wife Doris answered. I was almost in tears as I pleaded my case to her. She assured me that she would talk to Fritz. She seemed to get it. I certainly hoped so.

You can imagine my fear the day of the trip. Although Craig Peters tried to keep my mood light from New York to Dallas, I was a nervous wreck.

We rented a car and arrived at Texas Stadium early in the afternoon. As we entered the locker-room area, we were greeted by the Fabulous Freebirds, Michael Hayes, Terry Gordy and Buddy Roberts. Hayes's first words to me were not very welcoming.

"Hey, Billy Boy, you'd better stay clear of ol' man Fritz. He is more than pissed at you."

Gary Hart came down the hallway and approached me.

"Hey, mah man, I don't know what Fritz is gonna do about you," he said. "I couldn't really talk to him. There hasn't been any time."

Just a few yards behind Gary was my worst nightmare. Kevin, Kerry and Fritz Von Erich were walking toward us. Kevin and Kerry walked a bit in front of Fritz and came right over and greeted me. I sensed no tension from either of them. Now Fritz was standing directly in front of me. Before he could say a word, I started speaking quickly.

"Fritz, I am so sorry. Please understand. That story by Dan Shocket was written before David died. We would never do anything to hurt your family, Fritz. I hope you can find it in your heart to forgive me." I was apologizing for something I didn't even do, but I could not remain mute. I had total diarrhea of the mouth. I was about to continue, when Fritz put his hand up as if to ask me to stop talking. The 6'5" near 300-pound Von Erich leaned down to my 5'7" frame, and just when I thought he was going to put his hands around my neck or give me the "Iron Claw" on my face, he spoke ever so softly in my ear.

"It's okay, son," he assured me as his huge hands rested on my shoulders. "I forgive you. This is a big night for the family tonight and I'm glad to see you. Make sure you get a lot of pictures!"

I could not believe it. I could see smiles on the faces of Kerry, Kevin, Gary Hart and even the Freebirds, who had all been wondering if Fritz was going to break every bone in my body (he had quite a reputation of doing that to the people who crossed him).

Did Gary Hart finally get the heat off me by properly explaining the situation to Fritz? I don't think so. I had also implored many of the World Class Championship Wrestling workers throughout the week to go to bat for me, but none had proved successful. So who was it?

Just a few minutes after Kerry's dramatic win over Flair for the NWA World belt in front of 30,000 fans, I saw Doris Von Erich. As I got the entire family in line for a pose with Kerry and the belt, I hugged her and thanked her for letting me speak candidly with her about the Fritz issue. I told her that somehow he forgave me. She gave me a big smile, patted my left cheek with her hand and winked at me. That explained everything.

All of Fritz's horses and all of Fritz's men couldn't put my relationship with him together again.

Sometimes it takes the wife to get things done the right way.

Thank you, Doris.

My relationship with the Von Erich family continues to this day. When an ESPN 30-for-30 segment was being filmed in 2014, showing Kevin and his family life in Hawaii, they needed someone to talk about the Von Erich dynasty. Kevin suggested they talk to me. The program aired in February 2015, and I was proud to be included.

PUNK FAN BOOTED FROM SUNNYSIDE ARENA!

TWENTY-FIVE

In my teen years I lived in Maspeth, Queens, New York. My local arena was in a section of the borough called Sunnyside Garden. The arena hosted wrestling, boxing, dances and various community events. There was a weekly TV wrestling show broadcast from Sunnyside every Tuesday night on the DuMont Network— channel 5 in New York. On Thursday nights we got wrestling from Washington, D.C., and Saturday nights from Bridgeport, Connecticut. All these shows were promoted under the Capitol Wrestling banner, the company run by Vince McMahon Sr.

Somewhere around 1962, the very popular babyface team of Mark Lewin and Don Curtis shocked TV viewers by becoming heels. The handsome team made young girls cry and boys despise them. Police had to escort them in and out of arenas. It was that serious.

My brother, Paul, and a 12-year-old me as a budding tag team combo.

bring it to Sunnyside.

There was a rule in New York State that kids under the age of 13 were not permitted into wrestling or boxing shows. My dad had a friend on the State Athletic Commission named Pete Scalzo, who happened to be a former boxer. Although I was not yet 13, Pete told my dad, "Bring him in, it's okay—but keep a low profile." We went dozens of times, and I never made myself known to anyone.

As my dad and I headed to Sunnyside, he didn't ask me about the sign I had rolled up under my arm. We were just out for a night of wrestling and the usual stop for dinner at White Castle Burgers, just two stores down from the arena.

At the arena, we saw Pete, who gave me the "How ya doin', kid?" wink. He quickly escorted us to the bleachers where my dad and I sat in the last row, leaning against the wall. To get up there you had to climb over about 30 rows of bleacher seats.

We sat though a few prelim matches and then the main event was up, Lewin and Curtis against two fan favorites (I can't recall who they were). As Mark and Don were led to the ring by a throng of guards, I told my dad I'd be right back. Armed with my sign, I rushed

On one of the Saturday night TV shows emanating from Bridgeport, a fan was seen at ringside walking around with a homemade poster that read "You Are A Bum." He was directing it at Lewin and Curtis. It drove them mad. They screamed and yelled at the fan until arena police ordered the man back to his seat.

I thought this was so cool that I made a sign exactly like the one from Bridgeport and planned to down the bleacher benches as fast as I could and headed to ringside. As Lewin and Curtis got into the ring, I made my way closer, took the rubber band off my sign and opened it up. I envisioned myself just like the guy in Bridgeport—and I'd be on TV, so all my friends would see how cool I was . . .

The security guy ringside told me to go back to my seat, but I persevered and went right to the apron, holding my sign high. Lewin caught a glimpse of it, then pointed at me and yelled, "We are not bums!" The fans booed him loudly as he yelled at me. Now the guard had gotten off of his chair and was shooing me away. Curtis called to the guard and said, "Officer, give me that sign!" The guard confiscated my sign and handed it to Curtis. He ripped it to shreds, then he and Mark laughed as they threw the pieces back at me. Then Don questioned the guard, "That punk can't be 13. Throw him out." Lewin tried to get a chant of "Thrown him out" going, but the fans booed even louder as the bell rang for the match to begin. The guard asked me how old I was, but I just walked away.

As Lewin and Curtis brutalized

You Are A Bum.

their opposition, I turned back toward the bleachers, but before I could leave ringside, I saw Pete Scalzo walking toward me. He stopped me in my tracks and said, "Wait here for a minute." Pete went toward the bleachers and waved for my father to come down. I saw him talk to my father for a moment, throw his hands up as to say, "Sorry, but I can't do anything to help." My dad walked over and said, "Pete wants us to leave." I was devastated.

Outside the arena, my father told me that Pete was quite embarrassed when a few of the other commissioners questioned how "that kid" got into Sunnyside underage (I really did not look like I was 13). That was the last time we would go to Sunnyside for a few years, and it was all my fault. To make matters worse, on the Washington TV show two days later, Lewin and Curtis gloated about how they got some kid tossed out of Sunnyside.

* * *

In 1972, I met and interviewed Don Curtis in Florida. He was promoting a show in Jacksonville. I told him the story and he actually recalled the incident and said, "That was you? Holy cow, I hope you aren't here to seek revenge."

If you go to YouTube and search "Bill Apter Interviews Don Curtis" you will find what a great guy Don Curtis was.

As for Mark Lewin, I've told him the story many times, and he always gets a kick out of it.

But the person who always asks for this story is Dotty, Don's widow. To the lovely, sensational Dotty: This one is for you.

APTER HELPS PROMOTER WHO SUCCUMBS TO HIS OWN DEMONS

TWENTY-SIX

I t was 1977, and "Superstar" Billy Graham was at the apex of his popularity in the Northeast. I liked Graham, because he was one of the rare wrestlers, at the time, who loved the spotlight and would do anything to get his image in the magazines.

One time, we arranged a photo shoot in Times Square a few hours before a Madison Square Garden show. We had nothing planned and would just improvise.

After an hour or so of posing with fans on 42nd Street, hamming it up with the chefs in a few restaurants, and a couple of shots at the Mid-City Gym, we were ready to head back to the Garden. Before we got there, I saw a view of the entire Times Square area, and I thought it would be a great backdrop for a Graham cover photo.

I needed him to stand on something, and the

only thing available was a garbage can. Graham thought it would be an incredible photo and took off his shirt and mounted the garbage can. He began posing and a huge crowd formed around us. After a few minutes, the police asked us to finish, as we were disrupting traffic in the area.

As I put my camera back in my bag and Graham put his shirt on, a short, curly-haired man approached me.

"Hey, Mr. Apter, I'm a big fan of the magazines you work for," he said. "I own a dress shop in Flushing [Queens] and want to know if you can get some wrestlers to come to my store." I gave him my business card, told him I lived in Queens and asked him to call me. I would see what I could work out. He started walking with me and Graham, asking Superstar about an appearance as well. Graham told him to keep in touch with me.

The man was Herb Abrams, and he kept talking and walking with us all the way down to the Garden (about nine blocks). When we got to the Garden entrance and he said goodbye, his last words to me were, "One of these days I'm gonna be a wrestling promoter, and you'll see big things from me."

Herb called me the next day. He told me he wanted wrestlers to do an autograph signing in a recently opened store. Herb would pay each wrestler $50 and let him choose an outfit for his wife. He also told me that he would let me pick out anything I wanted for my wife as well—but no $50 for me.

I told Herb I didn't know if I could get anyone but that I would scope it out.

Two weeks later, I was covering a show at Sunnyside Garden in Queens, and Abrams was in the audience. He found me and asked if I could get the team of Billy White Wolf and Chief Jay Strongbow—who were on the card that day—to appear at his store when they came back to Sunnyside in a few weeks. I went down to the dressing room and they agreed to talk to Herb. Promoter Mike Rosenberg allowed me to bring Abrams to the dressing-room area and Herb did his pitch and booked them for his store. It would be a three-hour signing.

When the appearance took place, Strongbow and White Wolf drew a huge throng of fans and Herb was very happy. We all got our goodies and that was that—or so I thought.

A few weeks later I saw an ad in a local Queens newspaper that Herb's store was hosting another wrestling autograph day (I can't recall who the wrestler was). This disturbed me, as I figured I should have been in the loop since I hooked Herb up in the first place. I called Herb and he said, "I didn't want to bother you, so I had Strongbow and White Wolf hook me up." This happened a few more times and I eventually stopped calling Herb. Some of the wrestlers I saw at Sunnyside told me that Herb was talking about running his own wrestling show and was questioning them about their deals with WWWF.

Over the next few years, I saw Herb at Sunnyside shows and at Madison Square Garden. He would tell me that he was well on his way to promoting and had a financial backer in place. I had heard this same story many times from other hopeful promoters and I didn't think that Herb had a chance.

I lost contact with Abrams for what seemed like ages and then one day, at the magazine office, he called to let me know he had started a company called the UWF and that he already had a TV contract. He added that he had signed Bruno Sammartino as a commentator and wrestlers "Dr. Death"

Steve Williams, Paul Orndorff and others.

"I know I haven't been the best friend, but you helped me get my start that day in New York when you were taking pictures of Superstar Graham," he told me. "You are welcome to come to any of my shows and you'll have the red-carpet treatment."

That was nice of Herb, but I was quite turned off when I went to cover his first show at a hotel ballroom right across the street from Madison Square Garden. I arrived around three hours before the show and was headed into the dressing-room area when I was told by some faceless official I could not go back. I explained who I was and he said, "No disrespect, Mr. Apter, but Mr. Abrams says that he knows you talk to Vince McMahon and would rather you just cover the show and not be in the backstage area." It was like a slap in the face. I didn't even bother to cover the TV taping, I just left. The next day Herb called to say he was sorry and that it wouldn't happen again, but the damage had been done. One of the wrestlers on the card told me, "He didn't mean it, Bill. He was a nervous wreck, and I think he was all

> **It was like a slap in the face.**

messed up on drugs. It was a nightmare back there."

I did cover a few of the UWF shows in the months to come but had almost no contact with Herb. The rumors of his drug and alcohol abuse had by then overtaken any good the UWF had done.

I wasn't at all surprised that in 1996 he died of a heart attack while in police custody after an alleged incident with cocaine and prostitutes.

Welcome to Billy's Place—a show I did in broadcasting school.

A once-in-a-lifetime photo session with AWA World champion Nick Bockwinkel (left) and the NWA's World titleholder Harley Race.

Muhammad Ali can't believe I'm challenging him.

"Apter Chat" time in 1971 with Bruno Sammartino (left) and Eddie Graham (right).

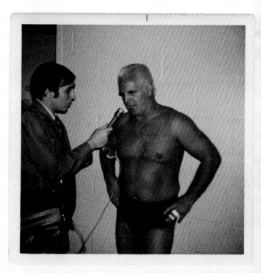

My first ring announcing gig. Sunnyside Garden, 1971.

Dick Van Dyke and me with our best "Stan Laurel" faces.

The "finger book" gets a great addition: "Nature Boy" Buddy Rogers.

Ric Flair and me posing in Puerto Rico. Why this team never succeeded is beyond me.

My best "Jerry Lewis" look as Ted DiBiase roughs me up.

———

One off my earliest meetings with Hulk Hogan.

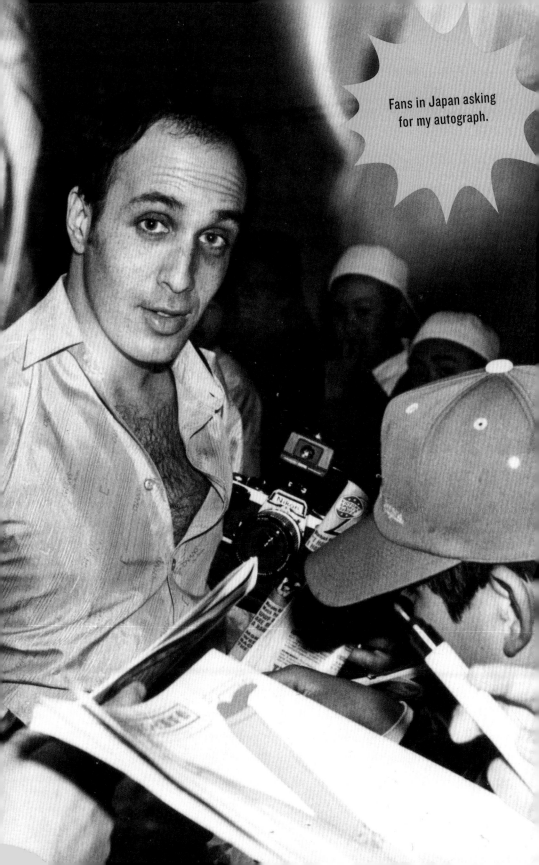

Fans in Japan asking for my autograph.

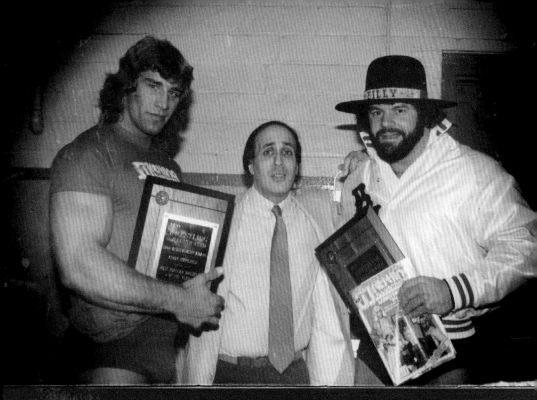

Presenting *PWI* awards to Kerry Von Erich (left) and Billy Jack Haynes (right).
[Photo courtesy of Buddy Myers]

Getting close to the action with my camera as Terry Funk battles the Sheik.

My friend Barry helps me attack Eddie Gilbert during a fun photo session.

That's Nikita Koloff choking me.

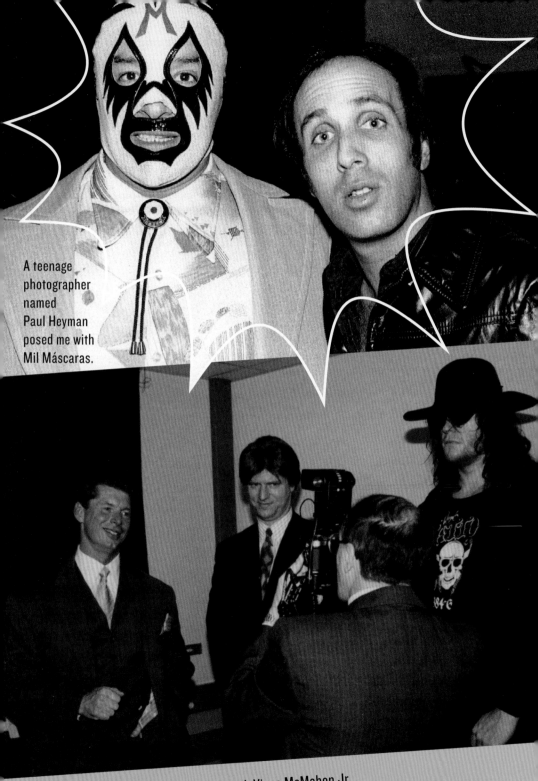

A teenage photographer named Paul Heyman posed me with Mil Máscaras.

One of the few times I ever got to photograph Vince McMahon Jr. This was at a *WrestleMania* press conference. Note the Undertaker and former WWE executive Basil DeVito looking on.

Boxing's Sugar Ray Leonard. He never did agree to fight me!

Mike (far left) and Kevin Von Erich listen to me speak
at a World Class Championship Wrestling function. [Photo courtesy of Buddy Myers]

Giving some attitude to "Stone Cold" Steve Austin.

The legendary Lou Thesz places the original World Championship belt around my waist when I visited his beach home in Virginia.

Joey Styles and I helped each other so much through the years.

Posing with Triple H— an old-school guy in a new-school world.

In my career I have covered Terry Bollea, Hulk Hogan and Hollywood Hulk Hogan.

The "Heartbreak Kid" with the "Heartbreak *Older* Guy."

APTER'S ASTONISHING NEWS: "I'M LEAVING *PWI!*"

TWENTY-SEVEN

My move from the *PWI* family of magazines to the upstart *WOW Magazine* in April 1999 happened very quickly, and in retrospect, it wasn't thought through. When the romance from the publishers at H&S Media in Chicago began, the negotiation went so fast it left me little time to ask, "Do I really want to leave the security of the company and the coworkers I have considered family for the last 29 years?"

It all started in early March 1999, thanks to Paul Heyman and Tazz. I had seen them at an ECW show and they told me that H&S Media would be producing the promotion's official magazine. Tazz pulled a magazine out of his bag—it wasn't ECW but another product. It was the first issue of *WOW*. Tazz asked, "Did you see this freakin' magazine on the stands yet?" I hadn't. He handed it to me and I was shocked at the engraved *WOW* logo, the thick glossy paper it was printed on and the overall glitz. "Bill, they got an editor there, but you should get in touch with these guys," he suggested. "Your name, with this mag . . . it could be the biggest thing to happen for you—and they got lots of money. I know, they're doing our *ECW Magazine*."

Heyman chimed in, "Let me know if you want me to make a call to the main guys there. I already put you on their radar. I told them they don't have a magazine unless they have Apter. It's up to you now."

On my way home, I stopped and picked up a copy at a newsstand. What impressed me was that this news dealer—as well as other bookstores I had visited this day—were placing it on the same rack as other high-class magazines, because of the way it looked. *PWI* and even *WWF Magazine* didn't grab your attention like *WOW*.

I brought a copy into the *PWI* offices and we sat around discussing how this magazine would not get anyone in the wrestling business to cooperate (ECW was the exception), because they broke kayfabe. There was even a glossary of kayfabe terms in the magazine! The sacred lingo used only in the business was now yours just for the price

of a copy. We were shocked that this could happen and felt that the days of *WOW* were numbered; we didn't think anyone would cooperate, and it looked expensive to produce! As we passed the magazine around, I recall our boxing editor Nigel Collins thumbing through the issue and then looking up at me and asking, "Hey, Bill, why aren't you working for these guys?" I'm not certain what my reply was, but I'm sure it wasn't positive. I was against everything they stood for. They might look better, but they broke kayfabe. In those days, that was not something I could easily live with.

A few days later, I received a call at home. The man identified himself as Mike Meyers (no, not the guy who plays Austin Powers). He said he got my number from Paul Heyman and wanted to talk. I listened. He told me they had an editor at *WOW* but were missing a "billboard name" and were interested in me coming aboard in that role. He offered to fly me to their offices in Chicago for, as he put it, an "informational meeting." Mike added that he would call me in a few days to arrange everything. He assured me that it would be totally hush-hush and that there would be no pressure if I decided against working for them after hearing their offer. He did add that he would offer me $20,000 more than whatever I was making and that there would be a three-year contract, with regular salary increases spelled out as well as bonuses. I had no contract with Kappa. I was an employee just like I was when it was Mr. Weston's G.C. London Publishing. I had never even been offered a contract before.

I thanked him and after getting off the phone, I talked to my wife about it. Her take: "It doesn't hurt to go and listen."

Hesitantly, I went into editor Stu Saks's office the next morning, closed the door and sat down. I told him everything.

"What are you going to do?" he asked.

"I'm going to make the trip—just to listen. I'm not leaving this place, Stu." That was the extent of our conversation. In my mind, there was no way I was going to leave.

There was another consideration. My relationship with WWF (soon to become WWE) was pretty good at this time, and the word in the business was that *WOW* was the enemy. Period. The end. The way the magazine looked and some of the things they did to get photos did not sit well. I had heard that they paid thousands of dollars to people like Rena "Sable" Mero and others to pose while still under contract to WWF. Shane McMahon was in charge of *WWF Magazine* (among so many other things in the company), and I was told that he did not appreciate the way H&S did their business.

WrestleMania XV came to Philadelphia a few days before our scheduled meeting (March 28), and there was a reception the night before—a *WrestleMania* "Rage Party"—that I was invited to attend. My goal was not to conduct interviews but to talk to one of the McMahons about this situation.

I was able to briefly meet with Linda McMahon. She was quite cordial until I mentioned the possible *WOW* offer. She became very concerned and said, "Those people are unscrupulous. They are paying huge amounts of money to our contracted talent to take photos, and our talent is accepting." (Note: To my knowledge, there was nothing in their contracts about not doing "outside" photos.) She continued, "They could have approached us, but they just went right to the talent. I cannot tell you what to do, Bill. You have to do what is financially right for you and your family. All I can tell you is that if you do go to work for them, we can't help you in any way. I hope you understand our point of view." Oy vey this was serious—the second-in-command of the biggest wrestling company in the world was telling me that this move wouldn't be good for my career.

On my drive home, I remember pondering what I would have done if the company was still owned by the man who gave me my start, Stanley Weston. The answer was easy. I would have never even gone to Chicago. When Mr. Weston sold the company, it was a totally different dynamic, and it changed the way I looked at where my career was going. I questioned my own loyalty to the new regime when the *WOW* offer was made. In the Weston days, I was like a family member; my wife and I went out with Mr. and Mrs. Weston on many occasions. In many ways, I felt like the son Mr. Weston never had. There were a few others through the years that had that same feeling, but I was the senior member. I was there before any of them, and I always stayed loyal.

A few days later I was on a flight from Philadelphia to Chicago and was driven to the small town of Bannockburn (near Dearborn) to meet with the staff at H&S Media. The red carpet was extended the moment I arrived. Meyers greeted

me, and as we walked through the office, he introduced me to all the editors and artists from all the magazines they produced, including a Beanie Baby monthly, which was a huge seller, teen mags and more. One man passed by me quickly and told me he had to leave due to some family emergency. He was very nice, very warm and introduced himself as Harvey Wasserman—the H in H&S Media. He told me, "Leave that other wrestling company behind. We're the new guys on the block and they won't even be around after a few more issues of *WOW*. We've got huge plans for you, Bill," he said. "Money is just the beginning." He patted me on the back and left.

Next we went into the office of the "S" in H&S Media, Mr. Steve Keen. He was far less flamboyant than Harvey, more businesslike and reserved. He had the personality of a teacher or an accountant. He was cordial in welcoming me and said, "I hope you like what you hear today and you will consider joining us. Your reputation is something we can really use, Bill." After a hearty handshake, publisher Meyers said, "We have a staff meeting for *WOW*. I trust whatever you hear will not be repeated to your current employer." I assured him it would not be.

I walked into a conference room and sitting around the table was managing editor John Delavan, managing art director Elliott From and art director Karen Kaltofen, Brad Perkins and Mike Berk from the editorial and production departments, as well as Tim Towe, who did just about everything at H&S.

Meyers opened the meeting with an introduction, although most everyone there already knew who I was. He said that I was an observer but would hopefully take the editor-in-chief role that they were offering me. That was quite a surprise: I didn't know about the title. The romance was heating up, and I admit I was loving it.

By the end of the meeting, I was thrilled with all the things I'd absorbed. I was treated royally by Mike and the entire team. Furthermore, I was told I would not have to move my family from Philadelphia. I could telecommute by phone and computer and come to the office perhaps once a month for three or four days. They would put me up in a hotel nearby and pretty much cater to any of my needs. Now I *had* to find out what the deal would be. Would it make me leave the security of Kappa? I wondered how the company would react. How would people in the business and the fans react?

Mr. Meyers invited me into his office, but before he talked business he said, "I'm told you know everybody in the wrestling business, is that right?" I assured him I knew most of the people, and he put me to a test. He said, "Get one of them on the phone. I just want to make sure you are who I hear you are before I make an offer." (I would soon come to understand he was a pretty brash and savvy businessman.)

"Hey, Hulk, it's me," were my first words into the telephone. "Willie-Willie," he replied. "Wassup, bruddah?" I explained where I was and told him that I had something to prove to the main man here. He told me to pass the phone over to him. Meyers looked puzzled, and as he began reaching for the phone, asked, "Which Hulk is this—Hogan?" I laughed, "Yes, he's one of my regular calls." Meyers got on the phone and they chatted for perhaps 10 minutes. Hogan told him all about me, and before the call ended suggested Meyers come down to his Tampa home and they go out on his boat one day.

Meyers was sold. To him, timing was crucial. They were starting the third issue and wanted me to take the helm ASAP.

I arrived home late that night, exhausted but also elated about everything that had taken place. As I walked into my house, my wife and kids were awaiting my decision—but I hadn't made it yet. While I said earlier that I was with the same family for 29 years, that wasn't really the case. There were a few editors through the years, like Craig Peters and Stu Saks, who were part of my inner circle. In 1996, Craig had left to work for Feld Entertainment (Ringling Brothers Circus is their most well-known event), spearheading their online marketing operations. So out of the "old-timers" who moved from Mr. Weston's company on Long Island, the only people left from the editorial department were me and Stu.

I talked it out with my family and came to a decision—as I was handing out WOW T-shirts and other gimmicks to the kids—I wasn't going to do this. I think they all felt a bit let down as the excitement had spilled over to them.

The next day, I went to work and walked right into Stu's office, where I told him about the trip (but nothing about what happened in the meetings). I also told him I was not leaving, and that was that. All was seemingly done with me and WOW. Then the phone rang. Someone was calling me and our operator said he didn't want to give his name but that it was important. It sure was. It changed everything. It was Mike Meyers and he spoke quickly and impatiently.

"Did you make your decision yet? We've got a magazine to publish and I want to send out a press release about you coming to work for us."

"I don't think it's going to happen, Mike," I told him. "But thank you for the opportunity."

"What the hell is stopping you?" he quickly asked. "We're offering you $20,000 more per year, and a three-year contract with big increases spelled out. It's an amazing opportunity."

I said thank you, but no, and he said, "I'll get back to you!"

Within 30 minutes he called back offering me a $25,000 signing bonus if I faxed him an agreement by midnight (it was 10 a.m. at this point). Another decision. Twenty-five thousand dollars. When I called my wife, she was thrilled but told me the decision was mine to make. I took a few deep breaths,

> Another decision. Twenty-five thousand dollars.

got up from my desk and went into Stu's office. He knew something had changed. I told him about the latest *WOW* offer. Similar to Linda McMahon, he told me, "You do what you think is best, Bill. I don't want you to leave, but $25,000 . . . I think you may have made up your mind already."

I called Meyers back from a pay phone, as I did not dare use the office phone, and asked him to fax the document to me. In a few hours it was all spelled out and in front of me.

At 11:45 p.m. that night, I signed the document and faxed it to Mike Meyers. I was officially leaving home, and they would find out about it the next morning. I had a special way to let everyone know what was going to happen. It would affect the magazines I had worked at for so many years, as well at the magazine I was now taking charge of. I was entering a new era. A lot of drama was about to unfold.

***

The next morning I went to the *PWI* office as usual, with just one slight change. Under my dress shirt I wore a *World of Wrestling Magazine* T-shirt. As I entered the editorial pool, I stood in the center of the floor and told everyone I had an announcement. Next, in a move that would have made the nWo proud, I opened my shirt to reveal an official *WOW* T-shirt. I recall some surprising applause (mainly from the boxing department) and then handshakes from the rest of the editorial department, with everyone wishing me good luck.

On April 27, 1999, I entered the *WOW* offices for the first time as an employee. I would begin working from my home office in Pennsylvania later in the week. After a few minutes of pleasantries, Mike Meyers popped his head out of his office and said, "Come in here, we need to talk." His tone was quite different from the romance period.

"Okay, now that you're here, this is what you're going to do," he said in a very stern tone. "We're paying you a lot of money and you had better be able to do everything. You are in charge of the magazine, the website and everything else to do with *WOW*. There's an editorial meeting going on in the conference room. Go to work." He turned away in his swivel chair and that was that, I thought. Then he swiveled back and said, "I need a press release stating you're our new editor by the end of the day. I also want you to start calling all of your contacts in the wrestling business and get them to work with us." Since I knew the WWF's feelings about *WOW*, I was not about to do that. I just said, "I'll work on all of this and get you the press release on time."

I went to the conference room and there, at the head of the table, was managing editor John Delavan. On either side of the long table were editors and art staff. Before I said a word, managing art director Elliott From asked, "How was your meeting with Mike?" Before I could answer, senior marketing rep Tim Towe said, "Intimidating, wasn't it?" That it was. Delavan chimed in, "Mike is under a lot of pressure. He has to make sure we turn a healthy profit. Let's go down the list of what we have planned for this issue."

We planned things out and it was a great meeting. The mood was wonderful. I was totally enjoying my new job.

The press release was done, I made a few calls to some wrestlers to let them know I had left *PWI* for *WOW* and the day was over. Elliott, Tim and John took me to dinner and then to my hotel.

The next few days were very invigorating. Elliott and Tim and I were a great threesome. Although Tim was the senior marketing rep,

he had been in charge of dealing with photographers and writers for the first two issues and continued that during my time there.

One of the things I didn't realize is that people in the business were looking at *WOW* in the same way that they had looked at Vince McMahon when he "raided" the territories. Freelance writers like Steve Anderson and several photographers jumped ship from *PWI* when I came aboard *WOW*. I never called to offer them anything. They called me, and I told them to deal with Tim. There was never an intentional "raid."

Tim and Elliott wanted to come to shows with me and wanted me to take them backstage. As you know, you can't just do that in the wrestling business. You have to be endorsed by someone for that privilege. I decided to do just that after I got to know both of them. I took them to many WCW shows where they got the royal treatment from Hulk Hogan and nearly everyone on the roster. We wound up going on wrestling trips to Las Vegas, Arizona and Florida, where I took Tim to Hogan's house. The most unusual *WOW* trip was with Tim to Japan. We had been invited by PRIDE (MMA) promoters to come and watch one of their shows. *WOW* didn't cover MMA so this made no sense. But they wanted nothing in return, so we took the trip. We did end up giving them some play in the magazine. To this day, I still wonder why the promoters spent so much money on our trip. I don't think I'll ever find out, but we had a great time!

One night when WWF was in Chicago, Tim found out what hotel the wrestlers were staying at. After the show, we popped into the restaurant and I would say that 90 percent of the roster was sitting there at a long table, having dinner. As the boys saw me, one of them (if I recall correctly, it was Chris Jericho) spotted me and called out, "Wonderful Willie. Get over here!" He was sitting right in the middle, so I went down the line shaking hands with Edge, Christian and everyone else. They were happy to see me and asked me to do my imitations of Dusty Rhodes, Superfly Snuka and a few others.

It was at this point that Tim came up with an idea. He excused himself and said he would be right back. At the same time several of the wrestlers asked for my telephone number so they could keep in touch. At another table I spotted a few people who worked for *WWF Magazine*. I could see by the look on their faces they were not too happy to see the main man

from *WOW* schmoozing with the talent.

As the group of wrestlers disbanded, they were all about to chip in for the check when the waitress informed them that it had been paid. She pointed to Tim and me. I had no idea. Tim called Harvey Wasserman and got his approval while I was "schmoozing." The guys were overwhelmed with joy—someone else had paid for their dinner in a classy restaurant. What happened next, as we were leaving the hotel, really surprised me. One of the wrestlers asked, "Do you have your camera with you?" I told him it was in the trunk of the car. He asked me to get it and come to his room, so he could pose for *WOW Magazine*. When I told him he would get in trouble, he said, "You let me worry about that."

A few minutes later, Tim and I were in the room with the wrestler as well as a few others. We snapped away. They wanted to be on the cover or even on the inside. They saw being in an independent magazine more compelling than the house magazine.

This wasn't a one shot deal. Whenever the wrestlers were in Chicago, some of them called and wanted to pose. *WOW* had become quite a force.

Word got back to me a few days

later that the *WWF Magazine* crew was furious that *WOW* picked up the tab for that night. That disturbed me, but I understood their point of view. The enemy was finding a way to break through to the troops. I was not very comfortable doing this—but it was my job!

***

WOW was selling well with knockout numbers. Everyone was very happy. Harvey Wasserman decided it was going so well that he ordered a new magazine to supplement the monthly *WOW*. It would be *Bill Apter's WOW Xtra*—every two weeks.

Although it was certainly the best of times, the worst of times were beginning to emerge. It was the second stanza of my three-year contract. While taking wrestlers out to dinner, my company credit card was rejected. The company assured me it was a technical issue and wouldn't happen again. After the third incident, I started to wonder. It was then that Tim and Elliott told me they heard the company was going through financial problems that weren't *WOW* related. Around this time, I got a copy of the latest issue of *WOW* and to my horror there was a "penis enlargement" advertisement. As the

magazine hit the stands, wrestlers, promoters and fans were in touch to express outrage or just make fun of it.

When I approached management, I was told that the company that bought the ad was paying good money. The wrestling magazine with a classy look just took a big step down.

It wasn't long after this that some employees were laid off. Finally a call came, telling me that the company was up for sale. Although *WOW* was selling well, some of their other publications were not. Money, which was so free-flowing for so long, was now a major issue. Soon complaints from photographers and writers came in that they were not being paid.

Then the company crashed, and I was in trouble. I needed to support my family.

***

Very soon after that news came, I received a call from Highbury House, the company in the U.K. that was distributing and publishing their licensed version of *WOW*. They were interested to see if I would take the reins of *WOW* U.K. should they continue. A week or so later I was en route to the U.K. to hopefully make a deal.

WOW U.K. lasted one or two issues more than the U.S. edition, but eventually Highbury ended *WOW U.K.*'s run. The publishers opted to continue the magazine with the name of *POW—Power of Wrestling*. Unfortunately, that became marred in legal issues (sounded like a copycat to *WOW*), and a new title was to be created. Ultimately Steve May, who was in charge of most of Highbury's entertainment periodicals such as *Total Electronics*, *Total Video* and more, suggested *Total Wrestling*. I loved it, and the editor who had worked on *WOW U.K.* and *POW*, Steven Ganfield, and I became the *Total Wrestling* team.

Total was another great experience. Not only did it keep me in the magazine business, but I was also able to make many trips to the U.K. It opened me up to an entire new world of wrestlers who were U.K. regulars. I quickly became friends with referee Steve Lynskey, Jonny Storm, Jody Fleisch, wrestler-promoter Alex Shane Greg Lambert and journalist Phil Austin. I must thank Alex, as he was kind enough to actually book me on several of the Frontier Wrestling Alliance shows he ran and tied in the *Total Wrestling* magazine to those events. There were so many great people I met—I don't have the room to list all of them here.

Like *WOW*, I thought this was going to last forever—but of course, it didn't. *Total* closed after the publishing company experienced a change in management and ownership. The powerhouses that kept the magazines going and who had a fondness for the wrestling genre were no longer there—and neither was Bill Apter. It was shocking. There was no notice. I was so shaken up I forgot to call the writers who worked for us, including my close friend and former *PWI* teammate Bob Smith.

It was the first time I was without a magazine tied to my name. My wife and I had just purchased a new car and still had a mortgage to pay. What was I going to do?

1WRESTLING TO APTER'S RESCUE

TWENTY-EIGHT

By 2004, *Total Wrestling* magazine was finished. I had no idea what I would do next. Around this time, I was doing some freelance work for 1Wrestling.com, at that time owned by Bob Ryder and Joey Styles. We'd all become friends, and I thought that perhaps I could pick up some steady work and get my feet wet in the internet world. I knew Bob from his days covering ECW and when he worked for WCW. As for Joey, he worked with me at London Publishing for a stint, and we always kept in touch. He became my key into 1Wrestling.com. I called Joey, who in turn called Bob. And then I got the answer I was hoping for: there was a permanent spot for me at 1Wrestling if I wanted it. With the bills mounting at home, this really took a lot of the pressure off. Joey and Bob had saved my life as far as I was concerned.

Besides writing, I brought audio and video

My basement has been turned into "Apter's Alley." It's where I tape many of my IWrestling.com video segments and, as you can see, keep my favorite memorabilia.

interviews to the site. We were the first pro-wrestling site to bring that kind of video content to fans—I am proud to be able to write that.

When Joey left to go to WWE in 2005, he sold his share of 1Wrestling.com to Bob. At this same time, Bob decided that I would become content editor. Since then, I have found contributors who have stayed loyal to the site; Jay Shannon, Big Ray Hernandez, Andre Corbeil, Neal Borenstein, Lisa Williams, Bill Schuyler, Billy Ray Valentine, John Osting and many others have helped me keep the content topical and fun. I talk

to Bob several times a week, and I am so glad that he has kept the site running. He remains a great person to work for and a very close friend. Through the years, Bob has kept me on the payroll. I have no idea how to express my appreciation. He and Joey gave me a platform that allowed me to remain visible in the business. He gives me free rein as editor of the site, and I will never break his trust.

We also have established followings on Twitter (@apter1wrestling) and Facebook. I truly love working 24/7 for 1Wrestling. It's become my home on the internet.

A POWERFUL LESSON LEARNED FOR TOMORROW

APTER FOR

ometimes I wish I didn't ask so many questions and just let things flow. A perfect example of this happened on November 5, 1975, and I felt the effects for months.

Through a friend of a friend, I found myself booked as a guest on NBC's late-night *The Tomorrow Show* hosted by Tom Snyder. It was recorded at NBC studio 6A in New York (keep that in mind for another major chapter in this book). I would be part of a guest list that included California-based wrestling broadcaster Dick Lane, "Superstar" Billy Graham, Gorilla Monsoon, Bruno Sammartino and Vince McMahon Jr. Two female wrestlers, Kitty Adams and Donna Christanello, would have a brief match on the program.

This was a huge deal for me. I was going to be on national TV for the first time, and I'd be able to give the magazines I worked for some great publicity. The show was to be taped at 5:30 p.m. for a 1 a.m. airing.

I arrived at the studio roughly two hours before the taping with a number of neighbors from my apartment building—I was able to get them tickets for that night, which meant that they were my entourage and I was their star. The kid from Maspeth, Queens, was going to be a big shot on TV for a few minutes, and they wanted to witness it live.

After saying goodbye, they were escorted to their seats and I was taken to the greenroom to wait for showtime. Already in the room were Graham and Lane, who greeted me warmly. I knew Superstar but had never met Lane, and he thanked me for using some photos in the magazine of him interviewing wrestlers.

I didn't seen Vince until just a few minutes before we went out to do the show. When I saw him in the hallway outside the greenroom—and to this day I still don't know why I did this—I asked, "Is there anything or anyone you don't want me to mention?" He smiled and said, "Bill, you know this is your home turf, my dad knows you'll take care of WWWF first and foremost. It's okay to mention

the other guys, of course, but we're counting on you to do the right thing here."

What I didn't tell Vince is that earlier in the day I called Verne Gagne to let him know I would be on the Snyder show and not to worry, I'd take care to mention his AWA (American Wrestling Association). I had also contacted the head of the National Wrestling Alliance and told him I'd put the NWA in the spotlight.

The producers lined us up, and we were escorted into the wings of the studio. Sammartino and Monsoon were on the first segment. Besides being interviewed by Snyder, a makeshift ring had been set up and Bruno sparred with journeyman Frank Monte while Monsoon called the moves.

The segment with me, Dick Lane and Vince was next. Snyder talked with Vince first, then Lane and finally started to interview me. His first query was easy, asking me about the dangers of being a ringside photographer and reporter for such a physical genre. I told him about a few incidents where I had been too close to the action and had my camera smashed. The audience seemed entertained, and then he asked his next question:

"Bill, who is the best wrestler you have ever seen?"

Here is Vince McMahon (far left), me, West Coast Wrestling broadcaster Dick Lane and the host of the *Tomorrow* show Tom Snyder in 1976. It was my first appearance on national network TV and the first and only time I shared the spotlight with Mr. McMahon. [Photo courtesy of George Napolitano]

"That's a tough question," I shot back. "I would say the three major association champions would all fit that category."

Then I heard this come out of my mouth: "First I would say the champion of the National Wrestling Alliance, Jack Brisco. Next would be the champion of the American Wrestling Association, Nick Bockwinkel, and third, of course, the World Wide Wrestling Federation champion, Bruno Sammartino."

That was Snyder's final question. The segment ended. I got off my stool and went to chat with everyone, but Vince wasn't in the mood. He just smiled and said, "Nice job, Bill," then he gave me a cold stare, a quick handshake and left. I felt it wasn't sincere at all.

My friends were so proud as we headed home on the subway that night. I felt good—until the next morning.

When I got into the office, I called Vince Sr. to see if he had watched the show. His wife, Juanita, answered the phone and said he was busy and would call me back later. Next I called Bruno to tell him how much I liked what he did on the program, and he was very grateful for my kind words. Though he did add a line that caught me off guard.

"Bill, this isn't coming from me, but I heard the old man [Vince Sr.] is very upset that you mentioned Brisco and Bockwinkel first and second and me, Vince's champion, last. He's really annoyed. It doesn't bother me, but I think you should know he's pretty hot about this. His son told him that you had asked him how to handle that question if it came up, and you did exactly the opposite."

I didn't know what to say. He was totally right. I screwed up, which was why Vince Jr. gave me the cold shoulder and why Senior hadn't returned my call.

I tried calling Vince Sr. a few more times, but he wouldn't come to the phone. He was upset. I gave Juanita a long message telling Vince that I was sorry if I offended him and it was not my intention to hurt my relationship with him or with WWWF.

He did call back a few days later and accepted my apology. For months, at every WWWF show I covered, there was always a wrestler throwing the Snyder show and the snub of WWWF in my face. Eventually it died down, but I never forgot it.

As for the NWA, Sam Muchnick, Eddie Graham and other promoters thought I was the best thing since sliced bread— and so did Verne Gagne and Nick Bockwinkel.

I learned a lesson about politics the hard way—and this would just be the beginning of more stomach-turning political adventures to come.

APTER NEARLY BOOTED OUT DUE TO MAGAZINE'S PAST

I walked into a horrible situation just a few days after I started working for Stanley Weston in 1970. I often wondered why he had not been to a wrestling show in years, and the ugly answer hit me the first time I tried to get an official interview for the magazine.

I had arranged to go to a local show at New York's Sunnyside Garden—my home base. On a nice day I could walk there in 90 minutes and when my dad came with me, it was only a 20-minute drive. I called ahead to let promoter Mike Rosenberg and WWWF associate booker Oscar Conill know that I would be covering the matches for *Inside Wrestling* and *The Wrestler* magazines.

When I arrived, both of them welcomed me and showed me the staircase to the locker rooms. Immediately I spotted Willie "The Wolfman" Farkas, Bill White, Chief Jay Strongbow,

Another photo from my rookie year. From left to right: Mike Conrad, Crusher Verdu, Lou Albano (before he was a "Captain") and me.

"Baron" Mikel Scicluna, Mike Pappas, Mike Conrad, manager Tony Angelo and the Mongols, Lou Albano, Victor Rivera, the Black Demon, the Grand Wizard and Gorilla Monsoon wearing a suit.

Gorilla shot me a quick look and came over to ask if he could help. He told me he worked for Mr. McMahon and was the agent for the day's show. I explained who I was and he was very businesslike, yet warm. It appeared he would be glad to help me get some interviews. After a few minutes of small talk, he waved several of the wrestlers over and told them that I would be doing some taped interviews for a wrestling magazine as well as for a radio show I did in New York.

Thanks to Gorilla, my day was going to be a real success—until I knelt down to unpack my tape recorder and camera and get some photos. A huge shadow came over me. It was Monsoon. I began to rise and he said, "You can finish what you're doing, but someone just told me something that has changed my feelings about you and what you do."

I rose to talk to him, face-to-stomach—but I did look up.

"Did I do something wrong?" I asked.

"Not you exactly, Bill. It's who you work for. One of the guys mentioned that the magazine you work for, *Inside Wrestling*, is owned by Stan Weston. Is that correct?"

I nodded yes.

He replied quickly, "Do you know what he did to some of us? If you want to make anything of yourself in this business, I suggest you work for anyone but Weston. He is on the outs with us. Vince doesn't want him around, so I guess that's why he sent you."

I told him I arranged this entire day myself. I had no idea what Monsoon was talking about. What could Mr. Weston have done? Gorilla continued.

"First of all, he sent a photographer to my house to do an 'At Home with Gorilla Monsoon' photo story. He took photos of me with my wife, my family, my gun collection and other personal things. When the story came out, the lead photo had me holding one of my guns and the headline read something like 'Gorilla Monsoon: I'd Like to Take this Gun and Shoot Sammartino.' You can imagine how furious and embarrassed I was. Although Bruno and I are enemies in the ring, our families are very close. They couldn't fathom that I would give a quote like that—and I didn't. Weston made it up."

I told Monsoon that I could not explain why Mr. Weston would do that and that I would never do something like that. He said, "I will give you a chance and if you're true to your word, I will make sure you get whatever you need. By the way, Bruno Sammartino is not only furious about the gun story, but also about a life story Weston published. It's all made-up crap. It's good Weston doesn't come to the shows, because there are a ton of guys who would love a piece of him."

Monsoon was referring to a

I rose to talk to him, face-to-stomach.

series of "This Is Your Life" features that Mr. Weston had been publishing, which were selling really well on the newsstands.

With all this weighing heavy on my mind, I went upstairs to a pay phone and called Mr. Weston.

"It was a great story; I don't know why Monsoon is complaining," he said. "As for Bruno, I can't believe it. That story was classic."

I knew I wasn't getting anywhere. I told Mr. Weston that I was going to photograph the matches and perhaps we could discuss it at work tomorrow.

It was a hard sell. Mr. Weston defended the story the way he published it. He admitted that he gave the story to editor Steve Ende to write and was very happy with it. They both chose the gun shot as the lead photo and the headline was "a work—a great angle to heat up the Monsoon–Sammartino feud." He just didn't latch onto the thoughts of Monsoon. "I am the publisher of the magazine and the wrestlers don't run me," he said.

I needed more ammunition. A few weeks later, Bruno was at Sunnyside. I went to the show and Monsoon introduced me to the "Living Legend," who would become, and to this day still is, a dear friend and ally of mine. I decided that I would ask Bruno to explain his feelings about the life story Weston penned. He was glad to do so.

Bruno talked about how hurt and embarrassed he was that whoever wrote the story didn't come to him to check the facts. He talked about how in the story his young sister allegedly killed a few Nazi soldiers when he and his family were hiding in the hills in Italy and other huge errors about his parents and other family members.

"I was so mad that when friends came to me to ask questions; I told them they were all lies."

I recorded my talk with Bruno and played the tape for Mr. Weston the following day. He was embarrassed. He drafted an apology letter to Bruno and asked me to personally deliver it the next time I saw him.

A few weeks later, I not only delivered the letter but also sat down with Bruno for nearly two hours and did perhaps the first-ever "shoot" interview with him. As a matter of fact, this was the first shoot interview that ran in any of Mr. Weston's magazines. I guess I can add "Pioneer of Shoot Interviews" to my resume. It was his real life story—this time verbatim. Two months later the issue came out, and that was my real in as far as I was concerned. It proved

Mil Máscaras was one of my favorite photographic subjects and one of my "must see" in-ring performers. I was thrilled to meet and become his friend.

to Monsoon I was a man of my word, and to Bruno as well. From then on I was treated very well at the WWWF shows.

There was one more "This Is Your Life" train wreck I had to deal with. It was when I came face-to-face with one of my wrestling heroes, Mil Máscaras.

"They wrote I was born in an adobe hut and came from a poor Mexican family," he told me. "That is bullshit!" He then went on to tell me how affluent his family is in Mexico and that he comes from a long line of university-educated professionals.

At this point, I want to add that

Mr. Weston did have tons of allies in the business: Eddie Graham, "Kangaroo" Al Costello, Mark Lewin, Don Curtis and Dory Funk Sr. just to name a very few. (I could go on for days.) They didn't mind the stories he put out and were glad to get any publicity. Sam Muchnick was also one of his dearest friends. Weston spent years on the road nurturing these relationships.

My next obstacle was Vince McMahon Sr. Why didn't he like Weston? I eventually heard Mr. Weston's side of the story.

My boss explained that on the night of January 24, 1963, Buddy Rogers was going to lose the NWA World Heavyweight championship to Lou Thesz in Toronto. The title change would not be recognized by McMahon, and he would keep promoting Rogers as champion. Since there was no internet back then, Weston's magazines were one of the only ways you could find out. Sam Muchnick, who was president of the NWA, reached out and invited Mr. Weston to cover the event. But McMahon also reached out to Weston, asking him to not publish the result, so that no one outside of the Toronto area would know about the change.

A few months later, Weston's name was poison to McMahon. The title-change story was published in Weston's *Pro Wrestling Illustrated*. McMahon had no recourse but to do damage control. Willie Gilzenberg appeared on the WWWF TV shows to say that the NWA title was no longer recognized and that Buddy Rogers won a tournament in Rio de Janeiro to become the very first champion of the World Wide Wrestling Federation.

Vince Sr. didn't go into much detail when I was introduced to him at a Madison Square Garden show in 1970. He did say, "You know, I haven't talked to Stanley since 1963. I'll let you do your thing at my shows and we'll see how it goes."

APTER CLAIMS CARDBOARD GOLD

THIRTY-ONE

'm not exactly sure when I created Championship Office Wrestling (also known as the COW title). I do know it was back in Freeport, New York, home of the magazines. Little did I know, after a few defenses, the belt became one that some professional wrestlers actually wanted to say they wrestled for . . .

During photo sessions with wrestlers, I sometimes had to do things to get them in the mood to pose. When my imitations of Dusty Rhodes, Bruno Sammartino or Jerry Lewis weren't working, I would playfully begin to scuffle with them. Most of the early victims I did this with would just laugh and push me away, but then, as I persisted, we'd actually have a playful match. Of course, they'd always let me—the underdog— win. Afterward I would become very cocky and do my best Buddy Rogers strut, holding my arms in victory over my head and proclaiming myself champion of the office.

After a few matches, my photo assistant Laura surprised me with a cardboard Championship Office Wrestling belt she'd made. It was now official. I was the champ—and I had the cardboard to prove it.

Through the years, word about the two ounces of cardboard Apter was defending during photo sessions became a kind of mild cult-obsession in various dressing rooms. I knew this, because when I went to the matches in New York, guys would come over and tell me they wanted a title shot.

Eventually every wrestler who came up to the office participated in a match—some of them just a minute or two—just to say they did it. (Naturally, they posed, hoping to get on the cover—sans belt.)

To make matters more fun, one of the staff photographers, Jason Lavin, wanted to get in on the action. I made him the commissioner of COW. When he wasn't available, one of the office business people, Dave Gerhardt, who loved what we were doing, would be an associate commish for the day. We had some editors take on the role of referees as well. Matches were held in the photo studio area and one or two drifted into other areas so we could do a file-room death match or the cardboard-belt-on-the-ceiling

"Wonderful Willie" strikes a pose with the gold COW belt. Mr. Reggie Parks hand-crafted this gem for me. [Photo courtesy Joel Perlish photography]

stepladder match. Most of the matches were videotaped but the tapes are now in the hands of various editors, who would prefer the tapes stay out of the public eye.

Perhaps my favorite defense was with Chris Candido and Tammy "Sunny" Sytch. It all began at the Brendan Byrne Arena at the Meadowlands in New Jersey. The National Wrestling Alliance was running a show, and I arrived at the building in the early afternoon to do some interviews, some audio and some video. When I got to the ring, Candido was running the ropes. His girlfriend, Tammy, was standing close by with her camera (she was once a photographer for the *PWI* family of magazines). I asked her if she would mind filming something for me. She was happy to, but had no idea what was coming. I ran into the ring and playfully caught Candido with a knee to the midsection. He flew over my knee and then landed on his back. Quickly, I grabbed his legs and put him in the figure-four leglock. He screamed "I quit, I give up!" At that moment I gave Tammy the cut sign to turn off the video camera. We all had a good laugh—and had no idea what would happen next.

A few days later, I had the extreme privilege of having Dory Funk Jr. and his lovely wife Marti visit my home. I showed them the Candido tape, which gave birth to another idea. I asked Dory if he would "train me" for an upcoming COW defense against Candido, who was livid that I made him tap out at the Meadowlands. So Marti took my video camera and we did about 10 minutes of footage of Junior getting me ready for my match against Candido.

I called Tammy and Chris and invited them to the office. The lure was for photos in the magazine, but they wanted some COW action as well. We did an hour or so of posed photos and then shot the angle after they viewed the Funk training session.

Tammy comes on camera with a masked man she says is Chris. She explains that Chris hurt his face in a match but is going to win my COW belt in a belt-on-the-ceiling stepladder match. One of our junior editors, Ed, is the referee.

The match begins and Tammy hits me with a paddleball racquet as I climb the ladder to get the belt. I take a bump to the floor, she pulls on the belt and a part of it tears off—but she keeps going and finally hands it to her masked man!

Then, as Tammy and the masked man revel about the title win, Chris Candido appears on screen. They all have a good laugh as Chris unmasks the new champion—commissioner Jason Lavin. My colleague then unleashes an amazing hatred-laced promo about how much he has always detested me.

His title reign only lasts a few minutes though, as associate commish Dave comes into view and says that I am still champ.

Another fun loop was when the boxing magazine department wanted to get involved, so we did an entire feud called COW versus BOW (Boxing Office Wrestling). Their champion was

Eric "Roundhouse" Raskin.

The belt went through several cardboard incarnations and then, one day, I received a call from my friend, the champion of all belt makers, Reggie Parks. A few months prior to this call, when we were on a tour of Hawaii, I had shown Reggie and his partner, Ed Chuman, my cardboard belt.

"Hey, that cardboard has to go," Reggie said. "I have been looking at the photo of me, you and Chuman over and over, and I want to make you a real belt." I remember when he asked me what the federation should be called, I instantly said, "Championship Office Wrestling." It had the right tone to it and the initials. Yes, it was the COW belt and it would be solid-gold plated. He asked if I wanted Bill or William Apter as the name on the belt. I didn't want either. I asked him to use the moniker one of my first opponents, Jimmy Valiant, gave me— Wonderful Willie.

I'm simply amazed when I think about who has challenged me for

This guy Dwayne figured he would get well known by posing with Bill Apter's son. I think it helped quite a bit!

the COW belt over the years. To name a few: Rob Van Dam, Dan Severn (who had a brief COW reign, as did the Blue Meanie), Diamond Dallas Page, Sabu, Tazz, Tommy Dreamer, Rey Mysterio Jr., New Jack, Scotty Riggs, Konnan, the Sandman and dozens more.

One night at an ECW show, Bubba Ray Dudley was in the ring battling an opponent. I was shooting photos at ringside. As he floored his adversary, he turned to me and yelled, "Apter, this is what is going to happen to you when I get a shot at that COW belt!"

I was backstage at a WWE show in the late '90s, after WWE had given us permission to photograph a few of their wrestlers with *PWI* plaques. The Rock came into the studio and asked me if I had brought the belt. I had it with me and he not only posed with it but cut a video promo for me.

I took the COW belt with me to my overseas bookings and defended it against the U.K.'s Jonny Storm and a few others, making the COW belt a true World title.

By the way, each defense out of the office took place in an office setting. That was the rule.

I regularly bring the COW belt to the wrestling conventions I host or attend, and there is always someone looking for a shot at the COW gold. In late 2012, I made D'Lo Brown tap out to my figure-four leglock at a wrestling convention.

Dan "The Beast" Severn was a gem of a challenger. He was so into what COW was all about. We had several matches. At one of them, he came to the office with a Vader mask and became "Big Van Dan." With the help of his manager Phyllis Lee, who hit me over the head with a bag of frozen bagels, "Big Van Dan" won the cardboard belt. For years he would proudly display it at conventions alongside his UFC and NWA gold belts.

Today, I still defend the belt, and when it's not in use, it is part of the permanent "Apter's Alley" set I use to tape my various TV segments for 1Wrestling.com and other media.

THE TRUTH ABOUT THE *PWI 500*

THIRTY-TWO

The *PWI 500* debuted in 1991.

I never created the *PWI 500*.

I never wrote the *PWI 500*.

I am totally happy with the above statements.

I t was a stressful task, a 24/7 job, and the editors who compiled it typically became short-tempered—it was just so draining. I witnessed it firsthand. Editor Bob Smith did the writing for the first few years, and when he left, other editors worked together to compile and write the "nightmare."

I recall many meetings with the entire editorial department in the conference room. It was there, together, where we would sit for hours every day trying to come up with at least the

Top 100. I would throw out an idea and it might be rejected by Stu Saks, while Craig Peters may have agreed. Other editors had their battles too.

The two most important spots in the 500 were of course number one—and number 500.

"I was number 500 back in 1994," Don E. Allen told me a few years ago. "Some guys might have been pissed about being on the bottom of the list, but I got more publicity and bookings from that one story than nearly any time in my career."

I recall in year one (1991) when Hulk Hogan was the number one man on the list, I was personally accused of "ass kissing" by a lot of wrestlers. Then the fans, who saw me at the matches, would argue about "my" choice. It didn't matter when I told them I was part of a committee that agreed. They only saw me—and I was the guilty party as far as they were concerned. On the other hand, there were legions who complimented the choices throughout the years, but the complainers outnumbered them. The wrestling community really paid attention to the *PWI* 500 and that issue is still important to wrestlers today.

I was never paid one cent by Dusty Rhodes for all the awards he won.

Now, let's deal with the *PWI* year-end awards. The first thing I want to say is that I was never paid one cent by Dusty Rhodes for all the awards he won. I cannot tell you how many people in the business thought that Dusty was in my pocket, paying me to make sure he won Wrestler of the Year or Most Popular Wrestler of the Year.

Allow me to take this one step further: Dusty's employers, whether it was Eddie Graham's Florida office or Jim Crockett Promotions, also never paid *PWI* for giving Dusty or any of their wrestlers awards. So how were the award winners actually chosen? It's best said in an interview Stu Saks did with kayfabememories.com. Here is an excerpt—and be sure to go to the website to read the entire interview.

KM: Was (is) the *PWI* end of the year award voting legit or is it worked?

SS: Every letter is opened. Every vote is counted. The winners are selected by the readers. The vote totals were proportionally inflated, I confess. Now, we present the totals as percentages, rather than actual numbers.

So there you have it, plain and simple. I was never paid to give out any awards—neither was the company. The winners were picked by . . . *you.*

I enjoyed presenting the *PWI* year-end awards on so many wrestling TV shows: Georgia, Mid-Atlantic, Florida, World Class and others. To see the glow on the faces of the award winners—even someone like a Hulk Hogan or Sting—was priceless. Today, when I cover shows and go backstage at WWE, TNA or any of the indy cards and see the former award winners, they always tell me how they treasure those moments.

TAKIN' A LICKIN' BUT STILL TICKIN'

THIRTY-THREE

One of the most exciting aspects of my career was photographing the matches at ringside. But it was also quite hazardous.

As a teenager, I would sometimes run down to the ring from the bleachers at New York's Sunnyside Garden and capture the action with either my little camera or an 8mm movie camera. I loved being so close to the ring for the brief few moments the security guard would let me stay there. A few times, the guys were slammed and almost landed in my lap. Little did I know it was the start of things to come.

Madison Square Garden was my local major arena. The ringside area was totally unlike the way it is today, with photographers stooped close to the action. Back then there was a long wooden board—sort of like a desk—that went around all four sides of the ring. This way, if

At ringside in 1971 with the Minolta camera I used to photograph Ivan Koloff's shocking victory over WWWF Champion Bruno Sammartino. That camera was eventually replaced by a more intricate Nikon F, which I used for both action and studio photography.

you were a writer you had a place to put your typewriter or pad and pen, or if you were a photographer you had somewhere to place your camera bag and film. There was also another row of wooden planks directly behind it, which meant you were pretty much locked in once you got to your assigned spot and were unable to get out once the show started. You also had a folding chair that just seemed to be in the way. You were scrunched in—it was very uncomfortable.

The next thing you had to deal with was the ring apron. It was about two feet away from the ring ropes. This meant that when taking photos—wrestling and boxing— you had to put the upper portion of your body on the apron and wedge yourself somehow under the bottom rope. If you didn't do this, all your photos would have the ropes going across the wrestlers' or boxers' bodies.

Changing film during matches was an arduous task. You had to slip back down to your seat, rewind the film, open the back of the camera, take out the film, put in a new roll, get back up on the ring apron and start shooting the action again. It was not fun on my stomach, arms, hands or ribs. For some reason, film-changing always seemed to occur when some 300-pound

wrestler was being tossed onto the ring apron right over me and the other photographers.

For years the photo crew consisted of me, George Napolitano, Frank Amato and a young upstart, who always pushed his way to try to get the best photos. His name: Paul Heyman. What a pain in the butt he was around the ring. The three of us always hoped it would be Heyman who'd get dumped on by the wrestlers, but it happened to all of us on a regular basis.

To this day, I can still imagine the velocity of Bruno Sammartino being kicked out of the ring right onto me by Bobby Duncum. And picture the splatter of our clothes from the overly bloody "Captain Lou" Albano as he ran away from Dean Ho and Tony Garea and dove onto the photographers. Or feel the spit that always seemed to find its way onto us whenever a guy was punched. Ah, what fun, to be a ringside photographer at the Garden!

I recall an incident when WWWF champion Pedro Morales was punched in the midsection with so much force by Stan "The Lariat" Hansen that Pedro's body came crashing into me between the ropes, knocking me onto the table and cracking one of my teeth.

The fans always thought it

This photo was taken the night that Pedro Morales won the WWWF title from Ivan Koloff at Madison Square Garden. Pedro was always "ready for any kind-o-action."

camera and would play to the lens until they knew I got the shot. "Superstar" Billy Graham was a prime example. He would lock up his opponent, stare at the photographers and yell, "Apter, Napolitano, make sure this gets on the cover!" And he would keep the guy locked up until he saw our flashes go off. Most wrestlers entering the ring would also stand and pose so they might get a shot published in the magazines. Some of them did this as well to get "heat," as they would demand we take their photo and argue with us until they saw our camera flash unit go off.

In my early days, many wrestlers made me part of the angle when I was at ringside.

It was 1972, and I was in Detroit at Cobo Arena, shooting photos of "Wild Bull" Curry against the Shcik. After the match, Curry leaned over the ropes, grabbed me by the hair and pulled me into the ring. No, I was not told in advance this would happen, and yes, he did hurt me as he was pulling. I also dropped my new Nikon to the floor. He began punching me in the face and before I knew it, babyface Tony Marino came to my rescue. Backstage, Curry made no apologies. He just said, "Don't get so damn close to the ring next time."

was hilarious when we became part of the action. Sometimes the fans became an issue as well. Unfortunately, the beer fans tossed at the wrestlers rarely made it to the ring. Instead it made it to the photographers' clothes and hair (I did have a good head of hair back then). I remember going home on the subway some of those nights smelling like a brewery, and I still can't stand the smell or taste of beer.

Some wrestlers adored the

In 1979, when Ricky "The

As the Sheik brutalizes Terry Funk in Texas, nothing could stop me from getting the best photo for the magazine readers. No matter how many times I got hurt, I always tried to get the perfect shot!

Dragon" Steamboat feuded with Ernie Ladd, we did this routine whenever I was at ringside. Steamboat would play to the fans while in the ring and would always come over and shake my hand. He knew the fans were watching closely. Ladd, also in the ring, would then make his way over to me and offered me his hand. I'd put mine up like I was going to shake his hand but instead would pull away and brush my hair back (similar to what Ric Flair would do years later). Then I'd walk away and shake Steamboat's hand again.

Ladd would go berserk. The fans loved the spot.

George "The Animal" Steele would always grab my camera and run around the ring with it, but he never broke it. Somehow, I always got it back intact.

Other people who broke—or tried to break—my camera were Bulldog Brower, "Crazy" Luke Graham, King Curtis and the Sheik.

The contemporary generation of wrestlers have generally stayed away from harming the equipment—or *me*.

A "KING" PLUS ANDRE THE GIANT EQUALS BIG TROUBLE WITH VINCE SR.

THIRTY-FOUR

For most of the years I had contact with Vince McMahon Sr., our interactions were uneventful—but there are some moments I will never forget.

The one that perhaps sticks out the most is when he sold his son the business. He called me at my office, which I considered a bit odd, because I was usually the one who called him.

"We're changing the name of the company from the World Wide Wrestling Federation to World Wrestling Federation," he said. "Also you can still call me whenever you want, but you should start to stay in touch with my son Vinny, as he's going to be playing a bigger part in the company."

I questioned Senior about the company name-change and was waiting for some sort of corporate line but instead he simply said, "World Wide Wrestling Federation doesn't sound right.

Everyone knows that the world is wide so we're taking the word 'wide' out of it. From now on, we're WWF." Really, that's what he said, people.

One of Senior's most prized commodities was Andre the Giant. If he sent Andre to a territory, it was made clear that Andre would not lose. That was part of his attraction—he remained totally undefeated.

In 1975, Jerry Lawler sent me a series of photos of himself against Andre. Somehow the story of the match had Lawler beating Andre. It was published and the headline was something like, "The Night a Midget Defeated Andre the Giant." Little did I know all hell would break loose.

The day the magazine hit the newsstands, Vince Sr. called. Rather than being calm, as he always was on the phone with me, his tone was hostile.

"Who the hell told you to do that story," he demanded. "Was it that guy in Memphis? Lawler?"

I was terrified.

"He sent me the photos," I said. "I asked someone who took photos of the match who won, and they told me that Lawler beat Andre, so we went with the story."

From there, the call only got worse.

"How could you run this without checking with me? It's horrible and unforgivable," he said. "Andre is undefeated and I want you to get those magazines off the market. You've ruined everything. I told you I didn't speak to Stanley for years and now look what you've done." I told him I would talk to Mr. Weston (he really didn't want to hear that either) and see what I could do.

I had a meeting with all of our editors and Mr. Weston, and the question kept coming up as to what Lawler had told me. I stuck to my guns. Mr. Weston snickered, "Now McMahon hates you too."

I called Jerry and told him what had happened, and I thought that was the end of the heat. A few weeks later at the NWA yearly meeting, Lawler was called on the carpet by McMahon and other promoters. Lawler said that he never told me he beat Andre and he didn't know where I got that result from. I was not there to defend myself. Either way, it was a sickening situation.

I tried to call Senior a few times, and his wife told me he did not want to speak to me yet and to call back in a few days. When he did agree to talk, he was calm.

"Listen, you're a nice guy. I don't want to stay mad at you," he said. "Why don't you retract the story? It'll straighten this whole thing out." I was so relieved and told him I would speak with the editors and Mr. Weston.

"So now McMahon wants to tell us what to do," was Weston's retort. "Well he's not getting his way." I was stunned. I explained to him that if we didn't do this, we'd be locked out. Mr. Weston would "sleep on it" and we would talk tomorrow.

The next morning couldn't have come fast enough. Weston agreed, and we wrote a full cover story proclaiming that Andre the Giant is the only undefeated superstar in pro wrestling.

I called Senior, and he was fine with it. Then he reminded me of what he told me the day we met.

"I remember telling you not to trust anyone, even me," he said. "I don't know who is telling me tales and who isn't and who gave you the result of that match. I just hope you learned a lesson. It was the hard way, but you'll think twice before you do something like that again." Whew . . .

More good times, and a *really* bad one . . .

In 1983, one of the distributors

> So now McMahon wants to tell us what to do. Well he's not getting his way.

of the Weston magazines informed us that Vince McMahon Jr. had been in contact to suggest they take WWF's new wrestling magazine, *Victory*. I was already aware Junior was going to publish a magazine. As a matter of fact, when it was just an idea, he called me to ask if I would like to be the editor.

"I can't give you any figures, how much I can pay, but I need to know if you are interested," he said. I told him that I was totally flattered, but I was well taken care of by Mr. Weston and did not want to leave. I suggested he call Les Thatcher, who had been publishing and editing the Mid-Atlantic/Crockett Promotions magazine. What I didn't know was that the newsstand magazines would be banned from covering the McMahon matches and that a brutal magazine war was going to take place.

I was at the National Wrestling Alliance meeting that year in Las Vegas. Ole Anderson, one of the most outspoken McMahon (Junior) haters, empathized with me and suggested I talk to the other promoters there, which I did. A lot of them had already been anticipating Junior's oncoming takeover and had stories of their own.

I was seated at a table for the premeeting dinner and when I looked a few tables over, I saw David Von Erich having dinner with Vince Sr. and wife, Juanita. I excused myself from my tablemates and went to their table. I put my hand out to say hello to David first, who got up and hugged me. Then Juanita McMahon put her hand out to greet me. As I extended my hand to Vince Sr., he took his thumb and index finger, put them firmly on my wrist and pulled me away from the table.

"What's wrong?" I asked.

"What are you telling these people about the way we are doing our business?" he demanded. I told him what I heard from our magazine distributor and how promoters have been telling me that Vince Jr. is trying to get their TV slots and more. He told me to talk to his son and find out directly from him what the plans are. He was very angry and told me, "If you want to stay part of this brotherhood, you can't go around telling people

things you hear that are not happening." To say I was blindsided is an understatement.

After the Vegas NWA meeting, I didn't see Senior until the funeral for David Von Erich in Dallas in February 1984. He was in a pew with promoter Jim Barnett. I went over and shook both their hands. Vince smiled and gave me a warm handshake. It looked like the heat had subsided.

I called him a few weeks later when I heard he was ill (he had been sick for a long time, but I hadn't known). I didn't realize just how ill he was. Juanita was wonderfully polite, as always, and when Vince got on the phone, I told him I had heard he was sick and hoped he felt better. He thanked me. And that was the last time I ever spoke with him.

He could have slammed the door on me way back in 1970, but he didn't. He let me go down the wrestling road and make a name for myself. That's the Vince Sr. I will always hold dear to my heart. I can't thank him enough.

178

I WAS A BACKYARD WRESTLER

THIRTY-FIVE

Around 1959, I decided to focus my energies on becoming a wrestler. I had the Buddy Rogers strut down pat, as well as the flying dropkick of Antonio Rocca. My mother warned me, "Billy, this is not a job for a nice Jewish boy," but it fell on deaf ears. All I needed was a ring and some opponents, and my career would be on its way.

At this point in my life, I was living in Ridgewood Gardens, a four-building high-rise development in Maspeth, New York. My family lived in Building 1. Most of my friends lived there as well. One of them, Robert, was also a rabid wrestling fan.

I recall Robert and I looking for a place where we could wrestle, and we wound up outside one day, in the back of our development. There, inside a thin chain-link divider, was plenty of grass to wrestle on. Although a small sign said "Keep

Billy Apter, a 12-year-old wannabe protégé of "Nature Boy" Buddy Rogers, faces the mirror and poses like his hero.

Off," it was the perfect place for the Maspeth Arena of our imaginations. It was easy to climb over the chain-link fence that became, of course, the ring ropes.

My obsession with the figure-four leglock was out of control. Robert and I would try different variations on each other, both arguing that the other hadn't got it right.

One night, Buddy Rogers appeared on TV and offered $5,000 to any man who could break out of his figure-four. I instantly took that idea to the Maspeth Arena and offered two shining quarters—a whopping 50 cents—to anyone who could break my figure-four. I also made a cardboard belt and proclaimed myself the Maspeth champion!

The challengers came: Bruce,

Mike, Eddie and Thomas (who all lived out of the building complex) and no one could do it.

For an entire summer, we had matches nearly every day. The grassy spot (which became a bald spot, perhaps foreshadowing my future trademark) was our playground until one day it all ended. My father had received a letter from the management office saying "his son and others were damaging the grass behind Building 1." They sent a bill for $25 along with the letter. The Maspeth Arena was going to shut down.

About two miles from the building was Maurice Park, and a big ball-field became the next site of the Maspeth Arena (although we ran the chance of being forced off the field by park keepers). I had several title defenses but lost the title when I submitted to my opponent—a kid named Joseph—who caught my thumb in his mouth as I had him in a headlock and would not release it from his teeth until I gave up. I still feel his teeth on my right thumb whenever I think of that match.

Throughout the years, people have asked me my opinion of backyard wrestling, and I have always been unwilling to give it. Now you know why. I was one of them—and possibly even the originator.

TV TIME

THIRTY-SIX

My main dream as a teenager was to become a pro-wrestling television broadcaster. Had this happened, I never would have gotten involved in the photography-journalism side of the business. Perhaps I didn't have the right look or the right voice, or maybe it was just bad timing, but I was never able to land that steady gig on TV. I was, however, able to make that dream somewhat of a reality, because of some great people who thought I would do okay on the tube.

Here are some of the places you may have seen me and the people or companies who got me there . . .

LONDON PUBLISHING: I have to lead off with the company I worked for for most of my life—the publisher of all the wrestling and boxing magazines I photographed and wrote for all those years. It was through my mentor Stanley Weston that I gained approval to begin traveling around the globe as the face of the magazines. Many promotions considered me a boost to their credibility, as I was an independent journalist from New York traveling all the way to cover their wrestling. As *PWI* publisher Stu Saks has (correctly) said on many occasions: "Without Stanley Weston, there would be no Bill Apter."

OLE ANDERSON: In the early 1980s, I approached Ole to see if he would be receptive to doing a three-to-five-minute *Pro Wrestling Illustrated* interview segment on his show, *Georgia Championship Wrestling*, which aired nationally on Ted Turner's WTBS Superstation. He was quick to say yes, and a few weeks later editor Craig Peters and I did the first set with Larry Zbyszko, Ole, Tommy Rich and several other stars. In the months to come we continued to host them and they became very popular. You can find many of them today on YouTube by searching "Bill Apter and Craig Peters interviews." Some of them have thousands of views. Thank you for continuing to watch them. The WWE owns all of these now, and I hope they show up somewhere

one day. Craig and I really enjoyed our time and Ole was always very appreciative.

GORDON SOLIE: Whenever I was covering the matches in Georgia or Florida, Gordon always made it a point to have me on TV, interviewing wrestlers or commentating matches alongside him. A highlight of mine was taping the VHS *Lords Of The Ring: Superstars and Superbouts* with Gordon in 1985. I had the pleasure of sitting next to him at the "news desk" introducing and recapping great matches in pro-wrestling history. To work beside this man, who was one of my all-time broadcasting heroes, was one of the highlights of my entire life. We got to do another one a short while later—*Ringmasters: The Great American Bash 1985*. To this day, I look back at that time in my career and can't believe it happened. Gordon became a regular for many years in the magazines as well, called upon when we needed a reputable source.

JIM CROCKETT/DUSTY RHODES: When WWF(E) tossed the independent magazines out, we reached out to the NWA's strongest promoter, Jim Crockett and his booker, Dusty Rhodes, to see if we could somehow market our mags on his local and WTBS-aired shows. Since Crockett was one of the main forces battling McMahon for TV and territory supremacy, a marriage would be beneficial to us both. Indeed it proved to be a superb relationship. We were given a "*Pro Wrestling Illustrated* Scouting Reports" segment that aired almost weekly and I was the host. I had my own talk show. I would fly to the Jim Crockett Promotions studio every few weeks and we would tape three or four weekly segments. Most of them were with Ric Flair. The segments proved so successful that after a few months, Crockett brought in top stars like Jerry Lawler from other warring promotions to be on the show. Due to my exposure on the Crockett product, rumors spread that I was working for him. I was not. But thank you Jimmy and Dusty for letting me live the dream under your roof. Dusty always told me, "Willie, we're gonna make you a stahhhhh!"

I have known Ric Flair since 1975 and maintained a great relationship with him.

JOE PEDICINO: Joe's nationally syndicated *Pro Wrestling This Week* was a unique program. It used a news desk format with Joe and cohost Gordon Solie reporting on and showing footage from promotions all across the globe. I was pleased to be picked by Joe to do weekly editorial segments taped either in his Georgia studio or at the *PWI* offices. Beside the editorials, I also read the weekly *PWI* rankings. Most major and indy federations cooperated with Joe, but he was not able to include WWF(E) clips on this show due to their exclusive agreement with their other TV vendors.

VERNE AND GREG GAGNE: Similar to what I did on Jim Crockett's TV, the Gagnes, Verne and his son Greg, offered me the opportunity to do "*PWI* Press Conferences" on their local and ESPN broadcasts. From Larry Zbyszko and Rick Martel to Sgt. Slaughter and Wahoo McDaniel, I got to interview everyone. At one point, Verne suggested that his new broadcast talent, a young guy named Eric Bischoff, cohost the *PWI* segments. I ran that past the publisher but he voted no, because he didn't want anyone who did not work on the magazine appearing on camera as if they were part of the publishing group. No offense Eric—it wasn't my call.

MARIO, ANGELO AND TOMMY SAVOLDI AND TONY RUMBLE: With Mario as the owner of International World Class Championship Wrestling, I was called on to do "*PWI* Press Conferences" not only at his local New York and New Jersey tapings, but also in exotic places like Bermuda and Puerto Rico. There were segments with guests like Dory Funk Jr. and Tony Atlas taped on these exotic beaches, all directed by another person who liked what I did on TV—their booker Tony Rumble.

MANY MORE: Afa Anoa'i let me do my thing in the ring as the commissioner of his WXW (World Xtreme Wrestling) promotion for several years. He also let me be a guest broadcaster beside regular Mike Mittman. J.J. Dillon was responsible for me being on TV in Florida so often. Bill Watts had me on the Mid-South UWF programs on occasion. Bert Prentice used me at many of his promotional efforts in the Tennessee area. Paul Boesch and Fritz Von Erich/Gary Hart in Texas. The videotape and DVD companies: Highspots, who I did so many shoot interviews for; RF (Rob Feinstein) Video, Kayfabe

Triple H "puts me over" at a spot show in the Memphis area many years ago. He was also a regular cover boy and he really knew how to pose without any direction.

Commentaries (Sean Oliver). A name none of you will know, Larry Tashman, who got me booked on Tom Snyder's *Tomorrow* show on NBC on a panel that included Vince McMahon Jr., "Superstar" Billy Graham, Bruno Sammartino and a few others. The late Billy Firehawk had me on most of his CyberSpace Wrestling shows as the backstage interviewer, as well as in the ring. Big Time Wrestling (California) let me be a part of their broadcast team many times. Marvin Ward made me one of his broadcasters at the announcers' table and in the "Okerlund role" through his various promotions in the Carolinas. Early Ring of Honor promoters put me in their broadcast booth at times and even let me do some skits with Colt Cabana. Tod Gordon had me in the announcer's position a few times in the glory days of ECW and 3PW. Bill Behrens let me do weekly segments for a long time on his NWA *Wildside* TV show. Alex Shane got me on TV in the United Kingdom both on his FMW TV shows and DVDs. That also holds true to Ingo Vollenberg in Germany and Roberto Indiano in Italy. Thank you for all the great exposure throughout the years. I also want to thank any of the independent promoters or filmmakers who had me as a guest on their work—just in case I forgot to mention you. Some others who believed in my TV skills from the get-go: Ric Flair, Kevin Sullivan, George Scott, Gary Hart, Fred Ward and the great Eddie Graham.

AND FINALLY . . . WWE: In the past few years, WWE has opened its doors to me. I have been a guest "talking head" on several of their network shows and also on a few DVDs. It has taken me nearly 40 years to get on their radar as a historian or journalist. This sudden change is due to the new era that Stephanie McMahon, Triple H and others have instituted, recognizing the people who helped the business way back when. (I'm not that old—am I?) It's a thrill for me to be called upon, and I hope this will continue for years to come. The gleam in my eyes for this kind of work is still the same as it was when I was dreaming about it.

HIS NAME IS PAUL HEYMAN AND HE WAS A WRESTLING PHOTOGRAPHER

THIRTY-SEVEN

ome well-known wrestling personalities kick-started their careers by photographing or writing about the matches and taking posed photos of the stars and upcoming talent. In my capacity as one of the editors at London Publishing, I was responsible for buying photos from them or saying "No thank you." Here are some of the people I regularly bought photos from for the magazines . . .

In the early 1980s, Paul Heyman was a semiregular photographer in the WWWF area. Along with me, George Napolitano and Frank Amato, he'd be at ringside trying to get the best photos possible. Sometimes, when one of us had a shot ready and set in the viewfinder, Paul and his knifelike elbows would push in and try to get the same photo. Despite this, he did get some really good pictures, and because of his relationship with the Grand Wizard, Freddie

Blassie and Lou Albano, he had an in to a lot of candid and backstage shots. Even though he was pushy, he had a contagious personality and would take photos of me with many of the wrestlers. Paul's photos were published and he didn't care if he was paid or not. "I just love seeing my photos in the magazine," he used to say. "I'll give them to you for free if it will make it easier to make a name for myself as a photographer." He was treated the same as the other photographers—$10 per shot.

Around 1991, Tammy Sytch was traveling with her boyfriend, Chris Candido, and documenting him breaking into the business, camera in hand. I remember meeting this lovely young lady at a few indy shows and complimented her on some of the photos she was selling at the gimmick tables. I suggested she send some to me. A few of her photos became centerfolds, and some were used for stories. She credits this time period as her first real job in the pro-wrestling business. She made a whopping $10 per photo and eventually became our main source of photography at Ohio Valley Wrestling.

To this day, Jim Cornette still contends I owe him about $30 for three photos. He was the guy we depended on for years in Memphis.

As a matter of fact, Cornette was the shutterbug who shot most of the classic photos of the historical Jerry Lawler versus Andy Kaufman matches. In later years, when Jim got into the business as a manager, a young man named Sam Lowe shot that territory. He also went on to become a manager in the area for a short period of time.

When he was 14 years old, Eddie Gilbert started sending in written reports of the matches in Tennessee. One day I decided to call him, as I knew his dad, Tommy, fairly well from photographing his matches. We started to talk a few times a month, and Eddie became one of my favorite correspondents. He also shot posed photos and many were used in the magazines.

Others: John Clark, who is now the head sports broadcaster on the NBC affiliate in Philadelphia, one of the largest markets in the United States, credits me with accepting his first photos for publication and states it helped inspire him to pursue a career in sports. I never bought a photo from this next person, because she wasn't shooting for the magazines, but at my request, promoter Vince McMahon Sr. eventually let my friend at that time, supermodel-to-be Christie Brinkley, shoot a few matches at Madison Square Garden. She was permitted to shoot some of the pre-lims at one show but moved out of the ringside area when the main matches took place. Mr. McMahon did not feel it was a safe place for a woman to be. I met Christie when I was shooting boxing matches, and we worked together many times.

THE McMAHONS

THIRTY-EIGHT

VINCE McMAHON JR.: Through the years, Vince has been called a lot of things by a lot of people. Although many have showered him with praise, others have used certain four-letter words to express their bitterness. At this point, none of that matters. Facts are what count. He took a small territorial company and navigated it through years of tumultuous waters. Today his company has probably exceeded even his wildest dreams. He is the ringmaster of a worldwide phenomenon.

No one can shortchange what he has done. The way it was accomplished may not sit well with some, and it didn't sit well with me at times either. But those days are gone.

Did a lot of people get hurt (both in their business and personal lives) when he went into the various territories to sign their best talent and secure their TV outlets? Yes. I witnessed a lot of this firsthand, and oftentimes I didn't approve of his business tactics. However, as the years went on, I began to think about the flip side of this story. Something positive was taking shape as WWF became bigger. I looked at how many performers, and even wrestling-company office staff, that were lured or moved to WWF and were able to earn livings far beyond anything they ever envisioned. This was due to McMahon's business expansion. The perfect example of this is Hulk Hogan. "Hulkamania" didn't extend beyond the AWA. It was the marketing expertise of McMahon's creative mind and his corporate machine that took hold of Hulk and made him into an international sensation.

Countless performers and support staff have McMahon to thank for their security and way of life. This is why someone like Shawn Michaels never strayed from the WWE family. McMahon took care of many of them, and they had a great life because of him. He couldn't do that with everyone, but that's true of any big business.

My relationship with Vince was always cordial. Even when the magazines I worked for were denied access, any time I came in contact with him, he never treated me badly, always offering a very hearty handshake and a smile. He realized that I knew the boundaries and appreciated that I never personally or purposely antagonized the situation between WWF and my employers.

Vince offered me a job in the magazine division of WWF several times throughout the years. I turned these offers down due to my loyalty to Stanley Weston. He understood, and I told him that I hoped I could work for his company sometime in the future.

In recent years, as WWF became WWE, I have had very little contact with Vince. I do get the occasional, "I spoke to Vince and mentioned I know you, and he spoke very highly of you," comment from mutual friends or business contacts.

Not long before this book went to press, I was backstage at a *Monday Night Raw* live show and happened to be outside a meeting room that Vince had just emerged from. He saw me, gave a big smile, extended a handshake and pulled me in for a hug. "It's been a few years, Vince," I said. "I just want to say how thrilled I am to see you. Thank you for opening the door to the WWE Network and the website. I've always wanted to work for you!" A huge grin came over his face and he said, "It's my pleasure." Another hug, a quick photo (it's on the cover), and he was on his way to his next meeting. I felt a great sense of accomplishment having finally had face time with him after all these years. I didn't know how he would react. Brian "The Blue Meanie" Heffron was nearby and saw the brief encounter. He patted me on the back and said, "Two legends, Mr. McMahon and Wonderful Willie, and I got to see them together!" Thanks, Meanie! That was certainly nice to hear.

I'm grateful for the opportunities offered and for the fact that when his business (and the other national federations) did well so did the sales of the magazines I worked for—so in an indirect way, he was always helping me make a living, even before I actually worked for him.

LINDA McMAHON: I remember Linda sitting at her desk in the late 1980s and offering me a job as an editor for *WWF Magazine*. She had a charming southern drawl and a glowing smile on her face, and I could easily sense her business acumen as she discussed the type of employee she was looking for. After weighing the offer and considering how long I had been at London Publishing, I graciously declined.

Through the years, like her husband, she has been nothing but polite to me. I came in contact with her several times during my *WOW* days, and she remained very sweet to me. She exuded class and does to this day.

SHANE McMAHON: I've had the least contact with Shane McMahon. During his peak years with WWE, the company did not allow the independent magazines into their matches. I got to know him at a few of the press conferences that I happened to be invited to, and he always greeted me with a smile and a hello. We never got to talk much, as he was a master of saying hello to everyone. He loved to work the room. I must say that I was a big fan of his ring work. I would have liked more opportunities to get to know him.

STEPHANIE McMAHON: She inherited the charm and class of her mother for sure—as well has her father's moxie. I really didn't get to know this terrific young lady, with such a buoyant personality, until I emailed her a few years ago to comment on something she did on *Raw*. She was quick to reply and that not only flattered me, but it also speaks volumes: she is willing to listen to the opinions of others and respond. As one of the key decision-makers in WWE, she seems to find time to juggle duties in so many departments, as well as keep her family (three kids and a Triple H) well intact. I've come face-to-face with her many times now and cannot help but be inspired by her undying energy and passion for the business and charitable causes. Stephanie is completely dedicated to the continued success of WWE—and is undoubtedly making her parents proud as she carries on the successful lineage of McMahons in the pro wrestling–sports entertainment industry. She may be a Levesque now, but she will always be a McMahon.

AN APTER "OLD SCHOOL" STYLE GOSSIP COLUMN

THIRTY-NINE

Throughout the years, fans have enjoyed my various gossip columns. So, in an effort to get some of that into this book, here are some items that might have not been worthy of a full story—but are definitely worth reading.

In 1972, I photographed a match in Florida between Mighty Igor and Bulldog Brower. On his way to the dressing room, Bower grabbed me and pushed me to the floor. I was wearing a baby blue leisure suit, and a lot of the blood that flowed in that match wound up on me. Unfortunately, this wasn't an overnight trip, and I had no change of clothing. As I tried to board my flight back to New York—in my bloody baby-blues—I was interrogated by airport security. I overheard some old lady thought I was a serial killer . . .

At a WCW show, I overheard Bill Goldberg

say to Eric Bischoff, "Let me ask Apter." It was the night of the Jewish holiday Yom Kippur, and Eric had plans for Bill to appear on TV. Goldberg, knowing I'm a person of the Jewish faith, wondered what I would do in that situation. I suggested it might be a good idea to do an interview but not to wrestle. I don't recall what happened after that, but it was nice of him to ask for my advice. Goldberg was invited to my son's Bar Mitzvah. He could not attend, but he sent a congratulatory videotape and a very generous gift.

When the Ultimate Warrior was in WCW, he became the only person in history to turn down a *PWI* year-end award. It was all due to some very sensitive issues, and although I can't go into detail, it's the truth.

In 1972, during one of the very first times I went out to dinner with a wrestler—it was at a Denny's in Upstate New York—the wrestler, who is now deceased and was a very religious person, shocked me when I showed interest in our waitress. He called her over and said, "Honey, my friend here is new in town and wants you to sit on his face after you get off work tonight!" What a line, huh? And by the way, she declined.

Of all the imitations I do, most people request to see Dusty Rhodes and Jerry Lewis.

The list of wrestlers I have put in my figure-four leglock throughout the years would take too many pages to fill. So some of the top victims have been Glenn "Kane" Jacobs, Shawn Michaels, Buddy Rogers, Steve and Colby Corino, Chris Candido, Bubba Ray Dudley, Rob Van Dam and CM Punk.

Some of the top social items: Around 1986, my wife and I chaperoned the Rock 'n' Roll Express on a date with the winners of a "Win a Dream Date" contest. Two giggly teen girls were flown to New York to see the Broadway musical *Cats*.

In the mid-'70s, along with "Captain Lou" Albano, I chaperoned (and photographed) a "Win a Date with the Valiant Brothers" contest. Lots of fun until the good Captain got a bit too intoxicated, and we had to get him home a bit earlier than expected.

Only a handful of people know this, but I was the videographer for Mick Foley's wedding. The stills were done by London Publishing's expert photographer "Judge" Roy London.

Owen Hart and I used to sing Collin Raye songs together whenever we saw each other (at least a few lines of them). We were both

Thank you, Darius Rucker for making me feel like the star you are. Not only am I a fan of his music, but I admire him for all the tireless charitable work he does.

huge fans of the country music star. Collin sang at Owen's funeral.

I was the person who got Bam Bam Bigelow his first and only MMA fight. It took place in Japan against Kimo Leopoldo. This happened when a promoter called me looking for a legit tough-guy wrestler. I suggested Bigelow, and against his family's wishes, he took the fight for a huge payday.

I am still knocked out by the fact that one of my favorite entertainers, Darius Rucker, is a fan of mine. That is very flattering. He and my daughter, Hailey, engaged in a conversation about wrestling on Twitter, and a few weeks later we were Darius's guests at his show in Atlantic City. I did an

"Apter Chat" video that you can see if you go to 1Wrestlingvideo.com and search "Darius." What a great guy. We even did a battle of Dusty Rhodes imitations and sang some Barry Manilow tunes. It's all on the video.

Back in the early '70s, I used to sneak this kid backstage at Madison Square Garden to get autographs. I did this because he was one of the nicest and politest people I had ever met. His name was Rick Rubin—and he became one of the most important and influential people in the music business. He was cofounder of Def Jam Record and former copresident of Columbia Records. He is the main man who helped popularize hip-hop music. LL Cool J, Kanye West, AC/DC, Metallica and hundreds more have all been blessed with his talents. It's worth a trip to Google to read more about this genius.

In Montreal in the mid-'80s, Craig Peters and I were headed to our hotel after the matches at the Forum. A young couple stopped us and said they were newly married and looking for a nice place to stay in town. We suggested our hotel. They walked with us a few blocks, and as we entered the lobby, there lying on a couch was Abdullah the Butcher with several bloody bandages on his head. Needless to say, the couple left the hotel very quickly.

I was in a hotel bar after the matches in Detroit. It was early 1971, and this was my first big trip out of town. I was shocked when one of the elder wrestlers, who had two sons and hailed from Amarillo, Texas, was highly intoxicated and told a very sexy lady sitting near us that I was a photographer for *Playboy*. She said she wanted to be a model and would love to have photos taken. I was ready to say, "No, I take photos of wrestlers," but he nearly kicked me off my bar stool as I opened my mouth. He invited her, me and my camera to his room to take photos. We got to the room, he told her to disrobe and I ran out of the room. I just couldn't go along with it. The next morning I saw him as we were checking out of the hotel. He put his arm around me and said, "She came out of the bathroom in the buff and asked where the photographer was. When she couldn't find you, she grabbed her clothes and ran out of the room still naked. And I never saw her again." We shared

> **She grabbed her clothes and ran out of the room still naked.**

197

a good laugh. That was some first night out of town.

In the mid-'70s, a very famous World champion boxer was in Las Vegas a few days before he was set to defend his title. He was known for being a party guy. He and I were friends, as I had known him for years shooting photos for the company's boxing magazines. I was in Vegas as well, staying at the same hotel. Two nights before his fight, he saw me in the hotel lobby and made a beeline toward me, passing by all the autograph hounds. "Bill, I just found out my wife is coming here tonight, and I was going to take my girlfriend to see the Diana Ross show. I wonder if you can help me out and take my girl to the show so I can take my wife?" (I guess that's what friends are for.) It was a great show, and I had the best seats and the hottest girl in town sitting with me. The boxer and his wife were not too far away. I'm still amazed I was the stand-in for this iconic champion!

When I was working for *WOW Magazine*, the company also produced a music magazine for teens. I was asked if I would like to photograph a Brittany Spears concert for a special concert issue. As a loyal company guy, I said, "Of course." The show was at an outdoor venue in Baltimore, and I was allowed

to take my daughter. I had to find the press contact a few hours before the show, so I was in the back by Spears's tour bus (my daughter was not permitted in this area). I knocked on the bus door but no one answered. I turned away only to see some man and a young girl coming toward the bus. As they got closer, I could see it was her. "Hey, what do you want and why do you have a camera?" the man with her questioned. He also added, "No photos back here, and you *did not* see her smoking—right?" I said, "Right!" I was warned that if I had any image of her smoking and they showed up anywhere, I would be "dealt with to the full extent of the law." They both went onto the bus, and a few minutes later a security guard came out to escort me to the photo area.

In the mid-'90s the publishing company that produced *PWI* decided to undertake a country music magazine titled *CountryBeat*. Craig Peters was the editor, and I asked if I could go on some assignments. I thought they would be fun:

My first assignment was to photograph and interview Willie Nelson. Willie was very nice to me when I got on his tour bus. I was taping the interview, trying to stay on topic about how country music seems to be like wrestling these days—exchanging old-school traditions for the entertainment bang. I had heard that Willie was friends with Dusty Rhodes and told him I was also close friends with Dusty. I was expecting a smile, but instead I got, "Oh, so you're friends with Dusty? Did he send you here to make sure he gets a cut of the money you'll make from this interview?" I had no answer. I laughed in a very uncomfortable manner, and he changed the subject, not back to country music or Dusty but to marijuana and why it should be legalized. To this day I still can't figure it all out.

Billy Ray Cyrus (Miley's dad) was one of the nicest people I ever interviewed and photographed. While he was on tour in 1995, I was on his bus and came up with an angle. I suggested putting a photo of him on the cover of *CountryBeat* with a shadow-like image of Elvis in the background. The reader might then interpret Billy Ray as the second coming of Elvis. I just thought it would be a

As one of the editors of *Country Beat* magazine, I met, photographed and interviewed some huge stars. Here I'm on Billy Ray Cyrus's tour bus watching his newest music video.

IS WRESTLING FIXED?

magazine seller. He had no objections. The next day, I received a call from his manager in Nashville, Jack McFadden, who threatened to sue me, the publisher and anyone else involved if we ran that cover. I transferred the call to Craig, who told McFadden that he can't tell us what to do and we will consider the pros and cons of the cover. We didn't go with the idea—it had barely been pitched to Craig. I saw Billy Ray a few months later, and he told me that "Jack went crazy when I told him what you suggested." He had no idea why, and we

never did find out.

I recently found out that Terry Funk tells people that I was his acting teacher. When Japan's "superfan" Masa Horie interviewed Terry about some of the movies Funk had appeared in, I was credited with helping his thespian career. This actually came about in a hotel room at 2 a.m. in Hollywood, California, in 1985, when I was covering a wrestling event featuring Funk. In the dressing room that night, he told me he has a reading for a part in a western TV series called Wildside. I wished him luck

TNA's president Dixie Carter is so very charming and always makes a huge "impact" when you meet her.

and told him to let me know how it goes.

I was dead asleep when the telephone rang at 3 a.m. It was Terry Funk.

"Apter, I'm in room 307," he said. "Come to my room. I read for the TV show at 9 a.m., and I need someone to cue me and read the other characters, so I can get a sense of how to react."

I couldn't say no. For three hours, I read aloud with him and, due to my years as a student of New York City drama coach Robert X. Modica, was able to fine-tune his reactions.

He got the part! I was thrilled, and now I can add "Acting Coach" to my resume . . .

When TNA wrestling was formed in 2002 and needed studio photos of their talent, they reached out to me. This was the first time I met Dixie Carter. What a fantastic woman who mixed charm and business just perfectly. It was a pleasure photographing Ken Shamrock and so many others on their roster.

APTER MAKES A HISTORIC MEETING HAPPEN: WHEN ANDY KAUFMAN MET JERRY LAWLER

FORTY

I met Andy Kaufman backstage at a wrestling show at Madison Square Garden sometime in late 1981. He was a fan of the magazines and knew who I was, which was quite flattering. I was a fan of his from the TV show *Taxi*, where he played Latka Gravas.

Andy had been at the Garden several times before I chatted with him. Back in 1979, he was actually interviewed by Vince Jr. at the broadcast table. He was on Vince's radar but nothing ever happened. It was known in the business that Vince Sr. didn't want too much showbiz on his shows. He was all about serious pro wrestling.

Andy was very polite and asked me for my telephone number so we could talk about wrestling. He was a huge fan of Buddy Rogers and Fred Blassie. I was glad to give him my contact information, and we started a nice phone relationship from the next day forward. There were times at London Publishing when I just had to cut him off. The publisher thought I was wasting my time and needed to get back to the business at hand—helping get the magazines done.

In those days, the company rented a photo studio in New York on West 46th Street. During one of my conversations with Andy, I mentioned that I was going to be doing a posed photo session with both Curt Hennig and Eddie Gilbert, who were appearing at the Garden later that night. He asked if he could attend, and I agreed. I got some great shots of them alone and with Andy. Curt's father, Larry "The Axe," happened to be there and he had a photo taken with Andy as well.

As the friendship grew, Andy invited me to be his special guest at one of his many *Saturday Night Live* appearances. He also brought me to the huge 10th anniversary celebration of the Catch a Rising Star comedy club.

One night before a show at the Garden, I saw him chatting with Vince McMahon Sr. backstage. I noticed Senior was very cordial to Andy, but his body language was a bit uncomfortable. Chatting with Vince before he had a show at the Garden was never a good idea. He was busy trying to run things, and

Andy was probably a distraction he didn't want at that moment. Finally he and Andy shook hands, and Andy turned away and walked toward me. He explained that he tried to talk to Senior about getting involved somehow, but Vince really wasn't interested.

Vince, still standing nearby, gestured for me to come over. Andy's back was turned and did not see Vince motion to me. I excused myself from Andy and told him I'd be right back. I walked with Vince and we stood in a corridor where we could not be seen.

"Look, that guy you're talking to is a nice guy, but I'm not interested in what he wants to do," he said. "I don't really like these show-business people coming backstage when we're trying to do business. See if you can just get him to go out to his seat already."

I went back out to the hallway and Andy was talking with Fred Blassie, Lou Albano and a few others. I could do nothing.

After photographing the show, I was backstage saying my goodbyes to everyone, and Andy was there as well. He asked if I was going anywhere special, and I told him I was going home.

"Oh," he said. "How do you get there?"

"The subway," I said. His next

Former Australian women's champion Susan Sexton became one of my closest and dearest friends. When we shared an apartment in Kew Gardens, New York, I shocked her one night by bringing Andy Kaufman home.

question really surprised me.

"Can I go with you, so we can talk about wrestling?"

Here I was, chatting with one of the most well-known TV stars and he wanted to take the train with me. I said, "Sure," and it was down to Penn Station, en route to my "pad" in the Briarwood section of Queens. He was very polite to fans who recognized him on the subway. We got to my apartment, and my next-door neighbor Alice happened to be coming in (we lived on the fifth floor of a six-floor

building). She was quite surprised when she realized who Andy was.

I shared my apartment with former Australian Women's Wrestling champion Susan Sexton. We had become best friends after I went through a divorce. Anyway, she came home, met Andy and we all began to talk. After an hour of wrestling talk, Susan looked at Andy and, obviously having had enough shoptalk, asked, "Can you talk about anything but wrestling?" He looked away and just kept going on about how much he wanted to wrestle at the Garden. At that point, Susan got up, looked at me, grabbed her headphones and her cassette player pre-loaded with her favorite Ramones tape and headed to her bedroom.

Andy kept questioning me about why Vince Sr. wouldn't give him a chance. No matter what I said, it didn't sink in. While we spoke, I thumbed through some magazines and noticed some photos taken in the Memphis area of a Frankenstein character. There was also a Freddy Krueger character. For some reason I recalled Andy's dead-on imitation of Elvis and said to him, "I know one of the promoters in this area," pointing out the photos to him. "Maybe you could go there as an evil Elvis or something," I suggested. My brain was racing.

"If you want, I can call my friend Jerry Lawler. He's a wrestler and promotes there," I told him. He said he knew of Lawler through the magazines.

"It's midnight in Memphis," he pointed out. "Isn't it too late to call?"

I assured him that the wrestling community is up all night, and if they aren't, they are always open to a wake-up business call.

Lawler picked up the phone fairly quickly.

"You've got Andy Kaufman, the guy from *Taxi*, in your little roach-infested apartment in Queens?" he asked.

I put Andy on the phone and they spoke for several minutes. When he hung up, Andy was so grateful he could not stop thanking me. He said that he and Jerry would talk again in a few hours. He was so excited. What I didn't realize is that this phone call would make history.

A few days later, Andy called me from Lawler's house. Plans were under way to make Kaufman the most hated man in wrestling. His promos insulting the people in the Mid-Southern area are classics. Alongside Kaufman was the "Mouth of the South" Jimmy Hart. What a duo of mouths!

I went into publisher Stanley Weston's office and asked permission to fly to Memphis to cover the match that was now signed and sealed. I was turned down.

"No one cares about this," he said. "A comedian against a wrestler? I would be embarrassed to run it in anything more than a column!" I called Lawler, and he told me that one of the house photographers, a kid named Jim Cornette, would get photos for us.

On April 5, 1982, Lawler versus Kaufman took place in Memphis's

Mid-South Coliseum. Andy's dream was happening. In his mind, he was Buddy Rogers and Fred Blassie.

The arena was filled to capacity and the match had amazing heat. The fans hated Kaufman and wanted to see Lawler destroy him—and that he did.

Guided by Lawler, Kaufman performed well. After a few minutes and several devastating piledrivers "The King" ended it. Lawler had won, but it would not be the end of the feud.

One month later, Andy showed up backstage at the Garden wearing a neck brace, selling the injury. To be honest, I thought that piledriver broke Andy's neck, though Lawler later let me in that it was a work. He was a master salesman! There would be more matches to come between the two, but now this rivalry was about to accelerate onto a national stage.

A few weeks later, Lawler called to tell me that he and Andy were booked on the *Late Night with David Letterman* show. Lawler and his wife, Paula, arrived a day

I am so proud to have been the person who kick-started the feud between Andy Kaufman (pictured with me) and Jerry "The King" Lawler. It all started with a subway ride, a visit to my apartment and a telephone call. As they say, "the rest is history!"

before this and editor Craig Peters and I met with them, taking them to several places for photo ops. We went to the Statue of Liberty, the Empire State Building and Rockefeller Center. Lawler had also arranged to make sure that Craig and I had total access at the Letterman show.

The next day, we were in the NBC studio's greenroom, and after mingling with Letterman, his band leader Paul Shaffer and some others, we were brought into the studio and told we could stand next to the TV cameras.

We didn't know what would happen. It's all history now, as after taunting each other for a few minutes, Kaufman went totally nuts and tossed a cup of hot coffee at Lawler. This precipitated Lawler to get up from his seat and slap Kaufman so hard he fell over. All this time Craig and I clicked away with our cameras.

When that segment was over, Craig and I rushed backstage to see both of them. Kaufman was gone—quickly escorted out of the building by security. Lawler stood in the corridor and looked at us in amazement.

"Did you get all that on film?" he asked. We told him we had gotten it all. Lawler was quickly taken to the elevator and down to a waiting limo to whisk him back to his hotel.

In the meantime, Craig and I wondered what to do with the film. We figured we had a huge exclusive story here and somehow we needed to find a place that could develop the black-and-white film. Perhaps we could get the images onto the Associated Press wire services. A call to the *New York Post* was all that was necessary. We rushed over to their offices. They processed the film, and the next day one of those photos wound up on the cover of the newspaper. Associated Press picked up the image and hundreds of newspapers published it.

We called Lawler and told him the good news, and he asked us to come to his hotel. We knocked on his door and found Lawler and his wife sitting on the beds. So who opened the door? It was Andy!

For the next hour or two, we talked about how well it all played out. They vowed to keep kayfabe. Although they were at the same hotel, no one knew they were together at this point—and this is the first time it's been revealed.

The next day, both of them were the hot topic. No matter where either of them went, they were asked about the incident on Letterman. And it all started with a simple telephone call in my "little roach-infested apartment in Queens!"

I went into Mr. Weston's office, told him what had happened and showed him a copy of the *New York Post*. He didn't seem impressed, but he did chuckle.

"You can use a few pictures in your column if you want," he told me. I informed him that Lawler was still in New York for a few days and wanted to visit our office. I suggested that we send a car to get him and bring him back to his hotel. Mr. Weston was old school like Vince Sr., and he said no. Jerry opted to keep the date and took the Long Island Rail Road from New York's Penn Station to the office in Rockville Centre on Long Island.

> No matter where either of them went, they were asked about the incident.

Jerry spent a few hours posing for photos, checking out the photo files and talking to the editors. I will never forget when he looked at me, shaking his head in disbelief, "I can't believe I took the train here. People on the train wondered what the heck I was doing there. I mean, it's the first time so many people recognized me, and it was on a dang railroad train!" I shrugged my shoulders and said, "It wasn't my choice!"

There was one more thing Jerry wanted to do before he left New York. He wanted to go to the comedy club owned by his favorite comedian, Rodney Dangerfield. I told him I would accompany him on the train and we'd venture to Dangerfield's together.

When we walked into the place, we were shocked. Standing at the bar was Rodney himself! He was known to stop by only now and then, and tonight was one of those nights. Redd Foxx was headlining, and Rodney wanted to catch his act. He recognized Lawler immediately.

"Hey, that gig you and Andy Kaufman did on the Letterman show last night was great," he said. "You're quite a team!" I snapped a few photos of them together. It was a great time.

Andy kept in touch with me during the next year. Then the calls became less and less frequent, and, at the time, I didn't know why. I later found out that he was ill and didn't want anyone to know. Andy died on May 16, 1984.

In 1986, Judd Hirsch, one of Andy's costars on the show *Taxi* was appearing in an off-Broadway production of a show called, *I'm Not Rappaport*. Walking downtown one afternoon, I happened to pass the theater, and Hirsch was just getting out of a cab. I stopped him and mentioned I was the guy who put Andy together with Jerry Lawler. I expected a smile. I didn't get it.

"The entire cast of *Taxi* hated that time," he said. "Andy was so wrapped up in wrestling that it hurt what we were doing. He showed up late, he would put on a wrestling persona. It just wasn't pleasant. I'm sorry I can't say thank you for hooking him up in wrestling, because it didn't work for us at *Taxi*." I was stunned. He started walking to the theater, but then turned around, walked toward me, shook my hand and said, "Sorry if I came across angry. It is just a sore subject. I'm sure you're a really nice guy,

and you were just helping him do what he wanted to do."

In 1999, Lawler invited me to the Letterman Theater in New York (known as the Ed Sullivan Theater back then) to see him and Jim Carrey recreate the entire incident. This was during filming of the Kaufman bio-pic *Man on the Moon*. I had another commitment that day and could not attend. When I did go to a screening of the movie, I was amazed at Carrey's uncanny resemblance to Kaufman in both appearance and personality. It was eerie.

Today, when I am interviewed for various shows or internet blogs, the Kaufman story is one I am always asked to tell. I am so proud to have been a small part of it.

MY PAL SAL

FORTY-ONE

There's an adage that teaches, "Be nice to the people on the way up the ladder of success, because you never know if you will need them on the way down."

In the late 1970s, Sal Corrente was just a teenage kid from Yonkers, New York. As a young wrestling fan, he spent all his money going to wrestling shows and buying wrestling magazines and pretty much anything else that had the word wrestling attached to it. Much like me when I was a teenager, Sal stationed himself near the wrestlers' entrance of any arena he went to, hoping to get a moment of time with one of them. An autograph, a photo or just a word or two would make his day.

Teenage Sal was one of the regulars standing outside the Madison Square Garden stage door right off 33rd Street and 8th Avenue. Along with a few others, he anxiously waited as the wrestlers walked into the Garden. For the most part, they whizzed past, perhaps waving, but mostly being hustled away by the MSG security guards.

I would go in through the same door as the wrestlers. I could see the "I wish I could get in there too" look on the faces of the fans, so being "Mister Social," I went to chat with them. One of those fans was Sal. He was thrilled, because he had seen me in the magazines, shooting photos around the ring and with the wrestlers. He told me how he wanted to get in the wrestling business, and I recall giving him my office telephone number and letting him know he could call anytime. And he did. We maintained a very good relationship that grew as the years progressed. However, I didn't realize what that one moment outside MSG would mean to my life until many years later.

Fast-forward several years. Sal is no longer a teen and through a relationship he developed with Afa (the Wild Samoan) Anoa'i was able to work himself into a spot in the business. He became a referee, a manager (known as The Big Cheese), a booker, a promoter and anything else you could become in the wrestling business—even, at times, a wrestler. Through all this,

he would call me or editor Craig Peters to give us results of matches and to tell us stories of the wrestlers he was working with in various territories.

Now, let's fast-forward a bit further. It's April 2004, and for the first time since I started in 1970, I thought my career was over. Just prior, I was the editor of the U.K.'s *Total Wrestling* magazine and was also supplying Italy's *Tutto Wrestling* and Germany's *Power Wrestling* magazines with a monthly column. Without any warning, the publishing company decided the magazine was no longer profitable and closed it down. I was at a dead end. The *PWI* magazines were not in need of my services, so I couldn't go back there. News of my unemployment was all over the internet, the "dirt" sheets and even some newspapers. I received a call from a gentleman named Michael Holmes—the senior editor of Canadian publishing company ECW Press, offering me a deal to pen my life story. I told him I'd get back to him. (I think you know the result of that call.) Then the phone rang. It was Sal Corrente.

"Listen, Bill, me and our old friend Rob Russen came up with an idea and think you're the guy that's going to make this project a success," he explained. "Everyone knows you, so we want you to be the face of a new website called All About Wrestling. We won't be able to pay you out of the gate, but let's get it going and get a following and maybe we can all earn part of a living with this thing."

It sounded great and I was thrilled—but it wasn't going to help pay my mortgage. It was worth a shot though. In the next few weeks, the site kicked off, but I could put only a few short hours a week into it, since I was still hunting for a paying situation. Eventually, the site fizzled. I felt sorry that I let my old friends down, but they understood. Little did I know that wasn't the end of their "Save Apter" campaign. A few days later Sal called back.

"No worries about the site," he said. "Rob and I are going to start putting on conventions with dozens and dozens of wrestling legends. We want you to host the events. The first one will actually have you and Diamond Dallas Page as the

hosts. It won't be steady money, Bill, but it will be something for you. The first one will be in Tampa in January 2005. Are you in?"

Of course I was. Prior to this, I had hosted a few very successful conventions for Greg Price in the Mid-Atlantic area. Rob and Sal called it WrestleReunion, and not only was I the face of the first convention, I also hosted three more after that. It gave me the opportunity to do live interviews and interact with the fans and talent. It was just perfect.

Today our relationship is still strong. We are in touch regularly on Facebook and sometimes he writes for me at 1Wrestling.com. He is still very well connected and anytime something major happens, he always calls to give me the scoop.

Amazing, and it all happened because I took the time to talk to him outside Madison Square Garden when he was a teenager. Thank you, my pal Sal.

DON'T GET TOO CLOSE—BUT I DID

FORTY-TWO

Relationships with wrestlers?

My mentor Stanley Weston insisted, "Don't get close to any of them . . . they are a bunch of pimps and hoowahs [his pronunciation for whores] who will wine and dine you, get you girls and more, just to make you believe they're your friend so you'll put them in our magazines."

Although some of what he said is true, there were two gems who didn't even give a damn if I brought my camera to their home or ever typed their name for publication.

I had casually met Lou Thesz at various events but never really got to bond with him. In 1982, I went on my first wrestling trip to Japan and was going with a bunch of wild guys like Terry Funk, Bruiser Brody, Stan Hansen and Haku. I was told that "the boys can get a bit out of hand at times" by Dory Funk Jr., who,

My parents schmoozing with Charlie and Lou Thesz. This photo was taken on May 16, 1983, the morning after my wife, Andrea, and I were married.

along with Terry, was a United States liaison for this tour with All Japan Pro Wrestling. A bit concerned by the stories I had heard from prior tours, I mentioned to Dory that since this was my first trip to Japan, I'd like to know who didn't have the wild-guy profile. "Just pair up with Lou Thesz," he said. "He's one of the finest gentlemen in the world, and he doesn't go out and get crazy like some of the other boys."

Dory was right. Lou and I met and became quick friends. He was a first-class gentleman and was like my personal tour guide. While many of the talent were out carousing after the matches, Lou and I, and a few others, would go to dinner, hit a few music places and then call it a night since we were usually scheduled to go to another town at the crack of dawn the next day.

Months after the Japan tour, my girlfriend, Andrea, and I were invited to Lou's home in Virginia Beach. There, along with his wife, Charlie, we were treated to their beach home, great weather and nightly barbeques for a few days. They were at our wedding and became special guests at our kids' birthdays when we lived in New York. The Thesz's were also special guests at our daughter's Bat Mitzvah.

Johnny "Mr. Wrestling II" Walker (left) poses with Mr. Wrestling II 1/2 (me)! Johnny, his wife, Olivia, and his three boys became a very close extended family to me.

When Lou passed away, we kept in touch with Charlie and still do. Charlie, along with best friend Dotty Curtis (widow of Don Curtis), make sure we're all connected these days through Facebook and Skype.

* * *

Johnny "Mr. Wrestling II" Walker was a huge star in Georgia. One night after a show at the Omni, he invited me to his home to meet his wife, Olivia, and his three sons, John Jr., Michael and Robert. He made it clear that he was not looking for publicity in exchange for the invitation. We had become friends on the road and wanted his

215

family to meet me.

Living in a large home on the outskirts of Atlanta, "Two" and Olivia had a wonderful relationship. They were the couple you talk about when you talk about people who are really in love. The first night I was there, Olivia cooked a meal that was better than any restaurant meal I had ever had. Braised beef, potatoes, string beans and more all topped off with mouth-watering desserts. After dinner came a few card games with the kids (Uno was their favorite) and then lots of business chat with Johnny as Olivia sat and took it all in.

For more years than I can remember, the Walkers refused to let me stay at a hotel. When I was in Georgia, they had a loft bedroom that was reserved for me.

Of course, I did convince Johnny (it wasn't hard) to get into his Mr. Wrestling II gear a few times, so I could take photos for the magazine I was working for. I also got a huge

scoop when I saw Olivia hard at work at a job she loved. She was a designer and seamstress. She made Johnny's robes, as well as the robes for Ric Flair, Greg Valentine, the Killer Bees and other stars.

When my first wife and I divorced, the Walkers invited me down to their home for as long as I wanted to stay, just to make sure I was okay. I took them up on it, touring with Johnny and going back to the Walker home nightly. I had a wonderful time traveling with him and referee-friend Ronnie West and then going back to Johnny's home where an Olivia-feast was always there for the hungry boys.

Olivia died in 2003. She was a fabulous lady, and I miss her dearly. Johnny wound up moving to Hawaii, and several years ago I went to visit. We went to Olivia's gravesite. It was a beautiful day to be in the presence of that great lady and my dear friend.

STRIKE A POSE

FORTY-THREE

I've lugged tons of clumsy photo-studio equipment to shows all over the United States. Most times I did that gig alone, posing wrestlers in a makeshift studio and then stopping to do the ringside photography once the matches began. On the real big shows, Craig Peters came along as another photographer-reporter, and we were then able to get all the show action and poses. In the studio, I got up close and personal with the biggest stars. And the wannabes. And some has-beens. (I won't write about them, as some of them are still alive and can still kick my ass.) On the run, sometimes I was able to use my trusty Nikon with a mounted flash. No matter, I was there to get the best possible images. I have to tell you, there were many complex personalities involved. I've posed hundreds of people so it's hard to recall them all, but here are some who were unforgettable . . .

Some were a dream to work with, like Ricky "The Dragon" Steamboat. No matter how much time I needed, he always made it for me. Curt Hennig, Chris Jericho, Harley Race, Nick Bockwinkel and the Road Warriors are in that category as well. On the other side of the coin, you will be surprised that one of the men who loved to be in the spotlight more than most also hated to pose.

"Give me five minutes, Bill," was the usual excuse. "I need to get out of this three-piece suit and into my ring gear . . ." That guy never came out until he was scheduled to get into the ring and then would only agree to a quick pose. Sometimes the promoter running the show twisted his arm, because he knew the publicity was important. And had promoter Bob Geigel not pressed the issue, I never would have gotten this man to pose for me after winning the NWA World title from Dusty Rhodes in Kansas City. That man is *Ric Flair*.

Flair's "cousins" the Anderson Brothers, Ole and Gene, were another posing problem. Quite typically, Ole would say, "Give us a countdown, Apter, so we can prepare for the shot." I would count down from 10. They would stand casually, waiting for the last few seconds to get into position,

I thought. Except that as I got to one, Ole would stick his middle finger in the air. Then they would laugh, turn and walk away.

In my early days, when I asked Bulldog Brower, "Wild Bull" Curry or "Crazy" Luke Graham to pose, they usually tossed a garbage can, an ashtray or whatever they could get their hands on to stop me from pursuing them.

Although you saw many poses of "The Living Legend" Bruno Sammartino on the magazine covers through the years, he was hard to pin down (not only in the ring of course) for a few standing poses. He did it, but you could tell it was because he was such a great guy he couldn't say no.

A real pose-hater was the Original Sheik, Ed Farhat. He was so true to his gimmick he *never* posed for me. He explained to me that his character would never just stand there. Many times his manager Ernie "Abdullah Farouk" Roth tried to convince him to do it just once, but Sheik wouldn't budge.

I never thought I would ever get to pose "Nature Boy" Buddy Rogers. I used to marvel at the studio photos I saw in the *Wrestling Revue* magazines I read when I was growing up. It was obvious he knew how to pose, and his body glistened under the studio lights. In 1979, when Buddy was working for Jim Crockett Promotions, I had the portable studio set up backstage in Norfolk, Virginia. That night Buddy was scheduled to wrestle Ric Flair. I made a request to Buddy to get him into the studio, even for a handful of shots. He gave me almost 30 minutes. I posed him exactly as I saw him pose in the magazines in my youth. It was a dream come true for me, as I was such a huge fan of Buddy Rogers. What an unforgettable time that was.

Unfortunately, one of wrestling's most iconic and loved performers recently passed away. This man made it clear that he was willing to pose only if he was compensated. That is why you never saw a posed photo of him on the magazine covers. I hold no grudge against him—that was his way of conducting business and he was always cordial. That man was Jim "The Ultimate Warrior" Helwig.

Andre the Giant was not crazy about posing but did it. Most of the time, I tried to find some regular-sized wrestlers to be in the photo to make him look even bigger. Whenever he saw me in the hallway looking for victims to photograph, Andre would always ask, "You need me to take a picture tonight, boss?"

Dwayne "The Rock" Johnson would playfully push whoever was in the studio away from the backdrop and joke, "Apter's not here to take pictures of you. He's here for me." His father, Rocky Johnson, was a pleasure to have in the studio. He was another one who knew how to pose and just looked great as a photography subject.

I'll never forget the time I chased King Curtis Iaukea back to the dressing room after a very bloody match against Chief Jay Strongbow. King Curtis's forehead had been split open, and I wanted to get a shot of the gore for the cover. Publisher Mr. Weston always believed that a bloody cover helped sell magazines. As I got to Curtis's dressing room, the blood was just trickling out. I told him I needed a real bloody image for a possible cover shot. He proceeded to take out a small razor tip and cut his forehead open, just so I could take the photo.

At the National Wrestling Alliance convention in 1998, at a hotel in Cherry Hill, New Jersey, I

> **A bloody cover helped sell magazines.**

"THE APTER CHAT"

THROUGH THE YEARS

IS WRESTLING FIXED?

had the studio set up in a ballroom. As I posed wrestlers and promoters, many watched from tables near my backdrop. In the middle of a photo session with female wrestler Strawberry Fields, she asked me to stop for a moment. She approached me and asked if she could borrow my tie. I had no idea what would happen next and neither did the handful of promoters and fans watching the photo session. She went back to the backdrop area, turned her back to us, dropped her top, somehow wrapped the tie around her breasts and then turned toward us. I almost dropped my camera, but the people in attendance urged me to click away—and I did. Some amazing photos came out of that session!

What started out as "shtick" sometimes ended up being something much bigger. I often shot cover photos at a studio that we rented on West 45th Street in New York City. On one occasion, the plan was to pose George "The Animal" Steele like he was destroying the place. It started like that, but George thought that the photos would be more convincing if he got into character. He told me to just keep the camera on him and it would "look good." He then kicked the seamless background supports down, sending the seamless paper crashing to the ground. One end of the paper brought down a light stand, cracking one of the studio lights. Thank goodness the studio owner, Jim Manley, came in and halted what could have cost us a lot of money. From that day on, the studio people were never too excited to have us back.

BENOIT

Chris Benoit and I were good friends, but my bond with his wife Nancy (née Toffoloni) was even stronger.

I first met Nancy in Florida in 1987, when she was being groomed in the business by Kevin Sullivan. At the time, Sullivan was the storyline leader of a group of Satanists that included Luna Vachon, the Purple Haze (Mark Lewin), Sir Oliver Humperdink and a few others. Nancy became the character "Fallen Angel." She was sexy and drop-dead gorgeous, and she also had an outgoing personality and very upbeat sense of humor. I was a married man, yet I was smitten by her. She wound up marrying Kevin, and I stayed married. An affair with her was only to be in my mind. I am certain that I am not the only one who felt this way about this alluring woman.

Nancy would call me, almost from day one,

"Mister Bill" in the same inflection comedians on *Saturday Night Live* would use. Then she would grab me by the chin and plant a kiss on my cheek. This was fine with me. I enjoyed the flirtation.

When she was at ringside or in the photo studio she was a photographer's dream. She had that certain look—she had "it." I don't think I ever took an unflattering photo of her. It wasn't possible.

Throughout her years with Sullivan, then as the manager of Doom—the team of Ron Simmons and Butch Reed—and then as she aligned herself with Ric Flair and The Four Horsemen, Nancy always made time to flirt and chat with me. Eventually, Nancy shed her rookie "Fallen Angel" moniker and became known as "Woman."

It was weird to witness some of the backstage interaction between her husband, Kevin Sullivan, and the man he was feuding with in 1996, Chris Benoit. Kevin was WCW's booker at the time and the storyline saw Nancy go from Sullivan to Benoit. That story became all too real when a romance between Nancy and Chris developed right under Kevin's watch.

I recall seeing Nancy and Chris come back from the ring one night, holding hands, smiling at each other, like lovebirds. As they continued

down the hallway I called out for them to turn their heads. They did. I snapped a photo, and after the flash went off I noticed that Kevin was standing right beside them. He didn't appear bothered at all. It looked like he had accepted what had transpired. Did I find seeing the three of them in the same photo frame strange? Yes, I did. It was not very comfortable for me, so I can imagine that deep down it could not have been comfortable for Sullivan.

As for my relationship with Chris, it was always cordial, friendly. I found him to be very intelligent as well. Most times in the dressing room, or in the hotel lobby waiting for a ride, Chris would pull out a book and read. He would often ask me to tell him some of the bad corny jokes (are there any good corny jokes?) I became known for with the wrestlers. On many occasions you could see the rigors of the road in his eyes. You could tell that the business was taking its toll on him, but he wasn't alone. His traveling mates, Perry Saturn, Dean Malenko and Eddie Guerrero, all shared that look. They truly loved what they did, but you could see they were doing it just too much back in the WCW days. The road trips seemed endless.

Although Chris was one of the

most quiet, reserved wrestlers I knew, he was always willing to pose for photos and even do some funny ones. One time I had the cardboard COW (Championship Office Wrestling) belt with me, and he asked if we could pose with it (this was the version I had when I was editor of WOW *Magazine*). We did a tug-of-war over the belt, and he laughed after the picture was snapped and asked for a copy. "It will go in my favorite memories stack of pictures," he said. Somehow I felt he wasn't kidding. In the ring, Chris was incredible. To this day, I point to his match against William Regal at the Brian Pillman Memorial Show in 2000 as one of the greatest wrestling bouts I have ever seen and photographed. They were both at the peak of their professional lives that night. It was magnificent.

Through the years I kept in touch with Chris and Nancy. We exchanged email and would often use AOL Instant Messenger. I saw them at a few events, and they even brought their young son with them. "Daniel, this is Mister Bill," is how Nancy introduced me.

One night, probably around late January or early February 2007, Chris's IM popped up on my computer. He wrote, "Hi, Mister Bill!" That was the first time he called me by that name. Moments later, Nancy revealed herself. We exchanged some pleasantries, a few jokes and then she was gone. A few minutes later the IM box came up again, and I initiated the conversation. "Are you there, Nancy?" I typed. The letters came up, "Hi, Bill, it's Chris. I'm sitting here with Daniel on my lap. How are you?" We typed away for a short time and then he asked, "How come you're not working for us at WWF?" I went on to tell him the various reasons (elsewhere in this book) and he chimed back, "You should be working for us. Do you want me to talk to Vince?" I was flattered and shot back, "Hey, whatever. Thanks, I appreciate it!" He told me he had to get offline to put Daniel to bed. We said goodnight and they were gone.

The worse than horrible events that occurred that year, from June 22 until June 24, are just plain sickening. Although I have my own theory, which I won't go into here, the world learned Chris allegedly murdered his wife and son and then committed suicide. It was something unthinkable. How could this have happened? There is no justification. I heard that Chris and Nancy were having severe marital issues but to take it this far was unfathomable.

There is one piece that, to this day, makes me question everything they say happened. Sometimes husbands and wives get into situations, and maybe one of them takes things too far. We see it in the news much too often. But to kill a young child—it just doesn't fit.

I was summoned to appear on MSNBC, HLN and many other news networks to discuss the Benoit murders. The press had a field day with it, most blaming it on steroids. Chris Benoit's exploits of his days in pro wrestling have been erased from WWE history, and when his name is mentioned by anyone it's so unfortunate that it is the murders they think of first. I choose to remember Chris Benoit as the consummate pro wrestler. It's saddening that the monster within him destroyed everything he strived for and loved. How very sad.

APTER AND THE ICE-CREAM BOY

FORTY-FIVE

I n July 1988, the boxing editors of London Publishing asked me to take the portable photo studio to a hotel in Atlantic City. They'd assigned me to photograph boxer Lloyd Honeyghan a few days before his fight against Yung-Kil Chung. For some reason, on that steamy summer's day, I decided that I didn't want to drive the 90-plus miles from home to Atlantic City. Instead I opted to take the bus that stopped near my house.

This was a mistake. Walking the three blocks from my home to the bus stop had me looking like the star of a Jerry Lewis movie (Jerry, of course). I was carrying an 18-foot rolled-up background to use as the backdrop, a huge case of studio lights that weighed about 60 lbs and my cameras. On the way to the bus stop, people offered to help and I politely said, "No thanks, I got it," even though my arms were killing me, and the backdrop almost hit everyone who came close to either side of me.

The bus driver looked puzzled. I explained what all this stuff was, and he told me it would have to go in the baggage compartment. I was able to take my cameras to my seat.

When the bus arrived at the terminal, the driver unloaded the baggage compartment and left all my stuff on the ground for me to schlep to the hotel. I asked a taxi driver to take me to the hotel, but he refused to put the long backdrop into his vehicle. I was stuck pondering what to do, when someone tapped me on the back. A teenage kid with a high-pitched voice said, "Are you Mr. Apter?" I said, "Do we know each other?" He told me he was a huge fan of the magazine—and of mine. He lived in Atlantic City with his mother and grandparents, and he was just hanging around with some of his friends when he recognized me. He was 15 years old and told me his name was Brian.

He saw my equipment on the ground and asked if I needed any help. I told him I did—I needed to get to a hotel 10 long blocks away and couldn't get a cab. He told me, "Mr. Apter, it would be my pleasure to help you. I am free all day."

This was great for me. I told him that I would take him up on his offer as long as he would let me buy him dinner or pay him later. He said, "That's not necessary. Just hanging out with you is plenty of payment if we can talk wrestling." He assumed I was taking photos of a wrestler, but he was also interested when I told him it was of a boxer.

We got to the hotel, and he helped me set up the studio and spent hours with me during the photo shoot. After that, Brian helped me pack all the equipment and we walked back to the bus terminal—but not before I made my final offer.

"Where do you want to eat, kid?"

"Truthfully, I don't want a big meal, Mr. Apter. There's an ice cream place right near the terminal. That would be great!" he said.

So that's what we did. We both had ice cream and afterward he helped me onto the bus. We also exchanged telephone numbers.

Back in the office the next day, Stu Saks asked how the bus trip was. I told him what happened and how Brian had helped me all day. As was custom, I handed in my expense report for the bus fare and a meal.

Looking at the receipt Stu said,

"What is this charge of $3.50?" I said, "I got away with murder. The kid who helped me could have eaten $35 worth of food alone!" Stu tossed the bill aside and said, "I am not paying $3.50 for ice cream. This won't fly with the publisher. No way. I'm glad it all worked out but your 'meal' with the ice-cream boy will not be reimbursed." I had to let it go. It was not worth a battle and Stu was not going to change his mind.

Brian and I kept in touch for a few months and then lost contact. The ice-cream boy story was one I was ribbed about in the office for years. I don't think anyone in the boxing department even believed he existed. Sometimes they would offer me a few bucks to "reimburse me" for the $3.50.

Fast forward to 1994. Al Snow was scheduled for a posed session at our office. He was to be part of an ECW show not far from where we published. On that day, he surprised us by bringing along a few of his successful trainees. He stood near my desk and introduced me to his rookies. I took them over to Stu to introduce them, when one

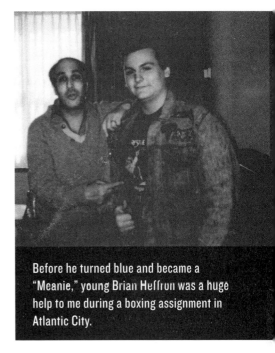

Before he turned blue and became a "Meanie," young Brian Heffron was a huge help to me during a boxing assignment in Atlantic City.

of them said, "Mr. Apter, don't you remember me? It's Brian from Atlantic City. I helped you at a photo shoot and then we had ice cream!'"

"Stu," I said, "It's the ice-cream boy!" Brian was now one of Al's prized students, and a year later he would debut in ECW. Yes, this was Brian "The Blue Meanie" Heffron.

While I never got my money back, having "Meanie" come to the office and confirm the ice-cream boy story was just too sweet.

APTER LOSES HIS PRO DEBUT

FORTY-SIX

BANG! is the Ocala, Florida, wrestling company owned and operated by my old friend and the legendary NWA World champion Dory Funk Jr. Besides it being one of the premier training centers, regular shows there draw quite a crowd.

Throughout the years, Dory has seen me playfully run in the ring at many arenas as the guys warm up. Many become victims of my figure-four leglock, others just get a headlock and punch to the face. Dory knew deep down I would one day have to satisfy my subconscious urge to get in the ring and wrestle in front of a crowd.

In August 2004, Dory called me with an idea.

"Apter, it's time for you to make your pro-wrestling debut, and I want you to do it here at !BANG!," he said. "My wife, Marti, and I, along with most of the roster, would love to

Editor Craig Peters and I were lucky enough to sandwich the lovely Missy Hyatt.
[Photo courtesy of Buddy Myers]

have you here." He went on to explain to me that an evil group called Royal Stud Enterprises was causing major problems for !BANG!'s good-guy competitors—Funk included. All this was happening because of their storyline-dastardly attorney James W. Gooding III, who controlled their matches and feuds. Dory said it would be good for me to come in and see if I could stop Gooding. I was told I could defend my COW title officially in this match. To add fuel to the match, I was made the official

!BANG! general manager. On my first day in office, I sent some stiff rules down that totally infuriated Gooding and this prompted Gooding to challenge me.

The day of the show, Dory pretty much gave me free rein to work it all out with Gooding, except for the finish. Also, a special referee was assigned to the match—Missy Hyatt.

It was a thrill to climb in the ring with the fans cheering me. The bell sounded, and Gooding and I locked up in a few holds and escapes we had worked out. It seemed very smooth. Of course he yelled at the crowd, and I encouraged them to keep the heat on him.

Finally, it was time for the finish that was worked out by Dory. I was knocked down by Gooding, lying flat on my back. Missy, who was wearing a dress shirt and *very* short skirt, stood over my body, counting to 10. Of course, my job was to just stare up her dress and make like I heard no count at all. As she was nearing six, a commotion took place as Claudia "The Claw" Reiff ran in and hit my opponent with a vicious low punch to the groin. Referee Missy called for the bell. I lost the match due to Reiff's interference. Gooding celebrated and waved my gold COW belt in the air as they headed back to the dressing room. Luckily for me, the belt was returned, as it was a disqualification—a belt can only change hands on a pinfall or submission.

Thank you, Dory and Marti and !BANG! for making all this happen. It was a key moment of my career, and I will never forget it.

Here is the official press release Dory ran on the dory-funk.com website:

Bill Apter to Step into the Ring
It is confirmed that Bill Apter will step into the ring at the Dory Funk Arena on Sunday August 29th. His challenge comes from a member of the Royal Stud Enterprises, attorney James W. Gooding III. Even though Bill Apter made his mark in professional wrestling as the premier wrestling journalist for the past 35 years, as a wrestler, Bill can handle himself in his own environment, the office. Apter, who holds victories in his office over Jimmy Snuka, Jimmy Valiant and myself, Dory Funk Jr., brings his Championship Office Wrestling belt to the Dory Funk Arena and will lay it all on the line against Windsor's attorney, James W. Gooding III. Recently, Attorney Gooding has been training with members of the Royal Stud Enterprises, learning all the dirty tricks of the wrestling business.

MEET THE PARENTS

FORTY-SEVEN

s a preteen, I was swept away by the action of professional wrestling on TV. I strutted around the apartment in Maspeth, New York, acting like Buddy Rogers. I wanted to have my legs insured by Lloyd's of London like the great high-flying inventor of the dropkick, Antonino Rocca. I practiced Johnny Valentine's Atomic Skull-Crusher elbow smash on unfortunate victims—my pillows. What an obsession.

My mother, Sylvia, who was a statistical typist for Metropolitan Life Insurance in Manhattan, and my dad, Nathan, let me know that they supported everything I had done thus far, but becoming a wrestler was "just not the right kind of job for a nice Jewish boy." Although my dad watched it with me, he never expected me to want to get into the ring. I told him that it would be an avocation then. He had his passions.

The formal Bar Mitzvah family portrait. From left to right: my brother, Paul, my sister, Judy, me, my mother, Sylvia, and father, Nathan.

During the days he worked as a mailman in the Garment District of Manhattan. On the side, he umped. He was an umpire for the Bronx Umpires Alliance. He would get home around 3 p.m. and a few days a week would drive 90 minutes to work the games in the Bronx. I remember him telling me, "Maybe you should become a manager or an announcer for wrestling, because you love it so much." My mother was in total agreement.

Throughout the years they supported me as I went from a job in the garment industry, to the mailroom of the Loews Movie Theatre chain, to the mailroom of Columbia Pictures and so many

other positions, as I tried to make my way into wrestling or show business as a singer/comedian/ master of ceremonies. I sang at parties, appeared at open mic nights and made it to the legendary "Borscht Belt" in the Catskill Mountains as an entertainer with The Charlie Lowe revue. For a few months, I even worked for Don Kirshner—"The Man With the Golden Ear." He discovered, produced and recorded superstars like Neil Diamond, the Monkees, Bobby Darin, the Archies and so many more. I worked as an assistant for a great guy named Myron Shrenkel. My job was to run coffee for the writers and entertainers who came to the office while

Myron did administrative work. I met all the huge stars of that era. It was a fun job.

As all of this was going on, I watched wrestling three nights a week. It was still my career target.

In 1965, with my parents' approval, I enrolled in the New York School of Announcing and Speech. There, I learned how to work the control board, produce a show, properly read commercials and star in my own program. That led me to buying time on New York's WHBI-FM a year later.

I used this as my entry into the wrestling business, sending photos and interview transcripts to the wrestling magazines I bought.

When I fully broke into the business in 1970, my dad, who used to go to live wrestling shows with me at Sunnyside and Madison Square Garden, came along. He was allowed to sit in the press row, and it was quite the bonding experience. He took photos of me interviewing wrestlers and got to know them. They really liked my dad. Ernie "The Grand Wizard" Roth dubbed him the "The Grand Nathan." My dad took a photo with a fez on his head—similar to the one Ernie wore as the Grand

Wizard—and gave it to Ernie. (I still have a copy.)

When my parents moved from New York to West Palm Beach, Florida, my dad was upset that our wrestling relationship would change. At that point, I called promoter Eddie Graham in Florida, who had met my dad a few times at MSG. Eddie did a wonderful thing. He told me, "Tell your dad to sit at the timekeeper's table every Monday night in West Palm. I'll set it all up with the local promoter Chris Dundee." My dad was so happy (and he even took my mom with him at times). He rang the bell alongside timekeeper L.B. Mitchell and became part of the wrestling family in West Palm. When wrestlers from New York toured that area, he would always call me after the show with something like, "Ernie Ladd told me he saw you a few weeks ago and wanted me to say hello for him."

To his last days of life in mid-1984, my dad was so enthralled to be part of the wrestling scene. My mom continued to play Mah-Jongg, Canasta and other "senior citizen" games until her passing a few years later.

APTER STUNNED BY RECOGNITION OVERSEAS

I was amazed that fans in other countries—I mean *a lot* of fans in other countries—recognized me. Even though some only knew me because they announced my name as I got into the ring, most of them knew who I was when they saw me coming into the arena or standing by the concession stands.

I've written this before, but if it were not for this business, I would not have become a world traveler.

I had a conversation with the premier pro-wrestling belt maker, Reggie Parks, in early 2003. He told me that he was making a few belts for a new company called Hawai'i Championship Wrestling. They were going to have a "blessing of the belts" in March, and I jokingly asked if he would take me with him. He said, "Sure, they would love to have you take photos and do interviews and put them in the magazines." He said there was one formality; he needed to okay it with NWA Midwest promoter Ed Chuman, who helped broker the belt deal for Reggie, and then with Linda Bade, owner of HCW.

In less than two hours, Chuman called and said that Linda wanted me there. Ed and his wife and daughter would be on the trip as well. There was one other hook. Ed told me that although Don Muraco was the face of the company and authority figure, Linda thought an outside source as commissioner would work better. So I accepted the job. I would not be shooting photos except at the "blessing of the belts," which would be done on a holy site miles from the show.

When we arrived, we were driven to the sacred area. The blessing was wonderful, and for the rest of the day we all went sightseeing and even climbed up Diamond Head— what a hike that was, but worth it to see the entire Honolulu area.

We did several more days of sightseeing, sang some karaoke, ate a few exceptional dinners and then it was showtime. All was perfect. I hated to leave. Hawaii is so wonderful—great weather, beautiful beaches (and women) and a lovely city right across from the beach. I was brought back again in 2004 and continued my role as the Commish.

Another conversation led to another great trip. I don't recall why, but Joe E. Legend and I were discussing his oversees bookings. He had an upcoming one in Germany. "Take me," I said.

"Okay, I will talk to Ingo, the promoter I work for at German Stampede Wrestling and see if I can make something happen." Again, just a few hours later I received a call from the owner of GSW, Ingo Vollenberg. He was very familiar with me and invited me to do an in-ring segment with Molly Holly and Bret Hart during GSW's version of *WrestleMania*, which was called *International Impact III*, on August 4, 2006.

Aside from my work for GSW, I was able to do lots of sightseeing. My friend Rick Peters, an elite fan who became a promoter, even made sure I got to see the Anne Frank house in Amsterdam, as I was taken to many different cities. Also, promoter Ingo and his mother were kind enough to take me to Berlin during one of my other trips to Germany (in 2009, as a broadcaster for the *International Impact IV* show), where we saw the ruins of many Nazi offices (Hitler's alleged office), Checkpoint Charlie and the remaining segments of the Berlin Wall. All this history I had read about in history textbooks when I was younger was now right in front of me. Steve Corino and his son Colby joined me for much of the sightseeing. Totally amazing. Thank you, Joe E. Legend, for getting me into the GSW world. Also thanks to the huge number of fans who recognized me all over Germany, and thank you, Steve Corino, for helping me find a karaoke place to sing at on the last night of the tour.

Special thanks to referee Gary Miller and his lovely mom, Chantel Tucker, for taking me from town to town—and Ingo's mom, who let me sleep with Joe E. Legend one night and her dogs another.

In 2005, Rikishi was booking for a company in Italy called Nu-Wrestling Evolution. This time, before I could even ask to go, Rikishi told me that promoter Roberto Indiano was interested in me going to Italy for a show on October 22. I couldn't have thought of a better date to do that: my birthday. A few conversations with Mr. Indiano and it was set. A few weeks later, I arrived in Italy and was taken to a studio where I would put an English commentary-track on several of their shows. Not knowing what the storylines were, Mr. Indiano did his best to clue me in. I wasn't ultra comfortable, but he liked the final result. It helped that

I knew some of the wrestlers on the tapes like Vampiro, Rikishi and Scott Steiner.

In January 2005, I received a call from Alex Shane. We knew each other well during the years I had been the editor of the U.K.'s *Total Wrestling* magazine. He was running his own promotion called Frontier Wrestling Alliance and had booked me on a few of the shows when I was visiting the U.K. magazine office. Alex, who had been a wrestler, promoter and radio and TV talk-show host, was trying to get the U.K. scene to a new level. So he partnered with the U.K. Wrestling Channel and went to work on a super-show that would take place in the town of Coventry. The show would be called *International Showdown*. He was very excited about the roster he had already signed, which included many U.K. talents, such as Jonny Storm and Doug Williams. On the U.S. side, he brought in A.J. Styles, Samoa Joe, CM Punk and others. However, there was one star he wanted but could not find—so he called me. The man was Mick Foley. I told Alex I could put Mick in touch with him and Alex said, "Get him to me, and I'll get you booked on the show too!" It all happened so fast. In March 2005, I found myself in the ring performing in a live Apter's Alley to present an award. I was cut off by hated manager Greg Lambert, who then had his man Alex Shane come out to try to take the plaque. Then Foley came to the ring as Shane and Lambert hopped onto the floor. Foley put me over and even had me do my Cookie Monster imitation in front of the huge crowd. The segment ended with Foley getting the plaque and bad-sport Shane running in and giving me a low blow.

It was in the U.K. where I also became dear friends with referee Steve Lynskey, who does regular interviews on 1Wrestling.com's "Face-2-Face" video segments. Oh, of course, Jonny Storm and Doug Williams made sure I got to sing karaoke at many places throughout England.

I also need to mention a man known to every wrestler who comes in and out of the U.K. His name is Phil Austin. Phil makes sure that everyone gets to where they are going, either in his car or by following him. He is *the* all-time super fan. He also made one of my dreams come true. I found out that Stan Laurel's hometown—which has a museum about Stan and his comedy partner Oliver Hardy—is about a six-hour drive from London. Knowing how badly I wanted to visit (as Laurel is one of my all-time favorites), Phil took an entire day off to bring me to the charming small city of Ulverston. It was one of the highlights of my entire life.

It was also overwhelming to be treated like a major celebrity each time I travelled with the wrestlers to Japan. The fans were wonderful to me, and the nightlife with friends like photographer Koichi Yoshizawa and promoter-manager Wally Yamaguchi was amazing. I hope to return to the "Land of the Rising Sun" at least one more time!

WAY BACK WHEN IT ALL BEGAN

FORTY-NINE

My older brother, Paul, stood on our parents' bed in our house in the Bronx. I was probably 11. He asked me to come up onto the bed. Then he directed me to "move a little to the left, now a little to the right." The next thing I remember is him yelling "dropkick!" I was knocked off the bed by Paul's powerful flying move—one he would tell me he learned by watching the amazing Antonino Rocca on TV wrestling on channel 5 in New York.

I was too smart to take him up on that a second time. However my curiosity about wrestling had been piqued. One night, I recall turning to channel 9 and watching a wrestling show called *Bedlam from Boston*. The announcer, a very proper-looking, well-dressed Englishman named Lord Athol Layton was doing a ringside interview with some bully-looking man named Dick the Bruiser. After asking a few pointed questions, Bruiser became angry, attacked Layton, tore off his suit, tossed him to the floor and repeatedly kicked him. Finally some other wrestlers came out and saved Layton. At that point, Layton took the microphone and challenged Bruiser to a match the next week. I was hooked.

When I was watching TV wrestling, I also did my own play-by-play on my Lafayette tape recorder. I also recorded many interviews of Buddy Rogers, Édouard Carpentier, the Kangaroos (and their manager "Wild" Red Berry) and studied them afterwards to develop my own interview style, just in case I became a wrestler after high school.

For nearly two years around 1961, I distanced myself from wrestling. Rocca had started his own promotion, and the shows just didn't capture my fancy like Vince McMahon Sr.'s company had. Also, my grandfather Sam (my mother's father) told me how ridiculous it was for me to watch wrestling—it was all fake. My friends (other than Robert and a few others) made fun of me, because they

I taught myself the flying dropkick after watching Antonino Rocca do this to his opponents. Here I am showing it to Matt Stiker at Johnny Rodz's World of Unpredictable Wrestling school in Brooklyn, New York.

all watched "real sports" like baseball and football, and I watched a "fake" event and believed it was real.

Of course, I eventually rekindled my love with pro wrestling, which continues to this day—and it all started with a flying dropkick off a bed in the Bronx!

KARAOKE AND A HORRIBLE JOKIE

FIFTY

"Now that you have made your first trip to Japan, you can honestly call yourself a world traveler in our business."
—Lou Thesz to Bill Apter, April 1982

I will never forget the telephone call from Dory Funk Jr. in February 1982. He and his brother Terry Funk were the bookers for the American talent roster of Shohei Baba's All Japan Pro Wrestling. A tour was coming up in April that would include the Funks, Lou Thesz, Ted DiBiase, Haku, Bruiser Brody, Stan Hansen, the Mongolian Stomper, Harley Race, Jimmy "Superfly" Snuka and Buck Robley. They wanted to know if I would like to go on the tour. Of course I wanted to go, but in what capacity?

"Baba has seen that his main competitor Antonio Inoki's New Japan Pro Wrestling gets a lot of press in the United States wrestling magazines, because they have invited George Napolitano over a few times. We think it's time for you to cover All Japan, and if you think it's worth the ink, you'll put the company over."

It didn't take long to check with my boss, Mr. Weston, and say yes. Although Mr. Weston did not want any promotion paying my tab—as he felt we would then be obligated to publicize them—he was not against this trip. He brushed it off as, "Good politics."

I had heard stories of how wild some of the wrestlers were while on tour in Japan. I was pretty straight-laced and the Funks knew it. I would travel with Thesz, who was not one of the party boys.

On the flight from Los Angeles, I was seated with Thesz on a giant 747. He told me to keep an eye on what Terry Funk would do—something he did on every flight to Japan. When the flight attendants would leave the galley, he would sneak in, swipe a few bottles of beer and then go back to his seat and drink it when they weren't looking. By the time the flight was about two hours from landing, he was conked out on the floor near the flight attendant station. No one tried to move him. If people had to use the restroom, they stepped over him. Those who knew who he

was giggled at the sight. The Funks were legendary in Japan, and Terry was certainly a legendary drinker on this flight!

When we finally arrived at Tokyo's Narita Airport, we were escorted to a large bus by referee Joe Higuchi. He was also Baba's right-hand man. I had never met Higuchi before, and as soon as he saw me he was very polite and told me that if I needed anything during the entire 10-day tour he would be there for me.

The next few days were exhausting. On day one, just a few hours after we were picked up from the airport, we were taken right to an arena. I could barely shoot the matches, as the jet lag had kicked in big time. I felt like I was in a twilight sleep. It was Higuchi who came to my rescue—he forced me to eat when I had no appetite and made me drink a lot of fruit juices. Within a few hours, I was back to my energetic self.

During the day, Lou made sure I saw all the must-see tourist spots. At night, he and I went out to eat, away from most of the crew, who were at the notorious Roppongi district (the area in Tokyo with bars, hookers and whatever else you desire). A few of the loyal married wrestlers had dinner and then drank Japanese beer and talked business in the hotel lobbies or various restaurants.

One night, as I arrived back at the hotel with Thesz, Haku asked if we wanted to go for a few beers. Lou wasn't interested and I don't drink. Haku told me I didn't have to drink beer—I could have a soda. I decided to go, having no idea that I would find my new obsession.

We walked into a bar a few blocks from the hotel. As we entered, I saw a dozen or more people sitting at the bar looking at books and one man with a microphone in hand at the bar singing an Elvis Presley song. It was the new phenom known as karaoke. Haku explained to me that there were karaoke bars all over Japan. He said it's a very polite form of entertainment. You stay in your seat and sing. We went to sit at the bar, and I thumbed through one of the books and asked to sing "My Way," the old Frank Sinatra standard written by Canada's Paul Anka. Keep in mind, I have been singing since I was a kid—in musical plays, in singing groups and on my own—most times with a piano player. This was different—a real big-band sound.

When my turn came up, I sat at first, and then climbed onto the bar for the finish. Haku laughed, and even though it wasn't "proper,"

he was cool with it. That night we went to four karaoke bars, and I sang "My Way" at each of them. I was over. By the time we got to the final bar, word had spread and the bartender just handed me the microphone and asked, "Please to sing 'My-A-Way.'" (That's how he pronounced it!)

In the dressing room the following night, Terry Funk said to me, "Apter, I heard you were a big star last night. Tonight, me and Teddy [DiBiase] are gonna take you out to see if you can sing like Haku says you can!" I was fine with that.

After the matches and my usual nightly dinner with Mr. Thesz, we went to several karaoke bars (Lou did not come with us) and I was a hit again. It was getting late, and I was ready to head back to the hotel, when Terry said, "We have one more place, Apter. This one isn't with recorded music. It's a live band. The place is run by the Japanese mafia. If you screw up they'll cut your dick off, so you better be good! I told them you were a big star from New York City!"

I clearly recall the two of them inviting some ladies over to our table as the club host handed me the microphone and said, "'My-A-Way' please!" As I was about halfway through the song, a lady dressed in traditional geisha garb came onto the small stage and started running her hands all over my body. Of course I kept singing as she opened the buttons on my shirt and rubbed my bare chest. I went right into my Jerry Lewis screaming voice and everyone in the place was laughing hysterically. I got over big time as everyone was applauding on their feet.

As a single man, I inquired about the availability of this geisha-style lady. I was told she was indeed single. At about 1 a.m., this lady, Funk, DiBiase and their guests planned to go to another bar. We left and were walking down a narrow alleyway, when the geisha stopped and asked me for a kiss. Funk and Teddy watched and were still laughing. As I was getting ready to lay a big one on her, Ted broke it up and said he couldn't let this go on any longer.

"Bill, the geisha lady is a guy!" Needless to say, I thanked her and politely left to go back to the hotel. I had been had!

The next night at the arena, the ribs didn't stop. Now I knew why Thesz didn't go out with this bunch.

But this didn't stop me from going out for a few more nights of karaoke with Haku. When I got back to the United States, I invested in a small karaoke machine and bought dozens of discs. To this day I still karaoke several times a week, either at bars, clubs or in my music room at home, where I have a nice, professional system.

Japan was quite an experience. I came back with 35 rolls of great candid and action photos that are still used in the magazines today. I returned to Japan a few more times, but it was because of this tour that Lou Thesz and I became extended family. I also got to make a dream of going to a country I never thought I would visit a reality.

I am totally indebted to the Funks for making all of this happen—except for the geisha-guy part!

YES, I WAS PAID BY WWF FOR TWO YEARS

I n 1970, I was slowly nurturing a relationship with Vince McMahon Sr. and his staff, which included Arnold Skaaland, Gorilla Monsoon, Angelo Savoldi and others. The relationships were businesslike, friendly and mostly positive.

When Vince McMahon Jr. took the reins of the company and began WWF's worldwide expansion, nurturing that relationship was the most challenging part of my career. Besides making it difficult for the regional promotions to survive, he had started his own wrestling magazine that debuted in 1983. His plan was to restrict any and all access to the outside wrestling magazines. As he was putting the plan together, one key element was to find an editor who was familiar with the business and who the wrestlers and staff would be comfortable with. That person was me.

I was flattered by his call. He asked if I was available. I told him I'd think it over. That night, I discussed it with my family and decided to turn down the offer. My mentor Stanley Weston was taking good care of me, and I loved working at the publishing company. I telephoned Vince the next day and graciously thanked him. I suggested he call wrestler Les Thatcher. Thatcher had produced, written, edited and done all the artwork for the *NWA Magazine*. Vince asked if I wanted to think this over a bit longer, but my mind was made up.

Through the years, I spoke with Vince on occasion and also became business-friendly with his charming wife, Linda, who I had met a few times at various WWF events.

In 1991, I received a call from Linda McMahon. She asked if I would consider joining the staff at *WWF Magazine*. I told her I would gladly listen to whatever she had in mind. A few days later, I was picked up in a town car from my home on Long Island and taken to WWF headquarters in Stamford, Connecticut.

Linda sat behind her desk and stood when I arrived in her office. She had a big smile and made me comfortable immediately. She spoke of the current direction of their magazine—which she was in charge of—and the desire to change the style to more of a "sensational" format rather than just the general bio-style material that the magazine was known for. Coming from a company with a tabloid image, she figured I could perhaps steer the magazine's image toward that direction. She said if we decided to move forward, the company would pay for my moving expenses and help me find a home. We spent a few hours talking about the magazines and my family and how they might react to moving from Long Island where most of our family and friends were.

That night, I came to the same conclusion as I had come to in 1983: I didn't want to leave Mr. Weston. I turned the job down. One of the main reasons for this decision was Linda's list of expectations—it would be an "in-office" job. I felt there might be too much pressure, and I didn't want my road trips— the part of the job that I loved so much at Mr. Weston's company—to become a thing of the past. I was comfortable where I was, and WWF just wasn't the place for me at that time.

I always wanted to be on the WWF TV shows, but I don't think that I ever made that known to the McMahons. In 1992, on a whim, I made a VHS tape of me in my basement. I had a dress shirt and tie on (pants too, of course!) and sat behind a desk with the video camera running. I had come up with a character called Mr. Fan Man. The concept was simple. Fans send in questions for wrestlers, and Mr. Fan Man interviews the wrestler to have the question answered. If the question is used, the fan who sent it in wins some sort of WWF merchandise. I called Vince's office and asked if I could make an appointment to see him and show him the tape. His secretary asked me to mail the tape, but I insisted on a face-to-face meeting. She set up one for the following week.

When I arrived, I was escorted into Vince's office. He didn't have much time and promised me he would watch the tape later that night. Although I drove nearly four hours to see him and he had only five minutes for me, I put it directly in his hands, so I know he received it. Later that night, he called and told me he wanted to run it past a few people and would let me know what "the collective team thinks." About a week later, I received the tape back in the mail with a thank-you note from Vince (sent by his secretary) explaining that they wouldn't be going with the idea.

Oh well, I tried.

The next WWF offer came in 1993. Mr. Weston's company had been sold to a publisher in Pennsylvania. I called my dear friend J.J. Dillon, who was the head of talent relations and Vince's right-hand man, asking if he could talk to Vince about me working for the magazine or the photo department—or anywhere in WWF. Mr. Weston was no longer my boss and my loyalty to him was unquestioned. Now that he was out of the picture, I was interested in working for WWF.

J.J. called and told me that there was nothing open in the company that I would fit into. It looked like Pennsylvania was a go for me.

Two nights before we were set to move to Pennsylvania, just as we were finishing some last-minute packing, the phone rang. It was Beth, Vince McMahon's secretary. She said Vince needed to talk to me. She put him on the phone and the first words out of his mouth were, "Did you move yet?" I told him it was just a few days away. He told me that he had an idea where I would fit in the company—after talking with J.J.—and asked if I would come to Stamford tomorrow. He said, "It's not a TV job, there is no on-air work with this position, at least not now, but we never know what the future might hold." He also said that I would not have to move. I would only be required to be in Stamford a few days a week, and the Apter family could remain in Long Island.

Early the next morning I was in a conference room with Vince, Linda and J.J. at Titan Towers. Vince told me that he had visions of a physical Hall of Fame and that they would need a curator once that was fully realized. He said he needed someone to procure personal items from wrestlers to kick-start this project, and he was hoping that would be me. After some back and forth, he said to me, "Do you or do you not want the job?" I asked, "What happens after I get all this memorabilia? What would my job be?" He was honest and said, "We will find something for you." That's when I started to doubt if I wanted the job. He suggested that I go to

lunch with some of the office people I knew there and the four of us would meet again in 90 minutes.

When we reconvened I was ready to say I was not sure, but they had their own idea. Vince and Linda thanked me for coming and said that J.J. would talk to me. They could see I was not sure, so they suggested I work as an independent contractor for the Hall of Fame. I would be paid $100 a week to gather memorabilia from the wrestlers, and I could still move to Pennsylvania. And that is what I did. The project lasted two years, and I got them Buddy Rogers's boots, trunks from several wrestlers and more. This was the first time I had ever received weekly paychecks from WWF, and I really enjoyed the work.

THE AWARD GOES TO . . .

FIFTY-TWO

Although I've presented dozens of awards to wrestlers, I have been honored to be on the receiving end several times. Here are some of the plaques that adorn "Apter's Alley."

My first honor was presented to me by the Wrestling Fans International Association, which was one of the most respected and prestigious fan organizations in the business. They held their first convention back in 1968. At this particular gathering in Kansas City, Missouri, on the weekend of August 7–10, 1985, I was awarded with the Writer of the Year plaque. It was (and still is) a thrill to have been chosen.

The next official recognition came from the Ladies International Wrestling Association. It was the Magazine Editor Award. The inscription reads, "In appreciation of personal and professional life achievements and for your

One of the happiest moments of my career was when Roddy Piper presented me with this Legend Award at the 2005 WrestleReunion convention. This magnificent plaque was hand-designed by Reggie Parks.

contribution to women and men." The award is dated June 20, 1998, and was awarded at the LIWA convention in Las Vegas, Nevada. I was not present for this one, but they did send me the plaque.

I worked in the role of commissioner for WXW (United States) owned by Wild Samoan Afa. My mantra was, "I'm the Commish and I get what I wish!" For my work as this character, the company was nice enough to give me an appreciation award at its annual dinner in 2002. I was also made an official member of the Samoan family: it was now Afa, Sika and Aptah!

In 2005, I was in the ring at a WrestleReunion convention and had just presented Roddy Piper with a Legend Award. He made his speech, and I tried to escort him out of the ring so we could present the next award. He refused to leave. Next, he grabbed the microphone from my hand and started ranting about what I mean to the wrestling business. All of a sudden, he pulled a magnificent Reggie Parks–crafted award out from under his kilt (I have no idea where he kept it) and presented it to me on behalf of WrestleReunion creator "My Pal" Sal Corrente. It had the WrestleReunion logo on it and was awarded to "Wonderful Willie." I was totally shocked and almost speechless—something that does not happen very often.

> I was totally shocked and almost speechless.

In September 2011, Maryland Championship Wrestling booker/wrestler Matt Bowman (aka "Wiseguy" Jimmy Cicero) called and told me that MCW wanted to induct me into its Hall of Fame. I was stunned, as I had never worked for MCW. "Owner Dan McDevitt and the rest of the office want to let you know that we appreciate everything you have done for the business and we're putting you into the Hall of Fame at our show on October 29. Can you be there to accept it?" Of course I was there, and it was wonderful of them to put me in their Hall of Fame.

To my dying day, I will never forget the telephone call I received from Lou Thesz's widow, Charlie, in March 2012. She told me that the Hall of Fame committee of the National Wrestling Hall of Fame and Dan Gable Museum would be awarding me the Jim Melby Award for "Excellence in Writing on Professional Wrestling." To say I was taken by surprise and totally knocked out is an understatement.

On July 14, 2012, at the reception in Waterloo, Iowa, the home of the Hall of Fame and Dan Gable Museum, I was flattered to be presented the award, alongside other honorees Road Warrior Animal, John "Bradshaw" Layfield, Baron Von Raschke, Dan Severn and the late Don Curtis (his lovely widow, Dotty, accepted on his behalf). Kurt Angle was also in this elite group but was not there to accept his award.

One very lighthearted note came when Severn gave his acceptance speech, and he chose to talk about me for a few moments. He called me a "cardboard champion." I knew that he was referring to the matches we had up at the old *PWI* offices for my cardboard Championship Office Wrestling belt. On one occasion, perhaps 10 years prior to this event, he beat me (he hit me with a bag of bagels, the cheater) and took the belt with him. For years I would see the belt alongside his array of gold at various conventions, and he told me,

"Wonderful Willie, you will never get this back." Standing at the podium, he reached for his briefcase, slowly opened it and pulled out the cardboard belt! I could not believe it when he gave it back to me.

These honors make me think of one of my favorite performers off all time—James Cagney. When asked how he felt about all the awards he had won throughout his lifetime, he said, "I am just another guy doing my job the best I can."

OTHER CAREERS MIXED IN WITH MY WRESTLING CAREER . . .

FIFTY-THREE

When the company that published the U.K.'s *Total Wrestling* shut the magazine down in 2004, for the first time in my career I thought I would have to find another way to earn a living.

My wife, Andrea, is overly sensible. The day we received the news from my assistant editor Stephen Ganfield, she suggested I go to the local Career Link office. One of the many services they offer—for free—is employment assistance. I told my wife I was nervous—I have a familiar face in the wrestling business and would be embarrassed if someone there recognized me. She shot back with, "So other than my salary, how are we going to pay this mortgage?" I was working at 1Wrestling.com and doing some freelance print and broadcast work, but it would not pay the bills. That sold me, and the next day I was at Career Link in Norristown, Pennsylvania. I signed in and was sent to a desk where a lovely counselor named Maureen took my information.

When she asked me what I had done in the past, I told her, "I wrote about and took photos of half-naked men in bathing suits making like they were beating each other up." She looked confused and then giggled a bit, asking me to explain. About one minute into my explanation, she cut in and asked, "Wait, you're with professional wrestling?" I said, "Yes." She wanted to know why I was in Norristown and not calling WWE for a job. I went on to tell her that I had tried WWE, but they had no jobs that were right for me. Maureen told me that there was a career fair for non-profit companies at Career Link the next day. Generally, non-profit companies do not pay at the level of compensation I received at *WOW Magazine*—but it was better than nothing.

After getting some great candy from dishes on recruiter tables, I stopped at a table with a sign for AHEDD Specialized Human Resource Organization. The man sitting at the table smiled, shook my hand and asked if this was something I might be interested in. Upon examination of their brochures, I found that this non-profit company provided employment

services for persons with various disabilities—both physical and intellectual. I was earning a healthy, near six-figure salary at *WOW Magazine* and wanted to stay in the same monetary range. Since AHEDD is a non-profit company, that could not be the case. I thanked him and it ended there. He gave me his card. His name was John Woodruff and he headed the Philadelphia-area office. As a polite gesture I gave him one of my "Bill Apter Enterprises" business cards and wished him good luck with AHEDD.

The next day, I called the local Montgomery County newspaper office in Ft. Washington, Pennsylvania. I asked to speak to the editor. They connected me with Mr. Mike Morsch, who was the head guy at Montgomery newspapers, which produced many regional newspapers. I told him I was a writer-photographer in the area, and he seemed interested—very interested—and invited me to come in for an interview the next day.

When I arrived, he gave me a tour of the editorial office and the printing-production area. Then I sat down across from him at his desk. It seemed like he was looking for the right words, and then they flowed freely:

"It's you, right, Bill Apter from

wrestling?" I nodded my head. "Why are you here? My God, I have been reading your articles and looking at your photos since I was a kid in Iowa. I can't tell you what a thrill it is to meet you." Mike went on to tell me that he would not offer me a job, because the pay scale was so low it would embarrass him to do so. He did have me speak with the advertising department as the commissions were a bit higher, but I didn't want to get involved in a commission-only job. I thanked him, and we kept in touch—and to this day, Mike and I are dear friends.

What to do? Okay, having a salary is better than not having a salary. I called Mr. Woodruff at AHEDD and asked if I could have a meeting with him. I was invited to the office in Jenkintown, Pennsylvania. We talked for over an hour, and I filled out an official job application. After one week, Mr. Woodruff called to let me know that another candidate had gotten the job.

This was a blow to my ego!

Once again, my wife chimed in and said, "Why don't you try one of the local hotels? You would be great at the front desk, greeting people and checking them in and out!" I envisioned myself as Jerry Lewis in the movie, *The Bellboy* (one of my favorites). I was interviewed and hired at the Days Inn on Route 611 in Horsham, Pennsylvania. That job lasted a very few short months. Yes, for me it was like Jerry Lewis. I screwed things up left and right. One time I put two people in nine rooms. This was not the job for me. I really liked all the staff, but when I was asked to leave it was okay with me. By the way, many people recognized me, and I had to tell them that this work was only temporary until I could get back into the wrestling world full-time.

As fate would have it, Mr. Woodruff called that night and told me that the person they had hired at AHEDD did not work out. Would I like to work there?

I've been at AHEDD for over eight years. I love my work there. It is so rewarding to be part of a team that positively changes a person's life—and in turn changes the lives of their family and everyone close to them. With the expert training of Mr. Woodruff, his assistant Mary Berry Shields, John Miller, Stacy Kyle, Lori Tyndall, Patti Hammer Judy Shear, Charlotte Butler and the president of AHEDD, Rocco Cambria, I was molded into a top member of their employment specialist division.

There is actually a lot of crossover with this career and my wrestling work. A lot of the people who come to us for employment services and job coaching are wrestling fans, and they can't believe that Bill Apter is their job coach. And I have been able to enlist many employers that I know through the wrestling business to open their doors and hire the people we serve.

A major career-crossover took place at our annual company meeting in 2011. The keynote speaker that day was my friend Matt Bowman ("Jimmy Cicero"). Matt is a professional wrestler with two young autistic children. He and his wife, Windra, were kind enough to accept AHEDD's invitation to do a Q&A interview with me as host. The entire staff was moved by their dedication to their children and Matt's "Bodyslam Autism" program. As I looked at the faces of coworkers and saw how awestruck they were, I felt a deep sense of accomplishment as my two worlds meshed so perfectly together.

I juggle my job as content editor at 1Wrestling.com, AHEDD, *Fighting Spirit* magazine (administrative), my "Apter Chat" Skype

Brett is one of the participants served by AHEDD, and he's been on my caseload for nearly eight years. When he's not at work, Brett loves taking scenic photos. He is an incredibly talented photographer. [Photo courtesy Mary Berry Shields]

show and more all day, every day. And not to mention the calls I get from wrestlers, promoters and other people in the business asking general "Can you help me?" questions. Then there is Facebook, Twitter, my lovely poodle, Lexi Rose, my two grown kids and my wife. Now I have to find something to do in my free time . . .

SING ME A SONG, WONDERFUL WILLIE!

FIFTY-FOUR

Somewhere in the mid-'70s, I happened upon a big, friendly guy who wrestled as the Concrete Cowboy. He had a great sense of humor, and whenever I was on the road in Long Island or Pennsylvania, he was usually wrestling in a show. We would often sit for hours talking about wrestling at a local diner.

My work with the magazines became more demanding and my trips to the areas that Concrete—real name Paul Swanger—wrestled dwindled. I saw him perhaps once a year for a few years and then not at all. I often wondered what became of him. Paul is also part Aboriginal, and most of his friends knew him as Paul "Big Bear."

In 2000, I was living near Willow Grove, Pennsylvania, and was driving down Welsh Road when I saw a sign "Karaoke Every Friday Night. Public Invited." Above it was a sign that said it was a VFW (Veteran's of Foreign Wars) club.

For as long as I can remember, I've loved to get up in front of a crowd and sing. So I went in, paid a few bucks, then went to the song books to choose my tune. The place was dark, and around the bar were some very attractive ladies, some near-out-of-control-looking guys drinking beers and, of course, some veterans exchanging stories.

I went over and told the karaoke DJ my first name (after filling out a song slip) and he said, "You're up after Bruno." I joked, "Bruno Sammartino?" He looked at me kind of strangely and then introduced Bruno, who did an expert version of "Monster Mash." My song would be "My Way."

As I sang, I looked at the people sitting at these large round tables, and they looked at me as if saying, "Who's the new guy?" or "This guy sucks." I definitely felt like an outsider.

At the end of my song, I got a bit of applause, and the DJ told me that I had won a prize. He had this small box with three doors and told me to choose one to open. I went right to the middle door and pulled out something rubber. It was a rubber WCW World championship belt. I looked at it and faced the DJ and said, "This is amazing. I work

My big (6′8″, 325 lb) adopted brother Paul "Big Bear" Swanger and I perform an old-school music and comedy show reminiscent of the Dean Martin–Jerry Lewis era. (I wonder who reminds the audience of Jerry?)

for a wrestling magazine—it's weird that I won this!" He looked me up and down and said, "Wait a minute, you're Bill—Bill Apter?" I was flattered that this big, bearded guy knew who I was just from my name. He walked closer and extended his hand. He smiled and then told me,

259

"You're shaking hands with the Concrete Cowboy."

Holy crap—I could not believe it.

Paul introduced me to all the regulars, and I went back week after week for years. Eventually, I became part of the gang. To showcase our musical talents, we put together a cabaret act a few years back and have been performing it all over the United States at benefits, clubs, private parties and old-folks homes. And I can't imagine doing it with anyone else.

It's rare that Concrete and I don't talk about 10 times a day. We're worse than two old ladies who talk for hours on end.

If I ever need a friend (and I have), he is always there for me—and he knows I've got his back too; although at 6'5", 380 pounds, it's hard to see me *behind* his back.

He's the Hardy to my Laurel. No matter what time of day or night, before we hang up the phone, the goodbye is always the same:

"Goodnight, Ollie!"

"Goodnight, Stanley!"

APTER SAYS WORK IS A GOOD FOUR-LETTER WORD

FIFTY-FIVE

In 2007, I was searching Craigslist for a freelance speaker job. I like to talk in front of people, and if it can bring my family some more cash, ever better. There was one ad from a talent agency that caught my eye. I called and told them who I was. Before I could tell the man, Michael James, my story—he said, "Bill Apter, I know who you are! If you're calling to speak at our VIP Talent Connect event at the Sheraton Hotel in Langhorne, Pennsylvania, you're hired. Be there next Saturday at 7 a.m. and look for me. I'm the president of the company." He offered me a very nice fee and told me I would be addressing about 250 show-business hopefuls who wanted to take the next step in their career.

The VIP (now also the iT Factor Productions) business model was as follows: people pay to listen to entertainment industry professionals speak for most of the day, and then they get to meet them one-on-one to give them their resume and photos and discuss next steps. Stars from Broadway shows, dancers, singers, songwriters, performers, acting teachers and so many other entertainment professionals are represented—even Tommy Dreamer, Andrew Anderson, Dawn Marie, Greg Valentine and Brutus Beefcake have been speakers.

When I saw the crowd of young beautiful people in the hotel lobby waiting to go into the main

Hand me a microphone and tell me to talk for three minutes and I will give you 20 or more! My daughter and her husband learned that the hard way on their wedding day in September 2014.
[Credit: Uncorked Studios]

ballroom for the festivities, I told Mr. James and co-owner Alycia Kayack that I didn't think this group would be interested in hearing about pro wrestling. I asked who the emcee was for this event. Mr. James said, "We don't have one. One speaker goes up and introduces the next one." I said, "I host events all the time. If you just cue me in one minute before each person goes on, I can do the job." He trusted me and loved my work.

Eight years later, I am still doing emcee work for VIP—and not in Langhorne. After the first event, the company moved to a venue in New York City and they still ask me to go on stage to do what I love to do.

I just realized that there is another "other" career that has not yet surfaced in this book. While doing my wrestling work for G.C. London publishing, I was also *very* involved in the boxing magazines. When I started at the company, the magazines were *Boxing International* and *World Boxing*. Then *KO* magazine was created, and finally, the company purchased *The Ring*.

From 1970 until the mid-'90s, I photographed some truly great fights. I also photographed some of the most iconic boxers in that portable studio I used to lug all over

I was so enthralled by the showmanship of Muhammad Ali, and I was fortunate enough to interview and photograph him dozens of times.

the United States. I was at ringside for Muhammad Ali's fights against Chuck Wepner, Jimmy Young and several others. I traveled occasionally with Ali and became dear friends with him, as well as with his trainer/mentor Angelo Dundee, publicist Gene Kilroy and cornerman Drew "Bundini" Brown. One time, when I was at Ali's training camp in Deer Lake, Pennsylvania, he asked me and another reporter to come with him as he tried to drive a huge bus down a mountain (it did have roads). He wasn't very steady, but I did get some great photos of him going down the mountain.

My all-time Ali highlight, though, happened at the press conference announcing his boxer versus wrestler match, which would be against Antonio Inoki on June 26, 1976. The press conference was about two weeks before the event and was held at the Waldorf Astoria Hotel in New

After I did a once-in-a-lifetime photo session with boxing's "Tomorrow's Champions" in 1984, I could not resist getting into a photo with them. Left to right: Tyrell Biggs, Meldrick Taylor, Mark Breland, Pernell Whitaker, and Evander Holyfield.

York City. As press from around the world was watching films of Inoki, I spotted a seat right next to Ali. I sat there, pressed record on my tape recorder and started to interview the champ. After a few minutes, I got the iconic ABC sportscaster Howard Cosell to join us. The press turned to us as I interviewed them both. Yes, I still have the tape—and the quality is great.

I met and photographed Mike Tyson when nobody knew who he was. Our boxing editor, Steve Farhood, told me to meet Mike at a studio we rented on West 45th Street in Manhattan. I had a great time when I found out he was a wrestling fan, and we traded imitations (his Dusty Rhodes wasn't bad). At the end of the photo session, he asked if he could borrow a few dollars to take the subway back home!

George Foreman was always a gentleman. I interviewed him right before his fight against Buster Mathis at Madison Square Garden, and when his trainers told him to stop talking and get in the ring to train, he kept talking. As well, Alexis Arguello was a charming fellow in the studio—so nice mannered and polite.

Joe Frazier and Mike Quarry both had issues with me. After Frazier's third fight against Ali, at Madison Square Garden in 1974, I went back to the dressing room and took a close-up of Frazier with his eyes closed and cheek bones a bit puffy. When it was published, someone from his office called and said he was very angry. Apparently, the photo made it look like more damage had been done than was actually inflicted by Ali. As for Quarry, he was leaving MSG after getting quite a beating, and I asked him if I could take his photo. He yelled out, "Why, Bill, why do you have to show this in the magazine? Give me one good reason." I told him it was my job. He angrily said, "Then take your damn picture and let me go home!" By the way, not only did I become good friends with Joe Frazier, I even wound up singing a karaoke duet of "My Way" with him at a benefit in Philadelphia about a year before he died.

I could write a lot more about my life in the boxing community, including meeting Joe Louis, Joe Bugner, Floyd Patterson, Oscar Bonavena, Evander Holyfield, Thomas Hearns, Buster Douglas, Larry Holmes and Sugar Ray Leonard—I have lots of stories that are just waiting to be told. Other random careers I've had?

I was a barker for the "Nickel Pitch" game on the boardwalk in Far Rockaway, New York, for three of the best teen-summers of my life.

I was a baby-clothes factory worker.

I worked as a messenger on Wall Street for a company called Loeb, Rhodes.

I worked in the mailroom at Columbia Pictures at 711 5th Avenue in New York.

Another mailroom job was at the Loews Theatre executive offices in Manhattan.

I was employed by two or three women's garment companies in the New York City garment district. My dad was a mailman in that area and he kept me working!

I sang in the Catskill Mountains with the Charlie Lowe Entertainers—one member of the group became a star for a short period of time—Linda Clifford. (Google it, kids.)

I was a "soda jerk" at the Hilltop Luncheonette, across the street from my apartment in Maspeth, New York.

In my late teens, I volunteered for the Carolians Club in New York City as an aide helping people with disabilities. I also did the same at Bird S. Coler Hospital on Welfare Island, New York City.

For nearly three years (because the money was wonderful), I did work on the side as a videographer (my own company—"Hocus Focus"—coined by my wife, Andrea), shooting weddings, Bar Mitzvahs and other occasions. It helped bring in the money when the magazines were drying up.

And, I was a full-time staff photographer for Apartment Wrestling. (Not! That's an inside joke to my dear love Missy Hyatt.)

THE FAMILY

FIFTY-SIX

Rather than write about my wonderful family, my taskmaster for this book, Greg Oliver, thought it would be interesting to hear from them firsthand. What was it like growing up around a father who was obsessive about pro wrestling? I had no idea what they were going to write, so here it is . . . unedited.

My wife also gets a chance to give her opinion as well . . .

HAILEY APTER

Bill's daughter. Occupation: Senior digital manager for a New York City advertising agency.

My brother, Brandon, and I grew up in front of our dad's cameras. From baby photos with Hulk Hogan, Don Muraco, Mr. Wrestling II and Ric Flair, to wrestling matches in our basement

How an Apter child learns to read.

against Dan Severn, professional wrestling was ever-present. It wasn't until maybe third grade that I realized how "cool" we were. Neighborhood kids would come to the house to talk to our dad and ask him about rivalries, tag teams and upcoming matches.

When I was in seventh grade, I interviewed Goldberg for the school newspaper and instantly gained boyfriends. I'll never forget that interview, when Goldberg told me I had huge feet for my age and a small stature. According to my dad, Goldberg asks about "his daughter with the big feet" every time they see each other. At Brandon's wrestling-themed Bar Mitzvah, numerous wrestlers recorded videos for him that were played during the reception, and you could just see his eyes light up and all of his friends' jaws drop. Basically, growing up with Bill Apter as a dad was the coolest, most eccentric *and* most normal childhood anyone could have.

BILL RESPONDS: Although she was not a huge wrestling fan, Hailey, who recently married David, loved being swept up in the show-business aspect of the sport—the spectacle—whenever she was taken to a show. These days, I see how she glows when I tell her about all the great things that are happening with my career (the WWE Network and the like) and how proud she is that I want to keep actively pursuing the dream.

BRANDON APTER
Bill's son. Occupation: Marketing and promotions manager for the Gwinnett Braves (Triple-A Affiliate of the Atlanta Braves baseball team).

Ever since I can remember, wrestling has been a part of my life. I don't really watch it too much anymore, but my childhood was consumed by it, and I wouldn't have had it any other way. The earliest memory that pops into my head is when our family relocated to Pennsylvania from New York. I

Yokozuna provides an uplifting experience for my son, Brandon, and daughter, Hailey. My kids loved being around the wrestlers.

had a rough time transitioning to a new school with new people. To make things run more smoothly for me, my dad got Yokozuna and Kevin Nash to record a "Good luck at school" audiocassette for me to listen to every day. It made me feel like the wrestling world was my world, and I loved it. It followed me throughout my life. My dad and I had regular matches in the living room as a nightly ritual before I would agree to go to bed. Of course, there was a stipulation that I had to win, usually by a Sharpshooter submission.

The mysterious "El Brando."

Getting to go with my dad to the matches was always an absolute blast. I soaked in the experience, and it still stays with me today. As an employee of the minor league baseball world, a lot of wrestlers from the 1990s, including Sgt. Slaughter, George Steele, Jerry Lawler, Ric Flair and others, visit stadiums across the country. Getting to see them as an adult and having conversations with them truly make me appreciate the amazing childhood that I had, thanks to my dad and the wrestling business. There are so many memories I will cherish forever, and my experiences with my dad and wrestling will be something that lives throughout generations of Apters to come.

BILL RESPONDS: For many years Brandon was the *total* wrestling fan, and there is one moment during those days neither he nor I will ever forget.

Brandon really wanted to meet Sting. He was probably 11 at the time, and he was no stranger backstage. I would take him to WCW shows when they were in Philadelphia, Delaware or Maryland, so the boys were used to seeing him. But he hadn't met his favorite wrestler yet. One night after a show, Sting had just returned to his dressing room after a long battle with some opponent, and I told Brandon, "Let's go say hello real quickly and head home." We entered the room, and there was Sting, sitting on a bench, filled with sweat and makeup nearly off. As we opened the door, he looked at us and perked up immediately.

"Who's this young man?" he asked, looking right at Brandon. He told him to come over, shake his hand and sit down next to him. For the next 20 minutes or so, Sting chatted with Brandon about school, his mom and me, wrestling, TV shows and more. It was the first time any wrestler really took interest in him. To this day, they have stayed in touch by email, text and the occasional phone call. Sting took the time and showed what a quality individual he truly is.

During his peak wrestling-fan days, Brandon refused to go to sleep at night unless we had a match in the living room. He would always be Bret Hart or "El-Brando," a masked man with a Rey Mysterio mask. I was just "Wonderful Willie," and he usually beat me with a Sharpshooter. As with Sting, Brandon got to meet both Bret and Rey and has stayed in touch with them on occasion too. Whenever I speak to either one of them, they always ask me to say hello to him. Kevin Nash was another one of Brandon's favorites, and they have continued to chat throughout the years.

Like with Hailey, Brandon tells me how proud he is that I am still "living the dream."

ANDREA APTER

Bill's wife: Admissions/marketing specialist for a Pennsylvania-based junior college.

In April 1982, I met my husband, William Stanley Apter, at a Benihana of Tokyo restaurant in midtown Manhattan. He had just finished covering a wrestling event with his associate, Craig Peters, at Madison Square Garden. I was reviewing the restaurant with a friend

and we were all seated at the same table—hibachi style. It was just the four of us and a conversation ensued, which then led to a date where I learned he would be traveling to Japan for a wrestling junket.

I had never been exposed to the world of wrestling nor had any particular interest in it. But I quickly learned it is a world into itself with a loyal fan base and a slew of interestingly named and colorful wrestling characters, like the Iron Sheik and Abdullah the Butcher. These names would become commonplace in household banter over the years, especially with our children at mealtime. Many matches were held with our children in the living room of our Massapequa Park, New York, home, where I would tell Bill, "Please watch the neck—the neck!" whenever he would pile-drive or throw our son over his knee. I was terrified our son would break his neck, or worse.

Through the years, I met such wrestling luminaries as Hulk Hogan, Sting, the Rock, "Nature Boy" Ric Flair, "The American Dream" Dusty Rhodes, "Superfly" Jimmy Snuka and the Rock 'n' Roll Express, just to name a few. I was fortunate to accompany Bill on some wrestling-oriented trips, like to the United Kingdom and

Nick Bockwinkel approves of my fiancée.

Hawaii—a no-brainer—which was always a nice perk.

Over the last decade, his interest and involvement in wrestling has remained steadfast and relentless as he discovers more ways, via digital, traditional and other media, to bring the news of wrestling to fans all over the world. My interest has waned a bit, because I am not in the thick of it, but to see Bill's continued drive for the passion that he was able to transform into a long-lasting career is very inspirational to me—and it should be to anyone who is seeking to turn an activity they love into a career.

BILL RESPONDS: Andrea was never a fan of the business. She's into baseball, football and the Olympics—not pro wrestling. She's met many of the stars at the many events I've dragged her to and is always pleasant around the wrestlers and fans, but it's certainly not her cup of tea. Give her some culture, a good conversation about current events, a Broadway show, a museum and especially a good book, and she's happy.

THE HUNGER FOR YOUNGER AND SOME LAST-MINUTE RANDOM THOUGHTS

FIFTY-SEVEN

Although this book is largely focused on my interaction with wrestling's greatest legends, I'm also quite impressed with the younger crop of "sports entertainers."

I've had the opportunity to visit the WWE Performance Center twice and attend NXT. Whether it's backstage or in the ring, I see the kind of enthusiasm and dedication that breeds success on so many levels. If NXT is what the future looks like, I hope I'm around for another 50 years to see what these new performers achieve.

As for the flagship products of the WWE, I have had the opportunity to meet the stars that have been brought to the forefront in recent years. Here are my impressions of some of them.

DEAN AMBROSE: I always joke that if Terry Funk and Dick Slater were wed and they had a kid, it would be Dean Ambrose. He has the fiery attitude, both mentally and physically, of both of them. This makes him a magnet, and you're drawn to watch his very unpredictable performances. Out of the ring, he's a fun-loving, pensive guy. He's a student of the business. At spot shows, he sits and watches the other matches on a monitor backstage.

ROMAN REIGNS: I shot so many photos and wrote so much about his father "Wild Samoan" Sika (along with his uncle Afa) that it's quite a kick for me to be watching this young warrior reach for the stars. He is totally different than his dad and uncle and has his own unique style. He's out to prove that he's more than just someone's son and he's done just that—not revealing his true Samoan identity until his WWE career was well underway. A quiet person out of the ring, with an infectious smile and a focus to succeed much further than a somewhat-doubting public can imagine.

SETH ROLLINS: An excellent heel with great mic skills and the talent to backup everything he has to say in the ring. I knew him when he was on the independent circuit and was telling people that he was

destined for the "big time." He's here and certainly making people take notice. I see him backstage culling advice from some of the veterans, as he is always trying to improve his game. He's friendly, outgoing, and super nice—it was a great idea to put the WWE World title on him.

ADRIAN NEVILLE: I have always been an advocate of wrestlers who soar way above their opponents to thrill their fans. Neville has taken soaring to the NXT (note the play on words here, folks) level. Now a member of the main roster I predict superstardom for this young man. He's a huge student of the business and loves to talk with me about the days he grew up studying all the wrestlers in the magazines I worked for.

DANIEL BRYAN: Here is a young veteran and one of my favorite in-ring-talents to watch. Bryan is a classic old-school style wrestler who loves to get in the ring with an opponent who can really mesh well with him and trade hold-for-hold. I've known him since his independent days and really took notice of him during his tenure in Ring of Honor. If anyone back in the ROH days would have told me that this pleasant, sort of shy guy, would be the biggest sensation in WWE even for a day, I would have called them "crazy." He was not the type WWE elevated to superstar level. They gambled, gave him the ball and he hit a homerun. Actually it was a grand slam. He is just a terrific person, and I'm glad to know him.

DWELLING ON SOME DIVAS: Paige has a totally charming and mystifying persona. She brings another level of competitive action to the DIVAS division. Natalya, the amazing daughter of Jim "The Anvil" Neidhart shines both in her ring work and as manager of Cesaro and Tyson Kidd. The Hart family has a lot to be proud of from this lady. The Bellas may have started out as eye candy, but they have certainly progressed athletically and as heel characters in the ring. Always there with some wide smiles and hugs for me backstage, they have shown nothing less than professional attitudes in WWE. AJ Lee announced her retirement, but you cannot take away her legacy in WWE. In many ways she helped changed the face of the Diva competitors with her characterization and very stiff ring-work (and I mean that in a good way).

CM PUNK: There is an old saying "What you see is what you get!" That is the perfect description of CM Punk. Although he has left the WWE, I have known him for many years. An outspoken, idea-driven, totally devoted to any cause he sinks his teeth in individual. He's got a great sense of sarcastic humor and is fun to be around. He is yet another person who totally immersed himself in wrestling business and respects its rich history. Like Daniel Bryan, he's an old school wrestler and loves a good "scientific" battle. Punk also likes to teach the art of pro wrestling and was a trainer at the Ring of Honor school many years ago. He has ventured into the world of mixed martial arts, but I predict he will be back in the role of a pro wrestler in the not too distant future.

BROCK LESNAR: I've only met this very imposing monster a few times. He's polite, quiet and focused backstage (at least he is around me). I would have loved to see Lesnar as challenger to Sammartino, Pedro Morales or Hogan in their prime.

RANDOM "APTER THOUGHTS . . ."

FIFTY-EIGHT

John Cena is one of the hardest working people in the business (if not *the* hardest working person)—both in and out of the ring. When he's not performing he's doing something charitable, usually involving kids. A huge thumbs up from Wonderful Willie!

As I write this chapter I just received the Jerry "The King" Lawler DVD. The good people at the WWE were kind enough to bring me to their studios for a day to record my story about Jerry and Andy Kaufman.

One of the "firsts" I am so proud of is that within the opening few minutes of the WWE Network launch, I was seen on the initial broadcast of the *WrestleMania Rewind* program. It's nice to know that I was there on camera when it all began.

Although he is mentioned in this book many times, I cannot overstress the part Bruno

John Cena is the hardest working athletic entertainer in the business. He gives way more than 100 percent of himself both inside and outside the ring. I have nothing but total admiration for this man!

Sammartino has played in my career. Bruno, although I never told you this, you were a mentor to me suggesting the way I should act around Vince McMahon Sr., and "the boys" in general. Your advice and putting me over to so many in the industry when I started my career opened so many doors for me. I am glad I could finally write how grateful I am.

Do I get some sort of award for seeing every Orton wrestle? In the '60s I watched Bob "Big O" Orton from the bleachers at Sunnyside Garden and Madison Square Garden. The '70s saw me cover matches of "Cowboy" Bob Orton and some of Berry Orton (he was named after "Wild" Red Berry) and of course these days Randy Orton. I don't think there are too many others who can say that!

Hey, I didn't forget. Thank you to all the fans who have supported me through the years—and continue to do so. I love interacting with all of you on social media (twitter: @apter1wrestling). To those of you who constantly ask how I would feel to be in the WWE Hall of Fame, my answer of course would be: "The accomplishment of a lifetime!" Perhaps one day they will open a "Media" division, and if so, perhaps I will be in that category. I want to thank Maryland Championship Wrestling for inducting me into their Hall of Fame several years ago, as well as WXW and of course the National Wrestling Hall of Fame/George Tragos/Lou Thesz/Dan Gable Museum.

One of the biggest regrets I have is that 50 years ago I gave an autograph book away to a guy named John when I was taking a night course at Bryant High School in Queens, New York. I had signatures of Buddy Rogers, Sweet Daddy Siki, Antonino Rocca and so many others. He was a huge fan, and for a short time, I quit watching wrestling because my grandfather nearly proved to me that wrestling was indeed fixed. So I gave my autographs away. It didn't make sense for me to keep the book any longer, and I knew John would love it.

Grandpa, if you're somehow reading this in heaven, I am sorry I didn't really believe you.

I DIDN'T KNOW IT WAS BROKEN!

BACK-WORD

By Joey Styles
The Voice of ECW
WWE Vice President of Digital Content

More than a decade before the internet and the era of instant information, pro-wrestling stars were made by the coverage and covers of national American magazines like *Pro Wrestling Illustrated*. In 1979, barely noticeable wrestling results in a handful of local newspapers (remember them?) were replaced by glossy, photo-filled magazines with everything and anything passionate fans like us wanted to know. I can vividly remember stopping by the local convenience store on my way home from school on the first Tuesday of each month to spend what little money I had on *Pro Wrestling Illustrated*.

The most important issue of the year was always the *PWI* Annual Achievement Awards.

Winning the fan voting for Wrestler, Tag Team or Manager of the Year, or Most Popular or Most Hated Wrestler carried weight with the promoters. *PWI* Achievement Award winners like Hulk Hogan, Ric Flair and the Road Warriors were beaming with pride when they posed with their plaques on the cover of tens of thousands of magazines across America. It wasn't long before the *Pro Wrestling Illustrated* Achievement Award plaques were being presented to the winners on national television, and it was *PWI*'s Bill Apter who was making the presentations and being introduced as pro-wrestling's premier journalist and ringside photographer. *PWI* had an all-star team of writers and editors like Stu Saks, Craig Peters, Eddie Ellner, Bob Smith, Brandi Mankiewicz, Roy London and many more, but it was Bill Apter who was the face of what would come to be known as the "Apter Mags" to promoters and wrestlers across America and around the world—and that was because of his national television appearances.

In 1991, Stu Saks, Craig Peters and Bill hired me as an unpaid college intern from local Hofstra University on Long Island, New York, and guided me as I worked my way up to becoming a paid contributing editor by the time of my graduation in 1993. During my time at *PWI*, it was Bill who arranged my first audition as a wrestling announcer for a local indie promotion, brought me backstage to WCW events in New York and New Jersey and, of course, introduced me to Paul Heyman, who would give me the opportunity with ECW that launched my career.

I am both very fortunate and happy to say that Bill and I have remained close friends for decades and now work together once again, as "Wonderful Willie" (as his friends call him) now writes columns read by hundreds of thousands of fans worldwide on WWE.com and is often interviewed for WWE Network programming and home-video releases. As with so many other things in life, pro-wrestling journalism has come full circle as a whole new generation of sports-entertainment fans have been introduced to the pioneer and measuring stick of the medium, Bill Apter.

A few weeks before my book was published, the world of wrestling suffered the death of the iconic Dusty Rhodes. On a personal level I lost a friend and mentor.

I would like to dedicate this book to the memory of his "American Dream" movement.

Dusty was passionate about many things he did in his life but none more than his family and charitable causes.

To learn more about two wonderful causes he talked about whenever he had the chance, please visit connorscure.com and joetorre.org.

GET THE EBOOK FREE!

At ECW Press, we want you to enjoy this book in whatever format you like, whenever you like. Leave your print book at home and take the eBook to go! Purchase the print edition and receive the eBook free. Just send an e-mail to ebook@ecwpress.com and include:

- the book title
- the name of the store where you purchased it
- your receipt number
- your preference of file type: PDF or ePub?

A real person will respond to your e-mail with your eBook attached. Thank you for supporting an independently owned Canadian publisher with your purchase!

Published by ECW Press
665 Gerrard Street East,
Toronto, Ontario, Canada M4M 1Y2
416-694-3348 / info@ecwpress.com

Library and Archives Canada
Cataloguing in Publication

Apter, Bill, author
Is wrestling fixed? I didn't know it was broken! : from photo shoots and sensational stories to the WWE Network—my incredible pro wrestling journey . . . and beyond! / written by Bill Apter ; foreword written by Jerry "The King" Lawler.

Issued in print and electronic formats.
ISBN 978-1-77041-154-8 (pbk)
ISBN 978-1-77090-751-5 (pdf)
ISBN 978-1-77090-752-2 (epub)

1. Apter, Bill. 2. Sportswriters—United States—Biography. 3. Wrestling—United States—History. 4. World Wrestling Entertainment, Inc. I. Lawler, Jerry, writer of foreword II. Title.

GV742.42.A78A3 2015   070.4'49796812092
C2015-902749-7

C2015-902750-0

Editor for the press: Michael Holmes
Cover design: Michel Vrana
Cover images: from the author's personal collection
Unless otherwise stated, interior images are from the author's personal collection.

Printed and bound in Canada by Norecob
5   4   3   2